Rethinking Peace and Conflict Studies

Series Editor
Oliver P. Richmond
University of Manchester
Manchester, UK

This agenda-setting series of research monographs, now more than a decade old, provides an interdisciplinary forum aimed at advancing innovative new agendas for approaches to, and understandings of, peace and conflict studies and International Relations. Many of the critical volumes the series has so far hosted have contributed to new avenues of analysis directly or indirectly related to the search for positive, emancipatory, and hybrid forms of peace. New perspectives on peacemaking in practice and in theory, their implications for the international peace architecture, and different conflict-affected regions around the world, remain crucial. This series' contributions offers both theoretical and empirical insights into many of the world's most intractable conflicts and any subsequent attempts to build a new and more sustainable peace, responsive to the needs and norms of those who are its subjects.

More information about this series at
http://www.palgrave.com/gp/series/14500

Nilanjana Premaratna

Theatre for Peacebuilding

The Role of Arts in Conflict Transformation in South Asia

Nilanjana Premaratna
Zurich, Switzerland

Rethinking Peace and Conflict Studies
ISBN 978-3-319-75719-3   ISBN 978-3-319-75720-9 (eBook)
https://doi.org/10.1007/978-3-319-75720-9

Library of Congress Control Number: 2018934627

© The Editor(s) (if applicable) and The Author(s) 2018
This work is subject to copyright. All rights are solely and exclusively licensed by the Publisher, whether the whole or part of the material is concerned, specifically the rights of translation, reprinting, reuse of illustrations, recitation, broadcasting, reproduction on microfilms or in any other physical way, and transmission or information storage and retrieval, electronic adaptation, computer software, or by similar or dissimilar methodology now known or hereafter developed.
The use of general descriptive names, registered names, trademarks, service marks, etc. in this publication does not imply, even in the absence of a specific statement, that such names are exempt from the relevant protective laws and regulations and therefore free for general use.
The publisher, the authors and the editors are safe to assume that the advice and information in this book are believed to be true and accurate at the date of publication. Neither the publisher nor the authors or the editors give a warranty, express or implied, with respect to the material contained herein or for any errors or omissions that may have been made. The publisher remains neutral with regard to jurisdictional claims in published maps and institutional affiliations.

Printed on acid-free paper

This Palgrave Macmillan imprint is published by the registered company Springer International Publishing AG part of Springer Nature
The registered company address is: Gewerbestrasse 11, 6330 Cham, Switzerland

*For Amma and Thaththa, Roland, and Wijesinghe miss.
And the artists and individuals who made this research meaningful
to me in numerous ways.*

Acknowledgements

This book is the result of several years of research and benefited from the generosity and support of many individuals as well as institutions.

First and foremost, thanks are due to Roland Bleiker who is an incredible mentor. Without his unwavering support and encouragement, this book simply would not be here. I am more grateful than I can ever express.

I also wish to acknowledge L. H. M. Ling, Shirin Rai, Morgan Brigg, Volker Boege, Cynthia Cohen, and an anonymous reviewer. All of these esteemed scholars provided feedback at different stages of the project, and their time, attention, and comments contributed towards improving the final manuscript. All imperfections in the book are mine.

I am grateful to the activists and theatre groups who inspired me to undertake this project. During fieldwork and even after, these fascinating individuals and groups welcomed me into their lives, shared their experiences, and allowed me to learn through their work. They bring meaning into the following chapters. All three theatre groups—Jana Karaliya, Jana Sanskriti, and Sarwanam—granted me the use of their photographs for the purpose of this publication. I am grateful for the generosity.

I was lucky enough to have many friends and colleagues who offered support in numerous ways. Janjira Sombutpoonsiri and Samanthi Gunawardena made rather timely visits and provided free consultations that helped me continue with the project. Sorcha Tormey, Joseph Hongoh, Luis Wiuff Moe, Jeyanthy Siva, Kathya de Silva-Senarath, Kerry Raleigh, Leah

Aylward, René Nessler, Chamila Udagama, Gayathri Bandara, Samanmalee Jayawardena, Olivia Fuchs, Theodore Mayer, Indrakanthi Perera, Vasuki, Nirrosion Perera, and Hannah Weigle engaged in many productive conversations and patiently sifted things through with me. My sincere thanks go to Constance Duncombe for editing an earlier draft, and to Harshadeva Amarathunga for contributing to this project in more ways than I can count.

My family deserves a special mention. My parents and sisters kindly forgave my long absences and silences, and the far too many hours spent in front of the computer; they shielded me from responsibilities of all kinds so that I can focus on the work at hand, and did their best to understand and provide companionship in the process.

I take this opportunity to thank the Department of Political Science and International Relations at the University of Queensland, where this project began; Australia Awards and UQ Graduate School for sponsoring the research; the wonderful editorial team at Palgrave Macmillan for their confidence in me and the efficiency and support throughout the manuscript preparation process.

Earlier versions and parts of some of the chapters included in the book are published elsewhere: Premaratna, Nilanjana, and Roland Bleiker. "Art and Peacebuilding: How Theatre Transforms Conflict in Sri Lanka." In *Advances in Peace and Conflict Studies* edited by Oliver Richmond. Basingstoke: Palgrave Macmillan, 2010; Premaratna, Nilanjana and Roland Bleiker. "Art and Theatre for Peacebuilding" In *Dimensions of Peace: Disciplinary and Regional Approaches* edited by Oliver Richmond, Sandra Pogodda, Jasmin Ramović. Basingstoke: Palgrave Macmillan, 2016. I acknowledge the contributions of Roland Bleiker and the respective editors and reviewers to the final draft, and thank them for the permission to include these in the book.

Contents

1 Introduction — 1

Part I Conceptualising Theatre for Peacebuilding

2 Peacebuilding and Its Critiques — 31

3 Theatre for Peacebuilding — 65

Part II Exploring Theatre in Local Peacebuilding Processes

4 Jana Karaliya: Inviting a Shared Future — 107

5 Jana Sanskriti: Transforming Through Empowerment — 153

6 Sarwanam: Speaking for the People — 187

7 Conclusion — 233

Index — 241

List of Figures

Fig. 4.1	People gather and stand in line outside the mobile theatre, waiting to attend the evening performance	120
Fig. 4.2	A scene from inside the mobile theatre	130
Fig. 4.3	A scene from Jana Karaliya play *Charandas*, featuring two long-term actors of the group: Logananthan Suman (right) plays the lead role, while Sumudu Mallawarachchi plays the lead supporting role (left)	137
Fig. 5.1	Last scene of the Jana Sanskriti play *Where We Stand*	172
Fig. 6.1	Sarwanam performing in a school during a national tour	205
Fig. 6.2	A scene from *Sakuni's Tricks* performed at the Sarwanam theatre	209
Fig. 6.3	A scene from *Remaining Page of History*	219

CHAPTER 1

Introduction

My interest in the arts goes a long way back: I was in primary school during the 1987–1989 insurgency in Sri Lanka. I have two vivid memories of that time: the first is the smell of burning human flesh one morning and the resulting fear and frenzy, trying to find out whether it was someone we knew. Being children, we were warned not to speak about these incidents in public, as they were intimately connected to the politics of the period. Even at home, state actions were questioned only in whispers, only among the family. Questioning the government openly was a guaranteed way to end up on a roadside pyre, so there were not many who dared to do it. The second thing I remember about that time is the arts: the songs and the dramas. These were the most vocal critiques of the senseless killings that had been going on in the country for so long. In fact, art seemed to be the only voice that broke through the curtain of silence that blanketed all other public spaces. A handful of artists toured the country, performing and singing in schools and public grounds, raising questions of justice, freedom, democracy, ethnic unity, and power. This made a lasting impression on me about the resilience of art: how it survives when nothing else does. And how it can speak when nothing else can. Also, looking back, I see that art gave people hope, a way to come together through the trauma, a way to reconstitute community separated by alienation and suspicion. This is when I started seeing the potential of art to reach into—and make peace with—the core of ourselves: to present a way out of the deadlock in which we find ourselves, during and after a conflict.

Motivated by this personal interest, I undertake a systematic study into the role of arts in peacebuilding through this book. As a Sri Lankan growing up during the war, conflict was just another part of life. Tallying death tolls was a nightly ritual mediated through the state television channels whenever active military operations were underway. At more than half a decade after the war, and several years of living outside the country, my first reaction to a backfiring tyre still remains an irrational fear and an urge to hold onto the person next to me. The unpredictable regularity of suicide bombs indeed leave scars. Exploring the nexus of peacebuilding and the arts is my way of embracing the sparks of hope, power, and connection that glimmer through the murkier feelings of resignation and apathy. Apart from the relevant and timely contribution it makes to the discipline, this book is meaningful to me in a deeply personal manner.

Key debates and recent developments in peace studies highlight the need for studying local and community-based approaches to building peace. This invites us to step back from the mainstream approaches and blueprints for peacebuilding, and to closely examine the practices that already exist at the ground level. Art is a powerful vehicle with established political significance. Despite this potential and the growing popularity of the arts as a peacebuilding approach among practitioners, there has been little scholarly inquiry into the area. The studies that do exist tend to be conceptual. In order to appropriately utilise the arts as a tool for peacebuilding, we need to better understand how the arts work for peacebuilding. What are the key elements in its peacebuilding process? What are the potentials and limitations of the arts for peacebuilding? Where can we find inspiration and gain pertinent empirical evidence? Using the arts to build peace, consequently, still remains an emerging area within peace and conflict studies.

This book seeks to offer answers to some of the above questions. It focuses on theatre as an art form, and examines its role in contributing to peacebuilding in South Asia.

To further unpack this phenomenon, I raise several critical questions: How has the art of theatre been used for peacebuilding in conflict situations? How does theatre open up possibilities of conversation between parties and narratives in conflict? And what potentials—or limitations—do different forms of theatre hold for peacebuilding?

The book draws on the insights of three theatre groups in order to answer these questions: Jana Sanskiriti from India, Jana Karaliaya from

Sri Lanka, and Sarwanam from Kathmandu, Nepal. Doing so, it offers a possible conceptualisation of how theatre works for peacebuilding: the multi-voiced and dialogic form of theatre is particularly suited to express local complexities and open up untapped possibilities of communication between former adversaries. Thus, the relevance of what is discussed here extends beyond the academic study of peace and conflict, into the practice of peacebuilding at different levels.

Approaches to Peacebuilding

The theory and practice of peacebuilding are largely dominated by approaches that stress institution building, democratic procedures, abstract rights, and neoliberal development.[1] Despite adopting a broader definition for peacebuilding that recognises the existence of a range of measures for peacebuilding working at all levels of the society in its May 2007 deliberations,[2] the United Nations Peacebuilding Commission still prioritises institution building through its mandate. The key areas of focus still remain reconstruction, institution building and development. Addressing the social and cultural aspects of a conflict does not receive its due emphasis within this framework. This becomes further evident with a closer look at the prevalent approaches to peacebuilding.

Oliver Richmond presents a four generational trajectory on how efforts to build peace evolved.[3] Albeit being a retrospective reading, this model succinctly captures the tensions in and in the development of the field. I provide a summary here.

Richmond argues that the first generation of peacebuilding was conducted within a "limited state-centric discourse", based on the assumption that conflict is "inherent."[4] Consequently, this phase excluded issues and actors that are beyond state parameters. The ensuing peacebuilding employed a generalised set of tools and structures that were developed based on western traditions and diplomacy.

The second-generation peacebuilding builds upon the first, but takes human needs as the focal point. It recognises concepts such as structural violence and individual injustice. The focus on a shared, universal set of human needs, opens up peacebuilding for engagement with non-state actors while still operating within the state-centric framework. The role of citizens and civil society are still limited to basic indicators of needs and are not seen as active agents of the process. Second generation peacebuilding, although it articulates a more mutual vision of peace, prescribes a universal formula that overrides local specificities.

Third generation peacebuilding takes a multilevel approach to address different dimensions of peacebuilding. It takes advantage of the breakthrough of second-generation peacebuilding and opens up the field to engage with a broader stakeholder base. It recognises the importance of engaging with both the top-down and bottom-up approaches to peacebuilding. The needs and perception of actors at multiple levels guide the process. International Organisations and bodies such as the United Nations Peacebuilding Commission worked within this framework in recognising the importance in bringing together relevant actors, marshalling resources, and providing "expert" advice on post-conflict peace-building and recovery. This format intends to bring peace through a transformation of key local institutions and practices relating to conflict, both from a state and citizens' perspective.

Despite the broader outlook, third generation peacebuilding is critiqued for emphasising western approaches at the cost of inadequate engagement with local practices and knowledge sources. Richmond points out that it allows context-specific renegotiation only at a marginal and superficial level.[5] The heavy emphasis placed on institution building and liberal-democratic practices, obstructs the potential for context specific adaptations. Stable political order leading to peace does not necessarily emerge from legislative frameworks or institution building. Protracted conflicts are often divided along social elements such as ethnicity, identity, or class. In addition to the establishment of institutions and procedures, sustainable peacebuilding requires the transformation of such root cases and social constructions. Furthermore, blueprints introducing democracy and liberal economic policies can have negative side effects. Hughes, Thompson, and Balfour observe that introducing such measures can profoundly threaten local initiatives working to create a communal foundation for a culture of peace.[6] Failing to appropriately take local practices into account when introducing liberal democracy in post-conflict situations can have serious consequences. It can challenge existing relationship networks and cultural patterns of a given context, that could have been the very threads that held the community together during conflict. Alienation and loss of community can possibly result. The relationship between liberal values and democracy is asymmetrical even though it is perceived to co-exist within the third generation approach to peacebuilding.[7] This fusion leads existing heterogeneity to be eroded in favour of creating a homogenous whole.[8] Therefore, pushing for democracy and free markets soon after a conflict can indeed destabilise a fragile post-conflict situation, undermining existing foundations of community and restricting the expression of minority voices. This often results in threatening local cultural shifts toward peace. Thus, pushing towards implementing western approaches to peacebuilding implies a disregard towards local agency, skill and knowledge.

Consequently, prevailing approaches to peacebuilding—primarily falling into the third generation of Richmond's categorisation—cannot adequately address local complexities and fails to satisfactorily include conflict transformation processes taking place at the local context. Ho-Won Jeong criticizes the discipline for its focus on liberal democratic solutions to a conflict at the cost of ignoring economic, institutional and cultural realities at the ground level.[9] These debates, previously located at the fringes of peacebuilding, have become central today. Formerly peripheral concepts such as culture, local practices and religion have become increasingly visible as salient factors in conflict resolution. Failure to allocate due significance to the social and cultural aspects of a conflict jeopardises the sustainability of peacebuilding, as many international examples like Democratic Republic of Congo and Liberia demonstrate. Thus, we need peacebuilding to embrace and preferably embody the diversity it encounters in practice. This increasingly insistent tension is the place from where Richmond articulates the fourth generation of peacebuilding.

Fourth generation peacebuilding presents a potential next step. Richmond argues that peacebuilding approaches should be more organic and context specific, thereby addressing the shortcomings of previous approaches. He identifies opening up to the "cultural, customary dynamics of the local environment" to be the "next big step" in peacebuilding approaches.[10] The "Sustaining Peace" agenda introduced through the United Nations Secretary-General's Report on Peacebuilding and Sustaining Peace in 2018 reflects a policy level step in this direction. Fourth generation peacebuilding, by prioritising communities instead of institutional peace, highlights the "grassroots." It does not aim to impose a liberal state upon the local. Instead, it aims to understand and blend with the existing political, economic, social and cultural traditions at the conflict context and work through these. As Richmond argues, this requires creating the space for the local and international to engage in flexible and open conversations about the unique peacebuilding process in each context. It recognises the need to focus on individuals in conflict contexts including how conflict is constituted within their lifeworlds. Seeing and addressing the conflict from this perspective is important for effective, sustainable peacebuilding. The focus on the macro level alone is gradually proving to be insufficient: the development of peacebuilding itself calls for focusing on an everyday, micro level approach to peace.

Statebuilding vs Societybuilding Debate

Having provided a chronological overview, I now examine peacebuilding from a contemporary perspective that captures current debates. I discuss two key themes in peacebuilding that are increasingly becoming visible: statebuilding and societybuilding. This juxtaposition captures the present tensions within peacebuilding.

The intersection of local and liberal approaches is a central point at which key debates in peacebuilding are located at present. The emerging discussion on peacebuilding as statebuilding and peacebuilding as society or community-building is a milestone here. Statebuilding generally comprises of the top-down, dominant approaches to peacebuilding that emphasises strengthening state institutions as the primary avenue for peace. Prevalent approaches falling within third generation peacebuilding, privileging democratic procedures and liberal values, largely reflect this.

The societybuilding approach to peace is more in alignment with the vision of fourth generation peacebuilding. With its focus on working directly with the communities through a bottom-up approach, societybuilding has the potential to address certain gaps in the statebuilding approach. As Andrieu argues, this is apparent in relation to societal legitimacy and the rebuilding of resilient post-conflict societies.[11] These approaches recommend focusing on people, drawing from the local culture, and merging peacebuilding with the existing local practices. Fourth generation peacebuilding accordingly takes an increased interest in the minute particles that make up the peacebuilding process: the particles that are made up of human beings and their lifeworlds. Societybuilding brings these hitherto neglected aspects within peacebuilding to the fore, emphasising the need to pay attention to and work with these in order to arrive at more effective and sustainable solutions.

The societybuilding model has also been challenged on a number of fronts. These overlap with some of the challenges of fourth generation peacebuilding.

Two areas from which fourth generation peacebuilding—and the everyday peacebuilding model it envisions—has been questioned are noteworthy. David Roberts critiques the viability and legitimacy of fourth generation peacebuilding. He problematizes the concept of emancipation featuring in fourth generation peacebuilding, on the grounds that it is unrealistic to expect this in practice within a globalised context where power relations are not responsive to the call for everyday life and local legitimacy.[12] However, Richmond asserts that we are yet to achieve fourth generation peacebuilding. This is partly due to the fact that fourth generation peacebuilding largely remains at a conceptual level, devoid of specific parameters that clarify its relationship with the local and resistance towards the liberal hegemony.[13] The attempt to bridge the dominant discourses with the local can disrupt or change the dynamics of conflict transformation arising within the local context. Such disruption, at times, results in a loss of legitimacy for the overarching peacebuilding process. From such a perspective, achieving the ideals of fourth generation peacebuilding and a sustainable local-liberal model become debatable. Baranyi agrees[14]; he notes that fourth generation peacebuilding becomes "even more problematic" when it is considered in terms of sustainability. He identifies the "mixed international motives" driving such operations and the absence of key local stakeholders within the peacebuilding process, as possible reasons undermining peacebuilding's sustainability. Thus, fourth generation peacebuilding also faces critiques for its inability to clearly outline a path for sustainable peace.

This book contributes to the development of fourth generation peacebuilding by exploring art initiatives that work to build peace. These initiatives take an everyday approach to peacebuilding, and effectively draw from and base themselves within the local socio-cultural context. Such community-based initiatives develop and fine-tune strategies to maximise their local agency and legitimacy, even within the unequal power relations that exist in a globalised context. Arriving at these insights from the case studies requires an exploration into the role of arts in peacebuilding.

The Role of Arts in Peacebuilding

Art offers an everyday peacebuilding method that draws from and works within the local socio-political background. Against the backdrop of prevailing debates in peacebuilding, there is a growing recognition that art can play an important role. Practitioners from different conflict situations are increasingly using art as a peacebuilding approach. However, there is insufficient academic literature studying this phenomenon. Even within what is available, there is limited empirical analysis of the ways in which art builds peace at an everyday level. As a result, we know surprisingly little about the exact issues at stake.

Art becomes a part of everyday politics as a fundamental element of life and society, and therein lies its significance for peacebuilding. The presence of art is evident throughout the evolution of human societies. Scholars argue it is a fundamental element of culture that exists in almost all communities, even at the most difficult of times.[15] Art's resilience testifies to its salience for human beings. Some go so far as to argue that art is a biological urge, leading to its integration as a cultural phenomenon.[16] The space art provides for expression is a space that is often absent in our regular communication: it works within the real and imagined, thereby opening dimensions that might not otherwise be possible within the day-to-day constraints of life. What is expressed within the imagination of art simultaneously constitutes and is constituted by the society; both a reflection of the society and a key agent of its transformation. In treading this fine line between the real and the imagined, art has the potential to elicit social residues and complexities of conflict. Thus, scholars recognise art as a powerful tool in shaping popular discourse as well as in constituting political beliefs,[17] and that it requires further study in this particular role in shaping politics.[18]

Peacebuilding needs to seep into these spaces where public discourse is formed, for peace is intricately bound up with interactions and perceptions on the ground level. As Paul Richards aptly notes, "[i]f war has spread from within, making its own cultural sense as it goes, then the search for peace may have to trace similar paths."[19] Incorporating the arts broadens the prevailing approaches to peacebuilding. It has the potential to encompass *and* transcend the limits of political, security, economic and development paradigms towards peacebuilding. The role of arts in peacebuilding sits within this dynamic transdisciplinary approach between culture and politics. Accordingly, there is recognition that art can contribute to peacebuilding.

Another advantage of art is its capacity to transcend the boundaries of rational deliberations to which peacebuilding is often limited. Elise Boulding and John Paul Lederach are early theorists to comment on the value of transcending the technical, cognitive or analytic approach.[20] Lederach points out that in our search for replicable, professional, technical processes to initiate social transformation, we have forgotten other sources of knowledge and ways of understanding, such as the creative.[21] Connecting with and working through the creative or the aesthetics enables innovation that is a hallmark of progress in peacebuilding. Boulding identified three modes of knowing through which peacebuilding has to work: cognitive/analytic or the rational, emotional/affective, and intuitive. She calls for the satisfactory utilisation of the latter two modes, as the prevalent approaches largely focus on the first. Both the emotional/ affective and the intuitive can work through imagination and, therefore, approaches to peacebuilding that draw from and cultivate imagination hold much potential for sustainable peacebuilding. The insights offered through art, as an approach that works primarily through imagination relying on the emotional and intuitive modes of knowing, "challenges the modern tendency to reduce the political to the rational."[22] Rational deliberations alone, therefore, are inadequate in restoring cooperative and harmonious inter-communal relations in post-conflcit societies.

These arguments do not idealise the significance of art: they only emphasise the potential of art in constituting politics. As Agathangelou and Ling assert, "art is not pristine. Nor is it ideal or devoid of its own politics."[23] It merely reflects the values and efforts we put into it, serving "as a site of struggle and labor, like any other productive enterprise."[24] Thus, working through the arts opens up and provides access to a creative space where everyday politics takes place.

Consequently, there is a growing academic interest in studying the nexus of art and peacebuilding. Practitioners have increasingly been using art as a peacebuilding approach over the last two decades, but academic interest in the area is more recent. Thus, the existing literature on the topic is somewhat limited. Scholars working on this area stress that art can effectively contribute to peacebuilding and while some call for exploring the connections between art and peacebuilding—or international relations[25]—others look at specific instances where art-based approaches have been employed in conflict situations.[26]

Not many authors provide an empirical analysis of the ways in which the arts initiate peacebuilding. There is some exploration of the outcomes of arts-based approaches, but studies that look deeper at the process through which art works are still absent. In a report on the arts and peacebuilding, Cynthia Cohen and Jonathan White emphasise the importance of researching the nexus of art and peacebuilding in order for the area to gain legitimacy as a tool for social change. Apart from more documentation, they call for work that identifies the "strengths and limitations of various approaches" and explores the "underlying theories of change in such approaches."[27] The empirical approach of this book, studying the process of theatre for peacebuilding, the issues at stake and the discursive practices through which the arts build peace, makes a concrete contribution here.

Theatre for Peacebuilding

While the theatre's capacity to script politics has interested scholars and practitioners alike, theatre for peacebuilding as an academic inquiry remains an emerging area. Discussions taking place in related areas shed some light on the potential that theatre holds as a peacebuilding approach. A number of theatre forms intentionally develope d for social engagement exist. Looking at these theatre forms offers insights on theatre's potential for peacebuilding and conflict resolution. I discuss this literature under two main overlapping themes: theatre developed for therapeutic purposes, and theatre developed for broader political engagement. This will be discussed at length in Chapter 3.

Theatre forms developed for therapeutic purposes aim for healing and reconciliation. While these can have a communal focus, often these theatre forms focus on individuals or small groups, and are used for personal healing and growth. Psychodrama, drama therapy and playback theatre are examples for this. Recent studies note the positive impact of such theatre forms, with some scholars particularly observing theatre's potential in helping autistic children to overcome their internal obstacles in communication and interaction.[28] Playback theatre, used at individual and small group levels, is also known for its potential for reconciliation. Cohen argues that playback theatre is effective in working with people from conflicting ethnic groups as it can facilitate the formation of cohesive narratives and closer relationships.[29] Although these theatre forms, with their therapeutic approach, call for well-trained practitioners and a case-by-case approach to be effective, they indicate the potential of theatre to bring about healing and reconciliation.

The theatre forms developed for broader political engagement focus on empowerment and development. Theatre of the Oppressed and applied theatre are two such widely practiced theatre forms. Theatre of the Oppressed specifically aims for the empowerment of those who participate, while applied theatre focuses on engaging with a given social issue or issues. Philip Taylor explores the community application of applied theatre in *Applied Theatre: Creating Transformative Encounters in the Community*, and Chinyowa notes its potential for initiating dialogue in "Emerging Paradigms for Applied Drama and Theatre Practice in African Contexts."[30] Such theatre forms demonstrate great potential in engaging with issues that go beyond the individual and personal, reaching out to the broader levels that peacebuilding calls for.

There is ample cause and room to develop the body of literature on theatre for peacebuilding, with a growing recognition of the role theatre can play in building peace. Practitioners from different conflict situations, as well as funding organisations increasingly use theatre as a peacebuilding approach. This growing attention has resulted in the documentation of theatre projects from some parts of the world and the production of some academic literature on theatre and reconciliation.[31] However, in order for the area to develop and to offer a comprehensive understanding of the potential of theatre for peacebuilding, we need systematic scholarly inquiry into the topic.

A noteworthy contribution is made through *Acting Together: Performance and the Creative Transformation of Conflict*, published in 2011. Organised in two volumes, here the authors Cynthia Cohen, Roberto Varea and Polly Walker present performances taking place during and after conflict in different regions of the world. The anthology also discusses ceremonies and ritualistic performances aimed at healing. The authors develop an analogy to explain how art works: they argue that art, or theatre, works as a permeable membrane between the everyday life and creative spaces. The factors regulating the filtering process through this permeable membrane are the ethical and aesthetic sensibilities of the artists or activists animated by their moral imagination. *Acting Together* presents an important starting point. For a deeper understanding of the way in which theatre works, we need comprehensive empirical studies that look at the conceptual underpinnings in using theatre for peacebuilding. *Acting Together*, as an anthology aiming to compile a practitioner's guide for using theatre in conflict zones, does not go into a detailed analysis of the groups systematically using theatre for peacebuilding in specific contexts. Understanding how and what elements in theatre contribute to peacebuilding is imperative to further develop and utilize the full potential of theatre for peacebuilding as an approach.

As an empirical study on theatre for peacebuilding, this book contributes to this task in a number of ways. Studying how local theatre groups come together and carry out their peacebuilding work, provides a deeper understanding of the role of theatre as a peacebuilding method, and strategies of group resilience over changing political conditions.

A common challenge to the sustainability of theatre and art for peacebuilding projects is the lack of resources. Given this background, studying long-standing local theatre for peacebuilding initiatives becomes salient. Insights from such studies can be replicated as models where it is appropriate and can serve as a starting point for contexts with inadequate resources. Empirical studies capturing these nuances can help in further refining theoretical positions[32] and furthering our understanding of how exactly change is produced at different levels of the society. Building such understandings can contribute to the successful implementation of theatre for peacebuilding initiatives. Different conflict contexts call for different peacebuilding strategies. Theatre's approach to peacebuilding is intimately bound with these differences. For the development of the field, it is imperative to sufficiently represent the diversity in the field and understand the nuances in the practice. Expanding the discussions to include as many voices as possible, and especially "participants from the Global South" is critical to expand this discussion in peacebuilding.[33]

The book attempts to bring voices from the ground level into the conversations on theatre and peacebuilding. Scholars comment on the persistent gap between the theory and practice of peacebuilding, where despite the increasingly heard critical voices at a conceptual level, the practice of peacebuilding continues to be framed within conflict resolution and management.[34] We can see peacebuilding initiatives that take a conflict transformation approach once we step beyond the mainstream peacebuilding processes. The empirical study presented in the book draws the theory and practice of peacebuilding into conversation with each other. The three theatre groups from South Asia—Jana Sanskriti from India, Jana Karaliya from Sri Lanka, and Sarwanam from Nepal—come from South Asia but respond to different conflicts, using different theatre forms. Despite their differences, certain underlying themes connect the process of transformation that takes place through each case study. Arriving here requires us to have an overview of the case studies and their work contexts.

Case Studies

This book focuses on South Asia. South Asia is noteworthy for its prevalence of conflicts and cultural diversity. Interestingly, scholars have also noted it as a part of the world where art forms "an intrinsic part of the daily life for the vast majority of the population", and where art is not just an individual activity but a "collective activity" to be "shared by all members of the community."[35] Peacebuilding activities by the local actors, although rarely studied, often reflect this diversity and creativity.

I carried out the primary field research for this book between May–October 2013, using observation, document review, semi-structured in-depth interviews, and focus groups as the main data collection methods. I travelled and lived with the theatre groups at times, and observed the everyday activities of the theatre groups, which included group processes, rehearsals, performances and interactions within and among research participants. This provided a third point of view from which to comprehend how the multivocality and dialogic of theatre works within the groups and their productions. The Sri Lankan case is an exception as there I also drew from previous data gathered in 2007 on a related research.[36] My primary interviewees were the theatre groups themselves. I also carried out complementary interviews with civil society leaders and audience members. I draw from altogether 59 interviews: A total of 18, 17 and 24 interviews were respectively carried out for the Sri Lankan, Indian and Nepalese case studies. I use pseudonyms to protect the identity of the participants, except for the cases where a participant explicitly requested the use of their own name. In the first instance of using a pseudonym, I clarify this in a footnote.

The case studies presented in this book all draw from and work at the ground level, and have an active, established and a widespread practice within the country. They differ from each other on their working contexts and the preferred theatre approach, and thereby facilitate comparison of these elements. Sri Lanka presented an ethnic conflict which was brought to an end through a military defeat; Nepal, a negotiated peace in response to the Maoist uprising against the monarchy; and West Bengal, India a context of structural violence. These different conflict situations required the case studies to develop different ways of approaching peacebuilding. The preferred theatre approaches is another distinctive factor that sets the case studies apart. Depending on their chosen theatre form, the theatre groups engage with the community in co-creating a play, or adhere to a didactic process of knowledge imparting to varying extents. In the first instance, consciousness shaping of the audience takes place through their personal offstage interpretations of the play. In the second, it can be a more collaborative, facilitated process between the performers and the audience. The Nepalese case study is closer to the first category, using an alternative theatre form that resembles proscenium theatre but draws from elements of street theatre. The Indian case study resembles the second category, primarily using Theatre of the Oppressed. The Sri Lankan case study fluidly shifts between both categories and carves out its own path in the process, being a mobile theatre group using applied theatre.

Jana Karaliya / Makkal Kalari / Theatre of the People

Jana Karaliya in Sinahalese, or Makkal Kalari in Tamil, is a multi-ethnic, bilingual mobile theatre group from Sri Lanka. This composition is significant in this particular conflict context.

The key parties in the Sri Lankan conflict are the Tamil ethno-nationalist group Liberation Tigers of Tamil Eelam (LTTE)[37] and the majority Sinhalese led Sri Lankan government. The main point of contention, as it emerged, is the demand for a Tamil homeland in the Tamil speaking north and east of the country. Ethnic tensions underline the conflict and emerge at different key points. The armed phase of the conflict started in 1983. It ended in 2009 with the government's military defeat of the LTTE, making Sri Lanka a case in point for a victor's peace.

Despite a regime change in 2015 that offered some opportunities for reconciliation, Sri Lanka still demonstrates the consequences of an enforced peace with its many ensuing complexities. The immediate postwar take on peacebuilding focused on resettlement and development, what Goodhand calls is a framework of "stabilisation and power-building."[38] Local and international peacebuilding beyond these delimitations were treated with suspicion and increasingly came under the scrutiny of the Ministry of Defence.[39] Activities that questioned or challenged the then power regime were discouraged and routinely suppressed. The root causes that led to or grievances that resulted from nearly three decades of war are still very much present. The rhetoric of militarisation and a victorious ethno-nationalist identity tied with Buddhist supremacy—both legacies of the military defeat—are strongly felt within the island. Ethno-religious tensions among the communities are increasing, as the violence against the Muslims in March 2018 indicate. Working to build peace between the different communities in Sri Lanka within this context requires navigating complex political sensitivities. It calls for unique, resilient peacebuilding strategies that evolve in response to changing political conditions.

Two artists, Parakrama Niriella and H. A. Perera, co-founded Jana Karaliya in 2003 during an internationally mediated ceasefire. The group continued working and travelling together throughout the changing phases of conflict. The team is diverse in its ethnic, linguistic and religious identities, and comes from different districts. A multi-ethnic cast performing in Tamil and Sinhalese is novel in Sri Lanka, given the limited exchange between these two languages. At present, Jana Karaliya is one of the oldest, most visible and committed theatre groups working for inter-ethnic harmony in the country. The group borrows from the theatre and music traditions of Sinhala and Tamil cultures, thereby initiating a cultural exchange between these two main bodies. This multi-ethnic collaboration models ethnic harmony and coexistence. Thus, at a conceptual level, Jana Karaliya initiates reconciliation between different theatre, music and performance traditions. At a practical level, the group brings together individuals from different ethnicities to perform and appreciate theatre.

The preferred theatre form of Jana Karaliya is "applied theatre." An umbrella term encompassing a number of theatre forms, applied theatre engages with contemporary social issues, embodying social change through its cast, performance, and performance space. Applied theatre is grounded on the contention that fiction and reality are interrelated and embedded in each other as narrative constructions. Thus, the assumption that narratives can be changed in fiction as well as in reality is at the "heart of practice in applied drama."[40] The process through which this change happens differs from context to context. An empirical study on Jana Karaliya allows us to understand the potentials and limitations of this particular application.

Jana Sanskriti

Jana Sanskriti from India offers another take on building peace through theatre at community level. Founded by Sanjoy Ganguly, Jana Sanskriti started in West Bengal and later spread to other states of India. It has a history of over two decades of using theatre as a method of social change. The group works in a context of structural violence. Instead of focusing on a specific conflict, Jana Sanskriti draws from the structural narratives of violence affecting the relevant community. Jana Sanskriti at present has 30 village level theatre groups, and the members come from and work within disadvantaged communities in remote areas. These groups perform regularly at the village level. The tension and conflict arising within their everyday life due to socioeconomic, caste, gender and religious discrimination form a part of these performances. Thus, the specific issues Jana Sanskriti engages with in a given performance vary, depending on the location and what is present during that period. Jana Sanskriti, consequently, sees theatre as a tool of social empowerment. Instead of the limiting culture of monologue seen in most aspects of life, Jana Sanskriti aims to establish a culture of dialogue that liberates and empowers the marginalised communities.[41] Jana Sanskriti contributes to the research by emphasising the ability of peacebuilding to address structural violence.

Jana Sanskriti presents an interesting case study as a local theatre group using Theatre of the Oppressed, a theatre form developed by Augusto Boal. Theatre of the Oppressed is also an umbrella term that includes a number of different theatre forms. Each of these has social action at its core, and initiates social change by giving a voice to the marginalised or the oppressed. Theatre of the Oppressed actively engages the audience in the performance, referring to them as "spect-actors". The audience explores the reality of their lives—and the stories they tell themselves about situations—through these performances and strive to create new narratives that are emancipatory, transcending the old and discriminatory stories. Theatre of the Oppressed presents interesting potentials for embodying dialogue and multiple voices. Also, Jana Sanskriti's extensive experience in working with communities has enabled it to develop unique mechanisms to address community reconciliation. Together with the use of Theatre of the Oppressed this makes Jana Sanskriti's contribution in the book relevant and novel.

Sarwanam

Ashesh Malla, a playwright from a rural district in Nepal, started Sarwanam in 1982 as a social movement. Formed to protest against the oppressive Panchayat system in place, the theatre group continued to be a voice for democracy, freedom and peace. The book explores how Sarwanam builds peace in a context of political insurgency.

The Nepalese conflict is a political insurgency led by the Communist Party of Nepal (Maoist)(CPN(M)) against the monarchy and the ruling classes, in a struggle for a fairer system of governance. The violent turn of the conflict started in 1996 and went on until 2005. In 2006, the parties formally entered into a peace agreement after signing the Comprehensive Peace Accord (CPA). Local leaders initiated the Nepalese peace process and invited the UN into the process in 2004. The presence of the United Nations Mission in Nepal—on a limited mandate—helped legitimise the role of the Maoists in stabilising the aftermath of conflict.[42]

In 2007 violence reappeared from the South Eastern regions of Nepal bordering India, demanding recognition and equal rights for ethnically Indian Nepali groups. The Seven-Point Agreement signed in November 2011 allocates more space for these marginalised groups through a state policy revision. In 2016, after a long-drawn process, Nepal adopted the country's first constitution drawn up on a consensus basis. Certain clauses of the constitution have led to further grievances among and protests by the minority communities. Therefore, the conflict background in which Sarwanam works, has undergone different phases. Yet, the country is relatively stable. Sarwanam has been active in the struggle for democracy in the country since early 1980's and consequently, throughout the Maoist insurgency.

Sarwanam's direct engagement with conflict issues through an alternative theatre form, sets it apart from other case studies and makes its contributions valuable to the book. Sarwanam has developed its own alternative theatre form in addition to using proscenium and street theatre. This theatre form is a stylised adaptation of street theatre that emphasises symbolic gestures and uses minimal props. Both these factors enhance the accessibility of Sarwanam plays. Using minimal props makes theatre more affordable. Strong emphasis on symbolic gestures and mime can break through language barriers and as such, Sarwanam perceives its alternative theatre to embody democracy and freedom. The group travels to perform in the regional districts of Nepal every year to reach a broader audience. According to the group records, there are over 50 affiliated theatre groups established in various communities practicing theatre for social justice.

The case studies bring in different perspectives and are yet connected through certain underpinning elements. Eliciting these enables the conceptualisation of how theatre works for peacebuilding and formulating the central argument of this book. The elements involved in the process also warrant a close examination.

Multi-voiced and Dialogic Form of Theatre

This book offers a conceptualisation of how theatre works for peacebuilding. To do so, it advances a two-fold argument: a conceptual argument and an empirical argument. It contends that the multivocal and dialogical nature of theatre is particularly well suited to express local complexities, and open up possibilities of communication between parties and narratives in conflict; thus creating an important precondition for sustainable peace. The case studies extend this conceptual argument to the empirical level, each demonstrating the aptness of theatre in a different way: Jana Karaliya creates a space where parties and narratives in conflict can come together in Sri Lanka. Jana Sanskriti uses theatre to bring out prevalent but less heard narratives of structural violence in India. Sarwanam makes excluded citizens' perspectives a part of the public discourse on conflict in Nepal.

Multivocality and the dialogic are important elements in theatre, as pointed out by a number of scholars. These elements come to the fore in eliciting underlying theories of change in theatre. Mark Chou speaks of a form of multivocality that contains deep democratic potential in its "ability to publicise multiple realities, actors and actions", capable of challenging the existing political order.[43] Dialogic, as Paulo Friere argues, is at the base of self-empowerment and transformation. This book builds upon these insights and suggests that theatre's capacity for peacebuilding is enhanced due to the multivocality and the dialogic inherent in its form.

This book establishes that multivocality facilitates expression of different and/or contradictory points of view in peacebuilding. Multivocality can bring out less heard voices, issues and groups into the public space of theatre; it can bring contradictory histories and narratives of conflicting groups face to face. The expression enabled through multivocality is of key importance when there is inadequate space for representation and integration for marginalised groups within the mainstream social politics.[44] Such expression can lead to healing and reconciliation at community level, becoming a crucial step towards nonviolent engagement with the "other."

The dialogic of theatre takes this expression forward: Bakhtin presents the dialogic as a feature of social discourse that is particularly relevant to the arts. It is recognised as a notion that is at the core, and facilitates the articulation of the processes embodied by theatre for social intervention.[45] The dialogic, as the book proceeds to establish through the case studies, takes what is expressed through the multivocality of theatre forward to a point of disquiet, learning, contemplation or empathy, from where the sustainable social action emerges. Multivocality starts from the expression on the stage, and together with the dialogic, it draws in the audience, making it a community activity. The voices that are expressed are not only the voices of the actors: it is a representation of the community, and it encourages the audience to express their voices, experiences and lifeworlds on and off stage. The ensuing dialogue is not limited to the stage. It takes place between and among all these different voices, continuing beyond the time and space of the performance. Communication within theatre goes beyond the vocal and is more powerful due to its emotional element. The multivocality and the dialogic of theatre facilitate peacebuilding to reach dimensions that are difficult to attain through the prevalent approaches.

Contributions and Disclaimers

The contributions of this book are twofold: It contributes to the academic discipline as well as the practice of peacebuilding. The systematic study addresses the need for an in-depth empirical study on local theatre groups that work for peacebuilding. It documents three longstanding and active theatre groups in South Asia, working in different conflict contexts, analyses the group processes and offers a conceptualisation of how theatre works for peacebuilding. In identifying the multi-voiced and dialogic form of theatre as a key element in peacebuilding through theatre, this book also offers a possible framework for the practitioners interested in using theatre for peacebuilding. Therefore, it contributes to the practical application of theatre for peacebuilding. This is but one-way of framing the contribution of art and in no way do I mean that this is conclusive, or even comprehensive. I merely offer a starting point that invites us to genuinely recognise the contributions the arts can make as a peacebuilding approach, and deepen our understanding of using the arts.

Though this book predominantly engages with using the arts for peacebuilding, it is important to acknowledge the risks of romanticising theatre. Theatre or art by and of itself does not necessarily imply peacebuilding. It is simply a tool that can be used either way—for peace or for war.

Theatre can be and has been used for pro-war causes. Just like any other form of art, theatre too has a history of being used to serve political purposes. While political theatre is a somewhat mild category resulting from this particular use of theatre, the category of agitprop or propaganda theatre offers clearer examples. Take "Holy Defense Theatre," a category of propaganda theatre emerging during the Iran–Iraq war as state sponsored productions that glorified the Iranian stance in the war and its soldiers.[46] Another example comes from Sri Lanka: the Tamil theatre artist K. Sithamparanathan used agitprop to mobilize people around the struggle for Tamil rights in the late 1980's. As the artist himself acknowledges, at that time, they performed to rally people around the cause of the rebel fighters.[47] As a member who worked closely with this group in the early 2000's confides, their theatre festivals focused on "healing the suppressed Tamil psyche and often were coerced to prepare and strengthen people's morale for war by the rebels."[48] There are ample instances where theatre was used to promote violence. Theatre is simply a malleable tool at the hands of the practitioner, and depending on how it is used, can be violent or peaceful. I acknowledge this aspect of theatre. Having done that, I purposely set out to look at the role of theatre when it is intentionally used for positive social transformation.

This book explores the relationship the theatre groups and the particular theatre forms they use have with the local context. It does not look at the politics or the relationship between locally inspired and externally introduced forms of theatre. Doing so is beyond the scope of this book. Therefore, while the book does explore such theatre forms, it does not explore this particular relationship. The groups showcased here are firmly rooted in their local contexts, being conceptualized, led and owned by people at the ground level.

Finally, this book does not claim these cases to be representative of South Asia. Rather, my only claims regarding representation are limited to highlighting the diversity of approaches and practices that exist in the use of theatre for peacebuilding.

Structure of the Book

The book has a total of five chapters that are organised into two parts: Part I conceptualises theatre for peacebuilding through existing literature and Part II presents the case studies and extends the discussion.

Part I: Conceptualising Theatre for Peacebuilding

Chapter 2 argues that engaging with the complexities in the conflict context and addressing the cultural impact of conflict is a prerequisite to sustainable peacebuilding. It looks at peacebuilding and its critiques, exploring key and relevant debates in peacebuilding literature. It provides an overview of the development of peacebuilding and the critical issues it faces at the moment.

Chapter 3 sets up why theatre warrants further study as an important but neglected area in peacebuilding. It explores theatre's potential and limitations for peacebuilding. Firstly, it presents conceptual evidence that theatre can contribute to peacebuilding. Secondly, it looks at the specific ways in which theatre can contribute to peacebuilding, including how multivocality and the dialogic relates to theatre. It proposes the multivocality and dialogic of theatre as key elements in theatre's potential as a peacebuilding approach and as such, warranting further study.

Part II: Exploring Theatre in Local Peacebuilding Processes

Chapter 4 focuses on the role of Jana Karaliya as a theatre group working for peacebuilding in Sri Lanka. It argues that theatre creates a space where parties and narratives in conflict can come together. The chapter first outlines the background of the ethnic conflict and fragile stability in Sri Lanka, and proceeds to discuss the ways in which these factors shape Jana Karaliya's activities. As a multi-ethnic, bilingual group borrowing from the Sinhalese and Tamil drama traditions, Jana Karaliya physically and metaphorically blurs the lines of conflict. This shared space created through theatre is where Jana Karaliya's peacebuilding takes place.

Chapter 5 explores the role of Jana Sanskriti as a theatre group working for peacebuilding at the community level in India. This chapter argues that theatre brings out prevalent but the less heard narratives of structural violence into the communal discourse. West Bengal consistently ranks among the highest in violence rates in India and presents a context of highly embedded structural violence. Jana Sanskriti works within this context, taking an embedded approach to address injustices the rural Bengal experiences at an everyday level.

Chapter 6 analyses the role of Sarwanam as a theatre group working for peacebuilding in Nepal, and argues that the group uses theatre to make excluded citizens' perspectives a part of the public discourse on conflict. While the People's Movements in Nepal emerged from the level of the ordinary citizen, the expected outcomes of the negotiated peace that filtered through to the lifeworlds of distant communities is marginal. This chapter also provides a conflict background first and then proceeds to discuss the ways in which Sarwanam uses the multivocality and the dialogic of theatre to highlight these issues.

Finally, the conclusion brings together the main themes of the book, outlining how these ran through the case studies. It elicits possibilities and limitations of theatre as demonstrated through the case studies, and points at some shared elements that are important or challenging in working as theatre groups at the ground level. This section, and the book, conclude having articulated implications for future research in using art for peacebuilding.

Notes

1. See Oliver P. Richmond, *A Post-Liberal Peace* (New York: Routledge, 2011); "Resistance and the Post-Liberal Peace," *Millennium* 38, no. 3 (2010); Roger Mac Ginty, "No War, No Peace: Why So Many Peace Processes Fail to Deliver Peace," *International Politics* 47, no. 2 (2010), for a further discussion.
2. See Erin McCandless, "Lessons from Liberia: Integrated Approaches to Peacebuilding in Transitional Settings" (Occasional paper 161, Institute for Security Studies, 2008).
3. Oliver P. Richmond, "A Genealogy of Peace and Conflict Theory," in *Palgrave Advances in Peacebuilding: Critical Developments and Approaches*, ed. Oliver P. Richmond (Basingstoke: Palgrave Macmillan, 2010).
4. "A Genealogy of Peace and Conflict Theory," in *Palgrave Advances in Peacebuilding: Critical Developments and Approaches*, ed. Oliver P. Richmond (Basingstoke: Palgrave Macmillan, 2010), 17.
5. Oliver P. Richmond, "Introduction," in *Palgrave Advances in Peacebuilding: Critical Developments and Approaches*, ed. Oliver P. Richmond (Basingstoke: Palgrave Macmillan, 2010), 23–25.
6. Jenny Hughes, James Thompson, and Michael Balfour, *Performance in Place of War* (Calcutta: Seagull Press, 2009).
7. Ibid.
8. Jason Franks and Oliver P. Richmond, "Coopting Liberal Peace-Building: Untying the Gordian Knot in Kosovo," *Cooperation and Conflict* 43, no. 1 (2008); Markus Fisher, "The Liberal Peace: Ethical, Historical, and Philosophical Aspects," in *BCSIA Discussion Paper 2000–07* (Kennedy School of Government: Harvard University, 2000).
9. Ho-Won Jeong, ed., *Approaches to Peacebuilding* (New York: Palgrave Macmillan, 2002).
10. Richmond, "A Genealogy of Peace and Conflict Theory," 31.
11. Kora Andrieu, "Civilizing Peacebuilding: Transitional Justice, Civil Society and the Liberal Paradigm," *Security Dialogue* 41, no. 5 (2010).

12. David Roberts, "Beyond the Metropolis? Popular Peace and Post-Conflict Peacebuilding," *Review of International Studies* 37, no. 5 (2011).
13. See ibid.; Oliver P. Richmond, "A Post-Liberal Peace: Eirenism and the Everyday," *Review of International Studies* 35, no. 3 (2009).
14. Stephen Baranyi, ed., *The Paradoxes of Peacebuilding Post-9/11* (Stanford, CA: Stanford University Press, 2008).
15. Rama Mani, "Women, Art and Post-Conflict Justice," *International Criminal Law Review* 11, no. 3 (2011).
16. Ellen Dissanayake, *What Is Art For?* (Seattle: University of Washington Press, 1990).
17. See Jacques Ranciere, *Aesthetics and Its Discontents*, trans. Steven Corcoran (Cambridge: Polity Press, 2009); *The Politics of Aesthetics*, trans. Gabriel Rockhill (New York: Continuum, 2004).
18. Girma Negash, "Art Invoked: A Mode of Understanding and Shaping the Political," *International Political Science Review* 25, no. 2 (2004).
19. Paul Richards, *Fighting for the Rain Forest. War, Youth & Resources in Sierra Leone.* (Oxford: James Currey, 1996), 3.
20. Elise Boulding, *Building a Global Civic Culture: Education for an Interdependent World* (New York: Teachers College Press, 1990).
21. John P. Lederach, *Building Peace: Sustainable Reconciliatin in Divided Societies* (Washington, DC: U.S. Institute of Peace, 1997).
22. Roland Bleiker, *Aesthetics and World Politics* (Basingstoke: Palgrave Macmillan, 2009), 11.
23. Anna M. Agathangelou and Lily H. M. Ling, *Transforming World Politics: From Empire to Multiple Worlds* (New York: Routledge, 2009), 109.
24. Ibid.
25. See Alex Danchev and Debbie Lisle, "Introduction: Art, Politics, Purpose," *Review of International Studies* 35, no. 4 (2009); Negash, "Art Invoked: A Mode of Understanding and Shaping the Political"; Debbie Lisle, "The Art of International Relations," *International Studies Review* 12, no. 4 (2010).
26. See Hughes, Thompson, and Balfour, *Performance in Place of War*; Cynthia E. Cohen, Roberto Gutiérrez Varea, and Polly O. Walker, eds., *Acting Together: Performance and the Creative Transformation of Conflict: Volume 1: Resistance and Reconciliation in Regions of Violence* (Oakland, CA: New Village Press, 2011); James Thompson, *Performance Affects: Applied Theatre and the End of Effect* (Basingstoke: Palgrave Macmillan, 2009).
27. Jonathan White and Cynthia Cohen, "Strengthening Work at the Nexus of Arts, Culture and Peacebuilding" (Search for Common Ground & The Program in Peacebuilding and the Arts at Brandeis University, February 13, 2012), 4.

28. Julie Beadle-Brown et al., "Imagining Autism: Feasibility of a Drama-Based Intervention on the Social, Communicative and Imaginative Behaviour of Children with Autism," *Autism* (Published online ahead of print, 13 September 2017). Available at 10.1177/1362361317710797 (Accessed 02 January 2018); Nicola Shaughnessy, "Opening Minds: The Arts and Developmental Psychopathology," in *The Wiley Handbook of Developmental Psychopathology*, ed. Luna C. Centifanti and David M. Williams (Hoboken, NJ: John Wiley & Sons Ltd, 2017); Lisa Richardson et al., "Imagining Autism: Evaluation of a Drama Based Intervention for Children with Autism-the Views of Teachers and Parents," *JARID. Journal of Applied Research in Intellectual Disabilities* 27, no. 4 (2014).
29. Cohen, "Creative Approaches to Reconciliation," 23.
30. Kennedy Chinyowa, "Emerging Paradigms for Applied Drama and Theatre Practice in African Contexts," *Research in Drama Education* 14, no. 3 (2009).
31. Hughes, Thompson, and Balfour, *Performance in Place of War*; Cohen, Varea, and Walker, *Acting Together: Performance and the Creative Transformation of Conflict: Volume 1: Resistance and Reconciliation in Regions of Violence; Acting Together: Performance and the Creative Transformation of Conflict: Volume 2: Building Just and Inclusive Communities* (Oakland, CA: New Village Press, 2011).
32. Bleiker, *Aesthetics and World Politics*.
33. White and Cohen, "Strengthening Work at the Nexus of Arts, Culture and Peacebuilding," 3–4.
34. Caroline Hughes, Joakim Öjendal, and Isabell Schierenbeck, "The Struggle Versus the Song—The Local Turn in Peacebuilding: An Introduction," *Third World Quarterly* 36, no. 5 (2015).
35. Mani, "Women, Art and Post-Conflict Justice," 550.
36. The research on Sri Lankan chapter draws from previous research I conducted with the group initially in 2007. I met with the group at least once a year from then on, and the chapter draws from insights and information gathered during this period as well as the data collected during fieldwork in 2012.
37. The LTTE, later labelled as a terrorist group, declared itself as the sole representative of the Tamils.
38. Jonathan Goodhand, "Stabilising a Victor's Peace Humanitarian Action and Reconstruction in Eastern Sri Lanka," *Disasters* 34, no. s3 (2010): 351.
39. Kristine Höglund and Camilla Orjuela, "Hybrid Peace Governance and Illiberal Peacebuilding in Sri Lanka," *Global Governance* 18, no. 1 (2012).

40. Helen Nicholson, *Applied Drama: The Gift of Theatre* (Basingstoke: Palgrave Macmillan, 2005), 16–63.
41. Janasanskriti, "Janasanskriti Centre for Theatre of the Oppressed: About Us," Janasanskriti, http://www.janasanskriti.org/aboutus.html.
42. Astri Suhrke, "Virtues of a Narrow Mission: The Un Peace Operation in Nepal," *Global Governance* 17, no. 1 (2011).
43. Mark Chou, *Greek Tragedy and Contemporary Democracy* (New York: Bloomsbury Academic, 2012), 52. See also Donald J. Mastronarde, *The Art of Euripides: Dramatic Technique and Social Context* (Cambridge, UK: Cambridge University Press, 2010) for a relevant discussion.
44. See Chou, *Greek Tragedy and Contemporary Democracy*, 52 for a detailed discussion on how multivocality in tragedy contributes to democracy.
45. Anthony Jackson, "The Dialogic and the Aesthetic: Some Reflections on Theatre as a Learning Medium," *Journal of Aesthetic Education* 39, no. 4 (2005).
46. Marjan Moosavi, "Dramaturgy in Post-Revolution Iran: Problems and Prospects," in *The Routledge Companion to Dramaturgy*, ed. Magda Romanska (New York: Routledge, 2014).
47. See Madhawa Palihapitiya, "The Created Space: Peacebuilding and Performance in Sri Lanka," in *Acting Together: Volume I*, ed. Cynthia E. Cohen, Roberto Gtierrez Varea, and Polly O. Walker (Oakland, CA: New Village Press, 2011).
48. Sivagopal Anandan (former Pongu Thamil leader), interview with author, Sri Lanka, June 2014 (pseudonym used).

References

Agathangelou, Anna M., and Lily H. M. Ling. *Transforming World Politics: From Empire to Multiple Worlds*. New York: Routledge, 2009.

Andrieu, Kora. "Civilizing Peacebuilding: Transitional Justice, Civil Society and the Liberal Paradigm." *Security Dialogue* 41, no. 5 (2010): 537–58.

Baranyi, Stephen, ed. *The Paradoxes of Peacebuilding Post-9/11*. Stanford, CA: Stanford University Press, 2008.

Beadle-Brown, Julie, David Wilkinson, Lisa Richardson, Nicola Shaughnessy, Melissa Trimingham, Jennifer Leigh, Beckie Whelton, and Julian Himmerich. "Imagining Autism: Feasibility of a Drama-Based Intervention on the Social, Communicative and Imaginative Behaviour of Children with Autism." *Autism* (Published online ahead of print, 13 September 2017). Available at https://doi.org/10.1177/1362361317710797 (Accessed 02 January 2018).

Bleiker, Roland. *Aesthetics and World Politics*. Basingstoke: Palgrave Macmillan, 2009.

Boulding, Elise. *Building a Global Civic Culture: Education for an Interdependent World*. New York: Teachers College Press, 1990.
Chinyowa, Kennedy. "Emerging Paradigms for Applied Drama and Theatre Practice in African Contexts." *Research in Drama Education* 14, no. 3 (2009): 329–46.
Chou, Mark. *Greek Tragedy and Contemporary Democracy* [in English]. New York: Bloomsbury Academic, 2012.
Cohen, Cynthia, Roberto Gutiérrez Varea, and Polly O. Walker, eds. *Acting Together: Performance and the Creative Transformation of Conflict: Volume 1: Resistance and Reconciliation in Regions of Violence*. Oakland, CA: New Village Press, 2011.
———, eds. *Acting Together: Performance and the Creative Transformation of Conflict: Volume 2: Building Just and Inclusive Communities*. Oakland, CA: New Village Press, 2011.
Danchev, Alex, and Debbie Lisle. "Introduction: Art, Politics, Purpose." *Review of International Studies* 35, no. 4 (2009): 775–79.
Dissanayake, Ellen. *What Is Art For?* Seattle: University of Washington Press, 1990.
Fisher, Markus. "The Liberal Peace: Ethical, Historical, and Philosophical Aspects." In *BCSIA Discussion Paper 2000–07*. Kennedy School of Government: Harvard University, 2000.
Franks, Jason, and Oliver P. Richmond. "Coopting Liberal Peace-Building: Untying the Gordian Knot in Kosovo." *Cooperation and Conflict* 43, no. 1 (2008): 81–103.
Goodhand, Jonathan. "Stabilising a Victor's Peace Humanitarian Action and Reconstruction in Eastern Sri Lanka." *Disasters* 34, no. s3 (2010): 342–67.
Höglund, Kristine, and Camilla Orjuela. "Hybrid Peace Governance and Illiberal Peacebuilding in Sri Lanka." *Global Governance* 18, no. 1 (2012): 89–104.
Hughes, Caroline, Joakim Öjendal, and Isabell Schierenbeck. "The Struggle Versus the Song—The Local Turn in Peacebuilding: An Introduction." *Third World Quarterly* 36, no. 5 (2015): 817–24.
Hughes, Jenny, James Thompson, and Michael Balfour. *Performance in Place of War*. Calcutta: Seagull Press, 2009.
Jackson, Anthony. "The Dialogic and the Aesthetic: Some Reflections on Theatre as a Learning Medium." *Journal of Aesthetic Education* 39, no. 4 (2005): 104–18.
Janasanskriti. "Janasanskriti Centre for Theatre of the Oppressed: About Us." Janasanskriti. http://www.janasanskriti.org/aboutus.html.
Jeong, Ho-Won, ed. *Approaches to Peacebuilding*. New York: Palgrave Macmillan, 2002.
Lederach, John P. *Building Peace: Sustainable Reconciliatin in Divided Societies*. Washington, DC: U.S. Institute of Peace, 1997.

Lisle, Debbie. "The Art of International Relations." *International Studies Review* 12, no. 4 (2010): 656–57.
Mac Ginty, Roger. "No War, No Peace: Why So Many Peace Processes Fail to Deliver Peace." *International Politics* 47, no. 2 (2010): 145–62.
Mani, Rama. "Women, Art and Post-Conflict Justice." *International Criminal Law Review* 11, no. 3 (2011): 543–60.
Mastronarde, Donald J. *The Art of Euripides: Dramatic Technique and Social Context*. Cambridge, UK: Cambridge University Press, 2010.
McCandless, Erin. "Lessons from Liberia: Integrated Approaches to Peacebuilding in Transitional Settings." Occasional paper 161, Institute for Security Studies 2008: 1–20.
Moosavi, Marjan. "Dramaturgy in Post-Revolution Iran: Problems and Prospects." In *The Routledge Companion to Dramaturgy*, edited by Magda Romanska, 68–74. New York: Routledge, 2014.
Negash, Girma. "Art Invoked: A Mode of Understanding and Shaping the Political." *International Political Science Review* 25, no. 2 (2004): 185–201.
Nicholson, Helen. *Applied Drama: The Gift of Theatre*. Basingstoke: Palgrave Macmillan, 2005.
Palihapitiya, Madhawa. "The Created Space: Peacebuilding and Performance in Sri Lanka." In *Acting Together: Volume I*, edited by Cynthia E. Cohen, Roberto Gtierrez Varea, and Polly O. Walker, 73–95. Oakland, CA: New Village Press, 2011.
Ranciere, Jacques. *The Politics of Aesthetics*. Translated by Gabriel Rockhill. New York: Continuum, 2004.
———. *Aesthetics and Its Discontents*. Translated by Steven Corcoran. Cambridge: Polity Press, 2009.
Richards, Paul. *Fighting for the Rain Forest. War, Youth & Resources in Sierra Leone*. Oxford: James Currey, 1996.
Richardson, Lisa, Beadle-Brown Julie, David Wilkinson, Nicola Shaughnessy, Melissa Trimingham, Jennifer Leigh, Beckie Whelton, and Julian Himmerich. "Imagining Autism: Evaluation of a Drama Based Intervention for Children with Autism-the Views of Teachers and Parents." *JARID. Journal of Applied Research in Intellectual Disabilities* 27, no. 4 (2014): 343.
Richmond, Oliver P. "A Post-Liberal Peace: Eirenism and the Everyday." *Review of International Studies* 35, no. 3 (2009): 557–80.
———. "A Genealogy of Peace and Conflict Theory." In *Palgrave Advances in Peacebuilding: Critical Developments and Approaches*, edited by Oliver P. Richmond, 14–38. Basingstoke: Palgrave Macmillan, 2010.
———. "Introduction." In *Palgrave Advances in Peacebuilding: Critical Developments and Approaches*, edited by Oliver P. Richmond, 1–13. Basingstoke: Palgrave Macmillan, 2010.

———. "Resistance and the Post-Liberal Peace." *Millennium* 38, no. 3 (2010): 665–92.
———. *A Post-Liberal Peace*. New York: Routledge, 2011.
Roberts, David. "Beyond the Metropolis? Popular Peace and Post-Conflict Peacebuilding." *Review of International Studies* 37, no. 5 (2011): 2535–56.
Shaughnessy, Nicola. "Opening Minds: The Arts and Developmental Psychopathology." In *The Wiley Handbook of Developmental Psychopathology*, edited by Luna C. Centifanti and David M. Williams, 61–86. Hoboken, NJ: John Wiley & Sons Ltd, 2017.
Suhrke, Astri. "Virtues of a Narrow Mission: The Un Peace Operation in Nepal." *Global Governance* 17, no. 1 (2011): 37–55.
Thompson, James. *Performance Affects: Applied Theatre and the End of Effect*. Basingstoke: Palgrave Macmillan, 2009.
White, Jonathan, and Cynthia Cohen. "Strengthening Work at the Nexus of Arts, Culture and Peacebuilding." Search for Common Ground & The Program in Peacebuilding and the Arts at Brandeis University, February 13, 2012.

PART I

Conceptualising Theatre for Peacebuilding

CHAPTER 2

Peacebuilding and Its Critiques

The theory as well as the practice of peacebuilding evolved over several phases. Having come into mainstream practice after the Cold War, peacebuilding today is a key agenda for foreign aid, international organisations, and non-governmental organisations. It works in diverse settings, driven by changing political objectives. Theoretical underpinnings of peacebuilding, therefore, constantly evolve in response to a range of sociopolitical contexts.

This chapter outlines two main trends in key debates to peacebuilding: peacebuilding as statebuilding and peacebuilding as societybuilding. These two camps arguably capture the extensive deliberations on peacebuilding in the recent period. Though there is some overlap between these approaches and the resulting critiques, discussing the key debates in peacebuilding under these two broad themes is helpful in providing a conceptual overview.

The critiques of each approach help further clarify the distinction. The criticisms of peacebuilding as statebuilding have been longstanding, characterised by an exclusive focus on top-down political processes. Consequently, approaching peacebuilding as statebuilding has gained increasing attention. This also has its drawbacks. As the chapter proceeds to illustrate, we are still at the early stages of exploring and outlining a more sustainable approach to peacebuilding.

The chapter starts with a brief summary of prevailing approaches to peacebuilding. The evolving conceptualisation of peacebuilding serves as an entry point to introduce the two main approaches in key debates to peacebuilding: statebuilding and societybuilding. The second and third sections discuss each approach along with their respective critiques and challenges. Drawing from and building upon the society building approach, the chapter proceeds to identify and discuss the parameters of an approach that can address these challenges.

Peacebuilding: Conceptualisation and Key Debates

Peacebuilding has been defined and conceptualised in a number of ways by different authors, but is yet to gain a commonly agreed upon definition. The large scope of actions involved in the process of peacebuilding and the differences of opinion regarding when, where, and how it is practiced, makes providing a definition a difficult task. The evolving definitions, however, capture the tension within the discipline.

As a starting point, let us take the definition provided by Boutros Boutros-Ghali in 1992. He defined peacebuilding as "action to identify and support structures which tend to strengthen and solidify peace to avoid a relapse into conflict."[1] This definition assumes and implies that strong structures are a prerequisite for peace, and places strengthening such structures at the core of peacebuilding. The particular structures advocated here are liberal democratic, which is why a decade later Roland Paris argues that peacebuilding is "the globalisation of a particular model of domestic governance—liberal market democracy—from the core to the periphery of the international system."[2]

Though it is still largely based on similar ideological principles, the UN's take on peacebuilding has gradually expanded over the years. The UN Secretary-General's Policy Committee provides a relatively broader working definition in its May 2007 deliberations: "Peacebuilding involves a range of measures targeted to reduce the risk of lapsing or relapsing into conflict, to strengthen national capacities at all levels for conflict management, and to lay the foundations for sustainable peace and development." This definition, despite still placing significant emphasis on building and strengthening structures, allows space for the myriad of other activities that fall within peacebuilding. The committee further recognises the steadily increasing call for peacebuilding to be more context-specific. It clearly specifies that "peacebuilding strategies must be coherent and tailored to the specific needs of the country concerned, based on national ownership, and should comprise a carefully prioritised, sequenced and therefore relatively narrow set of activities aimed at achieving the above objectives."[3]

The turn towards "sustaining peace" in 2017 indicates a trajectory that goes beyond the previous notions for peacebuilding in terms of content and implementation timeline. With over fifty percent of the cases relapsing into conflict and others unable to establish sustainable post-conflict socio-economic conditions, the success of the UN peacebuilding missions is debatable.[4] Sustaining peace, therefore, indicates a shift in the UN peacebuilding approach that goes beyond a security discourse towards a more inclusive take. With a focus on a broader range of actors and areas, this conception strives to address some of the challenges that prevalent peacebuilding faces.

Scholars have attempted to offer definitions and add emphasis to certain elements in peacebuilding. In his book *The Moral Imagination: The Art and Soul of Building Peace*, Lederach[5] reminds us of the salience of imagination and creativity in peacebuilding, as well as any other process of social transformation. Notter and Diamond[6] highlight another dimension in defining peacebuilding as "creating the tangible and intangible conditions to enable a conflict-habituated system to become a peace system." They identify three levels of peacebuilding: political, structural and societal. Political peacebuilding includes the formal processes aiming for political agreements. Structural peacebuilding sits below this level, focusing on the establishment of physical as well as social structures, institutions and behaviour patterns. Finally, social peacebuilding is a grassroots process and engages with the relationship-building component.

These recurrent attempts at conceptualising peacebuilding capture the emerging tension in the discipline: the tension between seeing structures as the focal point, and the call for shifting the focus towards local peacebuilding approaches that are more contextual. The chapter discusses these tensions under two broad themes: peacebuilding as statebuilding and peacebuilding as society building.

Peacebuilding as Statebuilding

Peacebuilding as statebuilding is increasingly discussed within the discipline of peace and conflict studies. As separate concepts that can stand on their own, peacebuilding and statebuilding do not wholly overlap.[7] Nevertheless in practice, a given set of standard patterns and activities characterise mainstream approaches to peacebuilding and international statebuilding.[8]

The statebuilding approach to peacebuilding takes a strong state as a prerequisite for peace. Consequently, it focuses on establishing or strengthening state institutions, with the expectation that the said institutions will effectively deal with conflict. This focus follows from the predominantly Western-led notion where a weak or a failed state is seen to be at the root of security issues. The peace instituted through this approach, consequently, is located in a "security discourse" that rests largely on avoiding "state failure."[9]

Accordingly, the statebuilding approach to peacebuilding works through security, political or democratic, and socioeconomic aspects to build peace. There are specific tasks involved in each aspect[10]: disarming, demobilising and reintegrating combatants into society, military and police reforms, addressing refugee issues and de-mining are seen as central to security transition. Establishing a system of elections and the supporting legislative and judiciary bodies is the primary action for democratic transition, which is complemented by encouraging a strong civil society. Socioeconomic transition aspires for the promotion of a thriving market economy in the stable space resulting through the previous actions. Some scholars identify transitional justice mechanisms as a fourth category that engages with social reconciliation.[11] This, despite gaining increasing attention, is yet to be seen as essential as the other three aspects within the statebuilding approach to peacebuilding.

The statebuilding approach assumes the system or social stability can be ensured through rationalising key aspects of social relations through a hierarchical state structure.[12] State-society relations are legitimised and enhanced through state institution and capacity building. Societal structures as well as relationships are assumed to be products of state institutions; not only at the formal level, but also at the informal level.[13] This is sound at a conceptual level. Nevertheless, the outcome of peacebuilding here relies on having a functional, reciprocal, and receptive state-society relationship.

The statebuilding approach to peacebuilding fails to address and accommodate the culture and complexities of local contexts. The chapter discusses these debates through three key areas: Firstly, the exclusive focus on liberal democratic institutions as the primary solution for conflict. Secondly, disregarding context-specific socio-economic organisation and thirdly, the unequal power relations embedded in statebuilding.

Though these critiques often arise in relation to the practice of peacebuilding, the tensions leading to these critiques fall largely within the statebuilding approach to peacebuilding.

Exclusive Focus on Liberal Democratic Institutions

The state institutions on which the statebuilding approach to peacebuilding relies are based on liberal democratic values. The statebuilding approach to peacebuilding works on the premise that constructing and/or stabilising state institutions is the most direct route for managing and resolving conflicts. These state institutions are constituted by a combination of liberal and democratic values, leading contemporary peace operations to be generally referred to as liberal peacebuilding. The potential of this approach is in the "symbiosis of its components," or the ways in which specialised forms of liberalism and democracy work together to jointly produce a particular form of peace.[14] These conceptual frameworks highlight the individual as the target social unit, and operate from a Western human rights discourse. Liberalism, in turn, encourages an open economic policy. The resulting notion of peace takes for granted not only the symbiosis between liberalism and democracy, but also the assumptions made under the democratic peace thesis—that promoting liberal forms of statebuilding is the preferred path to ensure international peace, for liberal states to refrain from warring with each other.[15]

There is growing concern and dissent around the effectiveness of this formula. The basic framework of statebuilding is critiqued at three levels: peacebuilding through building/strengthening institutions, promoting democratic procedures and liberal economic policies.

Institution Building

The exclusive focus on institution building in the statebuilding approach to peacebuilding can come at the cost of ignoring the root causes of conflict. Protracted conflicts often suffer divisions along social elements such as ethnicity or identity, and/or indicate power imbalances and structural injustices. Transforming these root causes is key for the actual resolution of conflict. The re-establishment of formal institutions and legal processes alone is insufficient in such cases. Thus, designing appropriate political institutions that can effectively mitigate conflict within ethnically plural societies remains a challenge within the statebuilding approach.

The current debate revolves around the two broad models of consociational (power sharing) and centripetal (integrative) institutions.[16] Despite the finer points of the recommended models, liberal democratic values still frame the institutions established under statebuilding.

The emphasis statebuilding places on re-establishing or stabilising state structures through institutions indicates a top-down perspective of peace. It often necessitates "expert intervention" from the outside, working in tandem with the state level representatives. If state institutions are not truly representative of the community at the ground level—as it so often is the case in conflict situations—this can have serious consequences, ranging from an inaccurate representation of communities to outright discrimination.

Some scholars call for prioritising institution building before democratization and privatisation, as a response to the challenges faced by the statebuilding approach. Newman observes that when societies do not "enjoy stable institutions," democracy is "arguably adversarial or even conflictual."[17] This period of stabilising the institutions can be indefinite. Further, continued external involvement poses a critical challenge to the local ownership of the peacebuilding process. Devoid of genuine local representation and participation, waiting for stable institutions to emerge hardly appears feasible.

Stable political order leading to peace does not necessarily emerge from legislative frameworks or institution building.[18] Accordingly, the strong emphasis placed upon institution building at the cost of ignoring the underlying social root causes of conflict, hints at the lack of sensitivity in the statebuilding approach towards the local conditions.

Democratisation

Democratisation has become a key component of statebuilding in contemporary peacebuilding approaches. The notion that political organisation has to be—in fact, can only be—legitimised through an electoral process is generally accepted within prevailing peacebuilding practices.[19]

However, given that externally led liberal democracy building is counterproductive, this assumption becomes problematic. Pushing through the democratic agenda as the primary solution, runs the risk of being oblivious to the ground level realities and preparedness in taking part in the decision making process. Depending on the existing demographic composition and the conflict dynamics of a given context, it can even be harmful. Elections can, more often than not, further inflame and politicise the conflict, if local politicians manipulate the divisions for short-term political gain. Democratic procedures can also aggravate socio-economic problems, instead of resolving them as expected.[20]

Thus, democratic procedures as they are, hold little actual promise for the communities in post-conflict settings. To be useful, the electoral process has to take place on a foundation that believes in and respects the rights of the individuals. The history of a conflict makes this long-term ideal almost impossible to achieve within the limited time period assigned by international peace builders.

A key issue with democratic practices is its tendency to silence minority voices. By placing the voice of the majority over the minority, democratic procedures implemented through statebuilding erode plurality. Thus, statebuilding results in an initial suppression of existing heterogeneity in favour of creating a homogenous whole.[21] It leads critics to perceive the liberal peacebuilding approach more as a "system of governance" than as a "process of reconciliation."[22] This mismatch between the so-called democratic governance and the needs and wants of the local community is evident in the diminishing electoral participation witnessed in many post-conflict situations.[23]

Thus, we cannot see democratic procedures such as elections as an end point; it is just the beginning of a process that is much longer. As Amartya Sen notes, a country does not become "fit *for* democracy", but "fit *through* democracy."[24] The latter is a process-oriented approach that indicates the gradual participatory development towards stability. The statebuilding approach is widely criticised for prioritising democratic procedures as a sole indicator of a successful conflict transformation process.

Liberal Economic Policies

Introducing liberal economic policies as a foundational strategy of statebuilding also draws a significant amount of critique. Peacebuilding as statebuilding relies on the introduction of liberal economic policies along with democratic procedures to ensure a stable societal and economic transition. Critics argue that this often has a markedly negative impact upon the communities at the ground level.[25] Hughes, Thompson and Balfour observe that the introduction of free market economies along with democratic reforms, profoundly threaten ground level peace initiatives that can bring a sustainable culture of peace for local communities.[26] Fischer argues that this approach challenges established relationship networks and patterns, leading to a sense of alienation and loss of community.[27] It unsettles the local economic practices that might be more or less sustainable; it disrupts the community trading patterns; and it opens the local markets and the community to external competition in goods and services. Drawing from empirical studies, Moore points out that liberal values result in the intensification of division instead of bridging the divides as expected.[28] This state of disorder intensifies if democratic practices are unable to address grievances at the ground level.

Even though the statebuilding approach to peacebuilding unquestioningly accepts the co-existence of liberal values with democratic procedures, the relationship between these two phenomena are asymmetrical.[29] Liberal practices imply democratic institutions but democracy, in turn, limits liberal values. As discussed in the previous section, it allows the majority's will to outrank that of the minorities' at different levels, eroding diversity. Thus, rushing for free markets and democracy soon after a conflict—without the required long-term resources and agenda to ensure it is fully embraced—can destabilise a fragile post-conflict situation. Therefore, introducing liberal democratic policies and establishing state institutions as recommended through the statebuilding approach to peacebuilding does not necessarily result in the expected self-regulating stable state, or consequently, in building peace.

Disregard Local Forms of Organisation

The statebuilding approach fails to give due recognition to the local context. A key area where this becomes visible is its disregard for local socio-political and economic organizations.

The statebuilding approach to peacebuilding places an assumed universal formula upon the conflict context, irrespective of the existing socio-political and economic organizations. The resulting disregard and lack of accommodation towards the local forms of socio-political and economic organization is a legacy of the liberal framework upon which statebuilding is based. The role of the local is to accept the offered transition. Local ownership, in the liberal peacebuilding narrative, is expected to be nothing more than acquiescing to and, in the end, owning what has been produced and marketed by the international actors.[30] In the guise of ownership, the local is told what its interests are, irrespective of the context-related differences.[31] This assumed universality is hardly neutral. Mac Ginty aptly observes this specific form of peacebuilding to reflect "the practical and ideological interests of the global north."[32] The liberal rhetoric it promotes is seen as the ideology upon which the social, political and economic structures happen to rest,[33] rather than a unique production of a specific socio-economic-cultural and political context.

Another negative of the statebuilding approach to peacebuilding—located specifically within the liberal approach—is the limit it imposes on alternative forms of representation. The liberal framework encompasses social, economic, and political spheres through its components such as liberal democracy, human rights, a centralized secular state, and a global market economy. Space for alternative modes of representation within this ideological web is severely limited.[34] Seen in opposition to the "universally appropriate" values and norms of liberal peacebuilding, different ways of organizing society are deemed "morally inferior."[35] This view marginalizes and hinders the space for other forms of representation.

The "inferiority" assigned to the local culture, in opposition to the "universality" of liberal values in the statebuilding approach to peacebuilding, leads to the justification of outside interventions. Culture became a "vital framing" tool to justify interventions in 1990s, which led to the legitimization of interventions through the liberal peace rhetoric.[36] This indicates that cultural differences within the statebuilding framework are often seen as part of the problem. By default, the statebuilding approach to peacebuilding disregards context-specific socio-economic and political organizations in favour of a liberal framework. Consequently, it is widely critiqued as a delimiting framework, instead of being emancipatory or transformatory.

Despite repeated calls for flexibility, the feasibility of satisfactorily incorporating context-specific socio-political and economic organization methods within statebuilding remains dubious. As discussed, peacebuilding as statebuilding is increasingly critiqued for its disregard of local contexts. The feasibility of attempting to effectively incorporate local approaches within the statebuilding approach as a component of the larger liberal framework is also questionable. Just as the peacebuilding approaches developed in the North reflect its dominant worldview of democracy and liberalism, local peacebuilding approaches reflect the local ways of seeing and meaning-making. To utilize authentic local approaches to peace, it is important to genuinely contextualise these approaches within their respective conflict contexts. Unfortunately, the attempts at paying heed to the local is often limited to a minor complementary role, run within or parallel to an overarching liberal peacebuilding mission. Therefore, local peacebuilding initiatives within the liberal statebuilding framework result in an uncomfortable hybrid. The authenticity of such initiatives, sponsored by liberal peace agents, is questionable in terms of how much they have been amended to fit in with the norms and values of the organizations and governments in the global north.[37] The end result is an overall failure that is often conveniently associated with local peacebuilding approaches. Thus, a genuine attempt at incorporating local approaches calls for an overall strategy that embodies and reflects the context-specific socio-economic and political organization.

Unequal Power Relations

Another factor problematizing the statebuilding approach to peacebuilding is its embedded power inequalities. Increasing awareness of the significance of accommodating and including the local culture and practices in peacebuilding, raises questions on the extent to which this is possible within liberal peacebuilding. Embedded power hierarchies in the statebuilding approach maintain unequal power relations. The political and resource hierarchies associated with statebuilding make this apparent.

Statebuilding approach places the state at the top of its political hierarchy as the key stakeholder of the conflict. The resulting action plan is top-down. Post-conflict contexts often lack the institutional balances required to ensure that citizens receive fair representation from their state. More often than not, the state itself is part of the problem, playing a key role in curbing the voices of local groups and undermining the ethical responsibilities of a democratic state.[38] By making such states and their components an essential part of the strategy for peace, the statebuilding approach creates a problematic power hierarchy in conflict contexts.

The authority associated with liberal peace is another factor that triggers unequal power relations within the statebuilding model. The external actors enter from power positions. This power derives from the material resources and international standing of the proponents of liberal peacebuilding. Mac Ginty goes so far as to note that the "moral authority" of liberal peace stems from "the power of its promoters, the intellectual heritage" deployed to justify their peace interventions, "and the co-option of major international organisations and international NGOs [non-governmental organisations] in the service of this vision of peace" as well as from the success it has had in delivering "humanitarian and development assistance."[39] Thus, the international peace builders wield a significant amount of overt and covert power in deciding some aspects of the peacebuilding process. The type of activities undertaken, target beneficiaries, implementation timeline and evaluation of programmes are a few examples.

It is hard to bridge this power difference between the local context and the international push for liberal peacebuilding, since the former does not have access to the sources of power on which the international draw. Cultural authority is a main source of power accessible for the local context. However, as discussed earlier, this is often co-opted within the statebuilding framework. Thus, the statebuilding approach for peacebuilding maintains a "hierarchy of compliance" running from the international to the local, with the national state in the middle.[40]

The unequal power relations embedded within peacebuilding as statebuilding jeopardises the possibility of achieving self-sustaining peace in post-conflict contexts. The statebuilding approach to peacebuilding often works to constitute and maintain asymmetrical power relations in the local context, including existing systems of political hierarchy. It is seen as a process that reinforces the positions of existing power-holders, while doing little for the emancipation of people at the ground level.[41] Scholars raise concerns citing concrete examples of where this power hierarchy comes into play in the process of implementing reforms by international officials through authoritarian means.[42] Peacebuilding has come to mean restructuring the structures and institutions that led to conflict, and this in turn invariably leads to a decrease in sovereignty.[43] Scholars agree that there is no way of doing this without resembling or replicating the colonisation process. Hence, statebuilding makes its subjects comply with an "anti-democratic" process bound to a state and institutions that fail to satisfactorily represent the local.[44] Inevitably, statebuilding undermines the local strengths and result in further weakening the state institutions it means to strengthen.[45] Consequently, the statebuilding approach to peacebuilding struggles to bring self-sustaining peace.

Inability to Address Local Complexities

This discussion on peacebuilding as statebuilding emphasises a central point: that peace instituted through the statebuilding approach runs the risk of being fragile and is at best, temporary. The reasons for this are arguably the attempts to impose a universal formula and the inability to address local complexities. The features of statebuilding discussed earlier in this chapter relate to this: The first—statebuilding's exclusive focus on establishing liberal democratic institutions as a solution results in imposing a universal formula. The second and the third—disregard towards context specific alternative socio-political organisation and unequal power relations embedded in societybuilding—contribute to the approach's inability to address local complexities.

The statebuilding approach focuses on superimposing a standard set of ethics, values, and practices upon the conflict context, irrespective of local realities. Even if we leave aside the assumed universality of the liberal rhetoric and its components such as liberal democracy, human rights, a centralized secular state, and entering into a global market economy for a moment, and consider statebuilding as a neutral tool kit, it may not be the best form of structuring a society divided by conflict. In its attempts to address the existing conflicts, it can intensify competition and cut off the limited support structures accessible to communities at the ground level. Most post-war societies suffer from a lack of resources and capacities. Implementing and maintaining the required political institutions in such an environment also makes post-war democratisation—despite being possible—extremely rare.[46] Since liberal democracy instituted through statebuilding is hardly an organic form of governance, sustaining a healthy liberal democratic state on the ground becomes difficult.

The peace instituted through statebuilding is hardly self-sustaining, for it cannot satisfactorily address complexities in conflict context. Lasting grievances and cultural residues of conflict at the ground level are examples for such complexities. Cessation of violence—voluntary or enforced—does not necessarily mean transformation of the conflict. Transformation requires addressing the root causes of a conflict that often stems from unequal or discriminating power relations at an everyday level. The superficial peace brought through statebuilding can neither be satisfactory nor lasting. In fact, it is more likely to further inflict damage by reinforcing existing power relations through statebuilding. The resulting intensification of the root causes of and factors that maintain the conflict, can lead to an escalated level of violence. The cost of peacebuilding through statebuilding is immediately seen and felt within the informal everyday reality of the citizen. For many citizens in post-conflict situations the everyday—despite on-going peacebuilding activities—remains underdeveloped, poor, violence-ridden, and challenging in terms of intergroup relations.[47] The statebuilding approach to peacebuilding is unequipped to address communal or intergroup violence.[48] Critics point towards the focus on formal statebuilding to be the reason for this failure. Peacebuilding through statebuilding, therefore, runs the risk of jeopardizing the fragile peace in post-conflict situations.

Thus, at best, the statebuilding approach to peace and its liberal associations connect with negative peace: a strategy that addresses the manifestation of conflict, while avoiding the deeper changes imperative for the transformation of conflict.[49] Scholars agree that statebuilding efforts often fail to deliver a satisfactory state or sustainable peace and suggest that it is time peacebuilding looked beyond statebuilding—and liberalism—for approaches that can go deeper than a surface level, negative peace.[50] The call for improving prevalent approaches to peacebuilding requires a shift in the focus of the ideological framework and practice of peacebuilding.

Peacebuilding as Societybuilding

Coined in opposition to statebuilding, societybuilding is the other main approach to peacebuilding. Societybuilding is increasingly discussed as an approach with the potential to bring about self-sustaining peace legitimised within a conflict context. It is developed as an "intellectual counterweight" to the prominent statebuilding focus in contemporary peacebuilding, with the capability of addressing its gaps.[51] The societybuilding approach to peace is called "communitarian in character," for it emphasises the significance of the local society and traditions in arriving at understandings of and determining the legitimacy of a particular version of political organisation, justice, or ethics for that particular context.[52] Unlike statebuilding, which focuses on the political process and advocates universally apt and desirable liberal practices and institutions as the primary avenues for peace, societybuilding focuses on working with the community. It aims for a bottom-up approach to peacebuilding. A social peace process is needed to restore fragmented relationships and develop a shared sense of community, togetherness, and responsibility, in envisioning the future.[53] Societybuilding aims to rebuild exactly this; a sense of society and social legitimacy for a peace process at the ground level. Thus, it is apparent that the discussion on peacebuilding as societybuilding is a significant point in the peacebuilding discourse.

In exploring the key debates on societybuilding, we need to pay attention to how these regard the local context and their capacity to address societal residues of conflict. As the discourse on societybuilding is still emerging, there are a number of areas warranting further study. The critiques of peacebuilding as statebuilding highlight the need to go beyond liberal democratic values and state centricity. It urges the discipline to ensure that the local context and ensuing meaning-making processes are acknowledged and respected. Thus, the societybuilding approach aims to address the need for a bottom-up method, that does not rely on international-local power hierarchies to coerce, leading peacebuilding towards positive peace instead of negative peace. These are the paths that peacebuilding—as a discipline and a practice—needs at the moment. All these revolve around an important point: that of taking into account the particularities of the local context and the need to satisfactorily address socio-cultural residues of conflict.

This chapter specifically look at three key debates on developing local representation and sustainability of peacebuilding: the call for peacebuilding to focus on people and thus, arguably, on civil society; the call to make "everyday politics" the focal point of peacebuilding rather than "high politics" and finally, the need to draw from the hitherto marginalised socio-political landscape.

Civil Society as the Mode of Representation

The societybuilding approach argues that the focus of peacebuilding has to shift from state politics to social politics: it proposes rebuilding post—conflict societies through working with the people in the local context.

The commonly proposed approach is that of working through local civil society. Civil society is seen as a space that represents the local and as such, bridges the community with the international. This is also the apparatus through which a cohesive political community—placed at the core of self-sustaining peace—can be mobilised. Civil society is generally perceived to be essential for legitimising the key values of prevailing peacebuilding approaches, such as democracy and human rights. Some scholars go so far as to argue that civil society must become the "foremost tool" in rearticulating peacebuilding.[54] Thus, the society-building approach recommends shifting the locus of peacebuilding to civil society.

The role of civil society as the primary voice of the local political community is problematic at least in two points, especially within the current understanding of the term: the capacity of civil society and its ethical standing. Complicity within the local-international power hierarchies and elite participation, restricts civil society's capacity to reach into the lifeworlds of people on ethical grounds. It is questionable whether civil society has the capacity to represent authentic lifeworlds of the local. Nevertheless, external donors tend to overestimate the capacity of civil society organisations in constituting peace. It is not uncommon to regard civil society as a "feature of western democracy promotion strategies" that plays a key role in defining the nature of peace processes in the post-Cold War period.[55] In a similar vein, Kappler and Richmond note that peacebuilding usually relies on a particular type of civil society that aligns with the norms and values of statebuilding approach and is somewhat free of ethno-nationalism.[56] Even when it is free of ethno-nationalism it does not necessarily represent a people's voice. As post-conflict situations demonstrate, civil society often comprises of the urban elite. In a society divided along class, ethnic and social lines, this "artificially created and externally funded civil society" can be "just as exclusive to wider participation as a government."[57] Thus, the dynamics that lead political elite in post-conflict situations to be compromised applies to this civil society as well. Liberal peacebuilding has become a source for creating and enriching this transnational group of elites.[58] Continuing to work through this group that is not really rooted in the local context, is a key reason for the disjuncture between what is being undertaken as peacebuilding and the perception of the wider community.

Thus, a mere transfer of focus from the institutions and economics to civil society is insufficient to transcend the ideology associated with statebuilding. Civil society in average has become a space that perpetuates a set of given Western ideologies instead of mobilising genuine political community. Chandler places the centrality of civil society to international peacebuilding in its compliance with the external values and influences that further extend the prevalent peacebuilding discourse.[59] As he argues, civil society is not the autonomous sphere of decision-making it is articulated to be; its accountability and loyalty is more attuned to the funding agencies and the global west than the community experiencing the conflict. Going further, Richmond claims that the "local" as seen, appealed to and accepted within the prevailing discourse of peacebuilding is largely a part of Western civil society's imaginary,[60] rendering civil society to "western normative veneer" meant to supersede the existing community at the ground level.[61] Thus, instead of an authentic representation, the existing civil society offers a compromised viewpoint made palatable for the international experts. Instead of acting as a bridge to the larger community, it works as an insular circle limited to the social elites. Consequently, assuming civil society as a universal force for good is problematic, and it is inadequate for providing an authentic representation of the local.

To move beyond the pitfalls of the statebuilding approach, societybuilding approach has to look deeper than the normative civil society as an apparatus. For instance, a politically-aware citizen's organisation has to be able to engage with the deep divisions that exist in a given context: such organisational forms have to be capable of bringing together the divided groups for a unified goal, with a shared vision for the future. While we cannot dispense of civil society, we can ensure that it represents the general population going beyond the transnational elite groups.

Tar's definition of civil society provides a workable starting point: "the participatory space between the formal apparatus of the state and informal settings of families and atomised individuals, whereby groups emerge to forge associational ties, articulate interests and participate in public affairs."[62] This definition emphasises the significance of self-organisation at the ground level and opens up the top layer of civil society to look at the more grassroots community-based groups. Considering the civil society as a space for co-creating a shared vision, instead of "handing down" a pre-defined formula is key here.

Communicative Action

Communicative action is an important aspect of articulating an appropriate civil society engagement within the societybuilding approach to peace. Andrieu proposes using Jürgen Habermas's concept of communicative action as a strategy to promote intercommunal reconciliation.[63] Here, the use of communicative reason is seen as a platform that can enhance coexistence and participation in the public sphere, leading to the eventual constitution of a shared lifeworld that is more conducive to peace. As numerous peacebuilding efforts around the world demonstrate, the primary challenge facing contemporary peacebuilding is not that of setting up a government or governing procedures, but that of getting people's support for these frameworks. Working within the community lifeworld can bring about ground level legitimisation for the peace process that will otherwise be an alien imposition upon the community. Such a process can, at best, elicit the multiple visions of future that exist at the ground level and work with these to create a cohesive vision of governance. At worst, it can allow the process to continue until the ground transforms into a cohesive voice that aligns with the proposed structures.

Dialogue at the ground level that arrives at a shared understanding between the parties, is vital for a self-sustaining peace in post-conflict situations. Achieving this is difficult due to the lack of intragroup dialogue and the collective insecurity about engaging with each other. In a post-conflict setting where fear, mistrust, and anger towards the other prevail, a process of dialogue that deconstructs the existing negative images and encourages positive attitudes towards each other is necessary. In identity-based or ethnic conflicts, this necessity is further emphasised. At the early stages in such a context, intergroup reconciliation led by a transformation in the emotional cultures of conflict pushes peace forward far more than structural changes can. Breaking through the stereotypes and identities created in opposition to each other over an extended period facilitates empathy, which in turn allow the parties to hear each other. This is the beginning of creating new identities that are no longer antagonistic.[64]

For effective communication leading to sustainable peacebuilding, we need to reach beyond the surface of a community. While recognising the need to go beyond taking the urban elites as people's representatives, scholars such as Yordan and Andrieu still locate the focus of statebuilding on the civil society. While this may seem an appropriate action in comparison with the statebuilding approach, it is insufficient. In order to reach into the community, communicative reason has to reach the people themselves and not just an upper echelon of society that often bends and distorts the message to suit their needs. Cohesive political community is necessary: but we need to seek it at the margins of the existing civil society, instead of at the centre. Thus, continuing peacebuilding within the prevalent discourse in fact hinders bringing about the transformation of emotional cultures required for sustainable conflict resolution.

We need to examine different peacebuilding approaches that allow us to reach into and draw from the community consciousness. This is where communicative reason comes to the fore. Habermas argues that the colonising tendencies of society, driven by strategic reason such as that of statebuilding, have eroded the integrative capabilities of the lifeworld in which we live. Therefore, to effect change through the lifeworld—the milieu of society in which we live—requires that we revive the vibrancy of the lifeworld. Instead of merely focusing on civil society, the societybuilding approach to peace has to take the community at large as its focus. Working with that widespread, vague mass of people has the potential to infuse vibrancy back into the lifeworld. For this, societybuilding needs peacebuilding approaches that can work at an everyday level while being firmly rooted within the context. It has to come from the lifeworld and carry out its work within the lifeworlds of individuals. It has to be able to reach people where they are and touch them at that point, instead of attempting to fit them into a framework that is already in place. Thus, the societybuilding approach to peace needs to focus on and be able to work with the lifeworlds of people in order to initiate self-sustaining peace.

A Lens of "Everyday" Politics

The debate on taking everyday politics as the focal point of peacebuilding is an important discussion pertinent to the societybuilding approach to peace. Proponents of the societybuilding approach to peace consider adopting a lens of everyday politics to be crucial. Some even go so far as to call the failure to focus on the question of everyday a "particularly blind spot" of contemporary peacebuilding.[65] While the decisions pertaining to peacebuilding might be made at the upper level of political processes, the actual work of peacebuilding is inevitably carried out among the ground level communities. These are the people who have to undergo a transformation of their political views and ideologies in order to coexist with their former enemies. The decisions made at the political level often fail at the stage of practical application if the communities are unwilling to go through with the proposed transformation. The focus on the ground level is therefore vital. An everyday lens puts the top-level negotiations back in perspective.

Adopting an everyday lens contributes to peacebuilding in three ways. It ensures that peacebuilding emerges through a local meaning-making process. It avoids the tendency of peacebuilding to either romanticise or essentialise the local, and it recognises and works through the agency and power of the everyday. Discussing each point in turn enables us to understand the role that everyday politics has come to play in the contemporary debates on peacebuilding.

Adopting an everyday lens ensures that peacebuilding works within the lifeworlds of the local and emerge as a result of everyday politics rooted in local meaning making. The social transformation of conflict requires a transformation of individual lifeworlds. Lifeworld is constituted, expressed and reshaped through everyday encounters. To work within the lifeworld for peace, peacebuilding needs to take everyday politics as its focal point. International Relations as a discipline is critiqued for its exclusion of the everyday, and the agency and interests of the communities and individuals who together form a state. Richmond defines the concept of "everyday" as "a space in which local individuals and communities live and develop political strategies in their local environment, towards the state and towards international models of order."[66] It is often "transversal and transnational, engaging with needs, rights, custom, individual, community, agency and mobilisation in political terms."[67]

It is important to note that the concept of "everyday" is different from the civil society found within prevalent peacebuilding discourse: the everyday level goes beyond civil society to represent a "deeper local-local" that consists of actual people behind the structured layers.[68] This space, therefore, is closer to the ground level and provides access to the lifeworlds of people. Here, there is space for the immediate expression of plurality and otherness at the same time, and is a source of collective creativity that facilitates the transcendences or change of existing conditions.[69] Thus it becomes a powerful analytical tool for peacebuilding. By taking everyday politics as the focal point instead of high politics at the state level, peacebuilding ensures that peace emerges through a local meaning-making process. It is an imperative for a self-sustaining peace.

Adopting a lens of everyday also facilitates reaching the local without being trapped in either essentialising or romanticising the local. Both these are commonly seen in peacebuilding debates. As discussed earlier in this chapter, prevailing approaches to peacebuilding continue to put forth a limited understanding of the local and local ownership in peacebuilding. Yet, others call for embracing the "pure", "traditional" practices of the local. These camps respectively essentialise and romanticises the local, preventing productive engagement with existing ground level conditions. The local is a complex entity that does not comply with narrow fixed definitions. The agency of the local manifests in different ways and indicates a range of divisions along power hierarchies.[70] Taking the everyday as the focus of peacebuilding calls for us to acknowledge the diverse nature of the local while avoiding any implied prejudices and inaccuracies.

Yet another reason to adopt an everyday lens is the acknowledgement of subtle forms of agency and power at the local level. This is crucial for a solid foundation for peace. Being the actual ground upon which citizenship rights are exercised, politics at the everyday level avoids the narratives of power and authority that privilege the elite, institutional, and state levels.[71] Individual actions in the everyday are free from hegemonic institutions and are too fleeting in nature to be categorized.[72] This transiency or flexibility is exactly what holds the power and agency in the everyday: it is fast, exercises agency in the present moment, and resists being pinned down. Not being institutionalised subverts the power associated with institutions, for the everyday politics has a decisive power to shape, stand up to, or approve institutions and strategies.[73] Unlike a fixed mandate, it can derive from the context and adapt to fit situations where it would not otherwise be accepted. Thus everyday politics are resourceful, makeshift and can bide their time.[74] This resilience produces a capacity to struggle for a just social order that goes beyond the capabilities of international liberal peace. In the act of conscious choosing, agency is exercised. It is a gradual process that leads to conscious political mobilisation through subtle actions of resistance and reconstitution.[75] Such a peace brought through the solidarity and the sense of community resulting from a shared lifeworld in the everyday is stronger than that which is brought through an external initiative. This approach to peace highlights the agency and power of individuals and communities. We, therefore, need to rethink how and where we perceive power and agency in peacebuilding; and the respective exclusions and inclusions this entails within the peacebuilding process.[76]

A shift in the focus of peacebuilding towards people and the community in general, and adopting an everyday lens in specific, can make peacebuilding sustainable. Scholars perceive that a focus on the people and communities will surpass that of state and institutions, providing alternatives that enable us to avoid the pitfalls and biases of liberal peace.[77] By focusing on people and society, peacebuilding reorients itself to deal with residual social and emotional cultures of conflict as well. Thus, everyday peacebuilding potentially holds a significant place in the societybuilding approach to peace.

Searching the Margins

Searching the margins of existing socio-political landscape for more sustainable approaches to peacebuilding is another suggestion within key debates of peacebuilding. Scholars note that it is important to go beyond and broaden the existing avenues of expression and identification, if we are to escape from the limiting, inflexible boundaries of the discipline of International Relations and the interests protected by these boundaries.[78] This opening up is especially relevant when it comes to peacebuilding as the process of peacebuilding calls for forging anew the fractured relationships in a given community. In the four generational model of peacebuilding outlined in the Introduction of this book, Richmond locates the "next big step" in peacebuilding at the margins of the peacebuilding discourse and practice.[79] It invites putting communities before institutional peace and focusing on the grassroots and the "most marginalised members" of the society, in order to address the shortcomings of contemporary peacebuilding approaches. Opening up to the so far overlooked local political, economic, social, and cultural traditions, and letting these direct the peacebuilding process instead of international agendas, is important within this framework. In the search for a more effective form of peacebuilding, the focus of peacebuilding turns towards what has so far been at its margins.

The margins here can point in two directions: at a conceptual level, the intersection of different disciplines with peacebuilding provides a fertile ground for exploration. From an empirical perspective, the intersection of local and international spheres holds potential.

Intersection of Different Disciplines

The transdisciplinary resources at the boundaries of peacebuilding hold much potential for the societybuilding approach. The disciplines of Political Science and International Relations largely encompass peacebuilding at the moment. These boundaries are reflected in the state-centric international approach to peacebuilding. Yet, complexities of violent conflicts cannot be adequately understood solely through these boundaries. Therefore, as the statebuilding approach amply demonstrates, addressing conflicts within the limited uni-disciplinary approaches is not feasible.[80] Peace encompasses different aspects of life and society at different depths. The discipline of peace and conflict resolution also has to embody this plurality to move towards and produce an authentic reflection of peace. To achieve this, we need to transcend the existing disciplinary boundaries. Such a transdisciplinary approach, drawing from and freely moving between the boundaries of different disciplines, associates with the principles of "empathy, creativity and integrated problem solving"[81]—features that are hard to see within the prevalent approaches to peacebuilding. Thus, the intersection of different disciplines at the boundary of peacebuilding provides a rich source to draw from in constituting a societybuilding approach to peace.

Different authors have pointed towards specific disciplines that can enrich peacebuilding: Spencer notes that due to the lack of attention given within the discipline of peace and conflict studies to everyday politics, literature on everyday politics has re-emerged at the boundaries of anthropology, post-colonial studies and sociology.[82] As fully-fledged disciplines focusing on societies, these hold much potential for insights. Richmond suggests the adoption of specific tools developed within these disciplines—namely discourse analysis and ethnography—as these facilitate access to everyday life. The politics of agency highlighted through these disciplines can provide different lenses to peacebuilding that has the capacity to address its existing weak points. Thus, exploring the intersection of different disciplines with that of peacebuilding holds much promise in shaping the societybuilding approach to peace.

Intersection of Local and International

The practices that take place at the intersection of local and international in peacebuilding are increasingly being seen and recognised as a rich ground for articulating a sustainable approach to peacebuilding. Exploring this hybrid space can meaningfully contribute to a societybuilding framework. Articulation of a post-liberal peace acknowledges the potential in this activity. Richmond observes that post-liberal peacebuilding "rescues and reunites" the liberal and the local, without aiming to "depoliticise the local or remove politics from the international."[83] The aim of post-liberal peace as he defines it, is to "highlight the evolving relations" between the local and international. This is apt, for given the pervasiveness of liberal practices and peacebuilding it is unlikely to expect an untouched local. Its material power and authority shapes not only peacebuilding frameworks at the international level, but also the language and the discipline along its preferred notion of peacebuilding.[84]

Thus, the principles of liberal peace have touched all actors in peacebuilding to varying extents. These power differences between the local and international results in an asymmetrical relationship. Hybridity emerges through this unequal partnership[85] resulting in unique forms of pressure and ways of interrelating. Exploring these particular forms of hybridity emerging in post-conflict situations allow us to recognise the agency and participation of the local, from an angle that has received little attention in peacebuilding so far. It encompasses a range of context-specific responses to liberal peace that provides a starting point for articulating a more self-sustaining peace. This hybridity is most visible at the margins of liberal peace that have remained "blind spots of the liberal peace" so far.[86] We need to explore the margins of peacebuilding where the local meets liberal for hybrid forms of peace that result in self-sustaining local initiatives.

Exploring the hybrid spaces at the intersection of the local and international reveals the agency of the local in shaping and claiming the process of peacebuilding. This is also referred to as resistance or contestation of the liberal model. Acknowledging local agency undermines the narratives about the local being powerless in the face of external intervention. It recognises the communities at the margins as active agents with the power to control, shape and ascribe meaning to the external frameworks that enter their arena. This reinterpretation and control indicate resistance. It entails a conscious choice and rejection of specific values and visions associated with the liberal peace package; cooperating with certain aspects of it while rejecting, ignoring or subverting other aspects.[87] Thus, it emerges from active agency stemming from the local population. These practices of subversion are at times seen as a negotiated hybridity between the local and the international. This negotiated hybridity can be seen as both a means and an end to successful peacebuilding.[88] However, these activities of resistance are highly context-specific and culturally bound, and therefore may not be visible for an external observer unfamiliar with the context. Thus, it is imperative to study the hybrid spaces and the forms of resistance in them from perspectives within the local itself.

The level of hybridity visible at different contexts could greatly vary. It might be less visible in contexts where there are strong liberal peace networks and frameworks in place, than in contexts where there is more space for discussion and acceptance for local forms of peacebuilding and participation. Mac Ginty proposes that hybrid peace emerges through the interstice between four factors: "ability of liberal peace agents to enforce acceptance of liberal peace, ability of liberal peace agents to incentivise local engagement with the liberal peace, ability of local actors to ignore, resist and subvert the liberal peace and the ability of local actors to present alternatives to the liberal peace."[90] The capacity for local resistance or subversion again depends on certain factors: "the extent to which local actors retain power during a liberal peace transition, the extent to which external actors are dependent on local actors …, the extent to which national, regional and local institutions are intact in the wake of a violent conflict, and the extent to which local actors … can marshal resources."[90] The first and last factors are seen as crucial in determining the level of hybridity in a society.[91] The constant flux into which the conflict contexts are often thrown into also accelerates hybridity. Exploring the different levels at which hybridity occurs will facilitate insights into its way of working.

Adopting a hybrid lens has much to offer to articulate a self-sustaining peace that can effectively deal with the complexities and socio-cultural residues of conflict. It can counter the power inequality in the peacebuilding discourse by helping us move beyond the underpinning binaries such as "liberal-non-liberal [or traditional], peace-war, developed-underdeveloped,"[92] towards more accurate understandings of a globalised society. This deeper understanding is necessary for us to recognise power relations and local agency at the ground level. The "unscripted conversations"[93] between the local and international, which Richmond sees as necessary for a future generation of peacebuilding, takes place within this hybridity. Adopting a hybrid lens requires putting communities first rather than institutional peace, and focusing on the grassroots and those who are most marginalised in the society.[94] The concept of hybridisation allows us to see the blowback suffered by the liberal peace. Neither does liberal peace always set the agenda nor the local actors always comply. Instead, local actors are able to use the liberal peace and the resources attached to it for their own agendas that might deviate from that of the prevalent approaches. The resistance of local actors and the hybrid forms of peace emerge through these interactions. Exploring these in-between spaces that have not been at the centre of peacebuilding discourse is necessary for the articulation of an approach to peacebuilding that can effectively counter the gaps of prevalent approaches. The intersection of different disciplines at the boundaries of peacebuilding needs to be acknowledged as a resource, studied along with the intersection of local and international in the existing peacebuilding initiatives. These hybrid platforms facilitate organic forms of peacebuilding that emerge through local meaning making processes.

The tension between the statebuilding and societybuilding approaches to peace stand at the centre of the key debates in peacebuilding. Recently, there are increasing calls for a shift in the focus of peacebuilding towards an analytical and empirical focus that refrains from privileging external actors, and instead focuses on examining the relationship between the local and external actors.[95] As a result, debates under the societybuilding approach are gaining prominence.

This chapter outlined selected areas within societybuilding approach that are key in further developing the concept. While varying and spanning different dimensions, these areas stand upon a shared foundation: the recognition and emphasis accorded to authentic engagement with people and communities in conflict contexts. The future approaches rest accordingly on peacebuilding's ability to engage the communities in the process. The sites where culture, community and individuals converge for alternative or complementary approaches to peacebuilding hold potential for articulating a more self-sustaining approach to peace. Exploring the margins of peacebuilding for initiatives that emerge from and are driven by the locals—instead of the local elite—is important in this process.

The key debates in peacebuilding have arrived at a critical stage: the prevalent approaches to peacebuilding pushing for liberal democratic procedures through statebuilding have repeatedly failed, resulting in a call for either being replaced or reformulated. The societybuilding approach indicates potential, but requires further exploration and development. It needs to draw from and emulate approaches and practices existing at the margins of peacebuilding, firmly situated within the local-international hybrid, and reflect societybuilding's fundamental feature of working within the community. For articulating the future directions of peacebuilding, we need to explore work that transgresses the prevailing boundaries of peacebuilding and the leadership, and particularities of a new discipline will arise in the resulting transdisciplinary spaces. Adopting new analytical layers that counter romanticised and essentialist understandings of the local and hybrid structures while delivering more complex understandings of the same, and studies that generate empirical evidence are important to arrive at this future vision.[96] The next chapter will explore theatre as a possible direction.

Notes

1. Boutros Boutros Ghali, "An Agenda for Peace. Preventive Diplomacy, Peacemaking and Peace-Keeping. Report of the Secretary-General Pursuant to the Statement Adopted by the Summit Meeting of the Security Council on January 31, 1992" (New York: United Nations, 1992).
2. Roland Paris, "International Peacebuilding and the *'Mission Civilisatrice'*," *Review of International Studies* 28, no. 4 (2002).
3. Erin McCandless, "Lessons from Liberia: Integrated Approaches to Peacebuilding in Transitional Settings" (Occasional paper 161, Institute for Security Studies, 2008).
4. Alvaro de Soto and Graciana del Castillo, "Obstacles to Peacebuilding Revisited," *Global Governance* 22, no. 2 (2016).
5. John P. Lederach, *Building Peace: Sustainable Reconciliatin in Divided Societies* (Washington, DC: U.S. Institute of Peace, 1997).
6. James Notter and Louise Diamond, *Building Peace and Transforming Conflict: Multi-Track Diplomacy in Practice*, Occassional Paper 7 (Washington, DC: Institute for Multi-Track Diplomacy, 1996).
7. See Susanna Campbell and Jenny H. Peterson, "Statebuilding," in *Routledge Handbook of Peacebuilding*, ed. Roger Mac Ginty (New York: Routledge, 2013) for a detailed discussion on the points where the concepts of statebuilding and peacebuilding converge into and diverge from each other's path.
8. "Statebuilding," in *Routledge Handbook of Peacebuilding*, ed. Roger Mac Ginty (New York: Routledge, 2013), 338.
9. "Statebuilding," 336.
10. Constanze Schellhaas and Annette Seegers, "Peacebuilding: Imperialism's New Disguise?," *African Security Review* 18, no. 2 (2009).
11. Richard Jackson, "Post-Liberal Peacebuilding and the Pacifist State," *Peacebuilding* 6, no. 1 (2018).
12. Carlos L. Yordán, "Towards Deliberative Peace: A Habermasian Critique of Contemporary Peace Operations," *Journal of International Relations and Development* 12, no. 1 (2009): 73.
13. David Chandler, "Race, Culture and Civil Society: Peacebuilding Discourse and the Understanding of Difference," *Security Dialogue* 41, no. 4 (2010): 379.
14. Roger Mac Ginty, "No war, no peace: Why so many peace processes fail to deliver peace," *International Politics* 47, no. 2 (2010): 155.
15. See "No war, no peace: Why so many peace processes fail to deliver peace," *International Politics* 47, no. 2 (2010) for a detailed discussion.

16. Adam Moore, *Peacebuilding in Practice: Local Experience in Two Bosnian Towns* (Ithaka: Cornell University Press, 2013), 18.
17. Edward Newman, "The International Architecture of Peacebuilding," in *Routledge Handbook of Peacebuilding*, ed. Roger Mac Ginty (New York: Routledge, 2013), 322.
18. Jeong, *Approaches to Peacebuilding*, 154.
19. Mac Ginty, "No war, no peace: Why so many peace processes fail to deliver peace," 156.
20. Michael Pugh, "The Political Economy of Peacebuilding: A Critical Theory Perspective," *International Journal of Peace Studies* 10, no. 2 (2005): 25.
21. Jason Franks and Oliver P. Richmond, "Coopting Liberal Peace-Building," *Cooperation and Conflict* 43, no. 1 (2008); Markus Fisher, "The Liberal Peace: Ethical, Historical, and Philosophical Aspects," (Discussion Paper 2000.07, Harvard Kennedy School, MA, 2000).
22. Oliver P. Richmond, "A Geneology of Peace and Conflict Theory," in *Palgrave Advances in Peacebuilding: Critical Developments and Approaches*, ed. O. P. Richmond (Basingstoke: Palgrave Macmillan, 2010), 23–25.
23. Roger Mac Ginty, *International Peacebuilding and Local Resistance: Hybrid Forms of Peace* (Basingstoke: Palgrave Macmillan, 2011), 85.
24. Amartya Kumar Sen, "Democracy as a Universal Value," *Journal of Democracy* 10, no. 3 (1999): 14.
25. See Timothy Donais, *Peacebuilding and Local Ownership: Post-Conflict Consensus-Building* (New York: Routledge, 2012); Moore, *Peacebuilding in Practice: Local Experience in Two Bosnian Towns*; Schellhaas and Seegers, "Peacebuilding: Imperialism's New Disguise?"; Stephen Baranyi, ed., *The Paradoxes of Peacebuilding Post-9/11* (Stanford, CA: Stanford University Press, 2008); and Franks and Richmond, "Coopting Liberal Peace-Building"; Oliver P. Richmond, ed., *Palgrave Advances in Peacebuilding: Critical Developments and Approaches* (Basingstoke: Palgrave Macmillan, 2010).
26. Jenny Hughes, James Thompson, and Michael Balfour, *Performance in Place of War* (Calcutta: Seagull Press, 2009).
27. *Performance in Place of War* (Calcutta: Seagull Press, 2009), 143.
28. Moore, *Peacebuilding in Practice: Local Experience in Two Bosnian Towns*.
29. Fisher, "The Liberal Peace: Ethical, Historical, and Philosophical Aspects."
30. Donais, *Peacebuilding and Local Ownership: Post-Conflict Consensus-Building*, 32.

31. See Eli Stamnes, "Values, Context and Hybridity: How can the insights from the liberal peace critique literature be brought to bear on the practices of the UN Peacebuilding Architecture?" (working paper, Norwegian Institute of International Affairs and Centre for International Policy Studies, University of Ottawa, 2010).
32. Roger Mac Ginty, "Hybrid Peace: The Interaction Between Top-Down and Bottom-Up Peace," *Security Dialogue* 41, no. 4 (2010): 393.
33. Roger Mac Ginty and Oliver Richmond, "Myth or Reality: Opposing Views on the Liberal Peace and Post-War Reconstruction," *Global Society* 21, no. 4 (2007): 493.
34. Mac Ginty, "No war, no peace: Why so many peace processes fail to deliver peace," 156.
35. Stamnes, "Values, Context and Hybridity: How can the insights from the liberal peace critique literature be brought to bear on the practices of the UN Peacebuilding Architecture?," 8.
36. David Chandler, *International Statebuilding: The Rise of Post-Liberal Governance* (London and New York: Routledge, 2010), 175.
37. Roger Mac Ginty, "Gliding the Lily? International Support for Indigenous and Traditional Peacemaking," in *Palgrave Advances in Peacebuilding: Critical Developments and Approaches*, ed. Oliver P. Richmond (Basingstoke: Palgrave, 2010).
38. Oliver P. Richmond, "A Post-Liberal Peace: Eirenism and the Everyday," *Review of International Studies* 35, no. 3 (2009).
39. Mac Ginty, "Hybrid Peace: The Interaction Between Top-Down and Bottom-Up Peace," 399.
40. Ibid.
41. Tim Jacoby, "Hegemony, Modernisation and Post-War Reconstruction," *Global Society* 21, no. 4 (2007); James Mayall, "Security and Self-Determination," in *The Empire of Security and the Safety of the People*, ed. William Bain (Abingdon: Routledge, 2006).
42. Moore, *Peacebuilding in Practice: Local Experience in Two Bosnian Towns*, 28. Also see William Bain, ed., *The Empire of Security and the Safety of the People* (London: Routledge, 2006); David Chandler, ed., *Peace Without Politics?: Ten Years of International State-Building in Bosnia* (Abingdon: Routledge, 2006); Gerhard Knaus and Felix Martin, "Travails of the European Raj," *Journal of Democracy* 14, no. 3 (2003).
43. Michael Pugh, "The Problem Solving and Critical Paradigms," in *Routledge Handbook of Peacebuilding*, ed. Roger Mac Ginty (New York: Routledge, 2013), 21.
44. Richmond, "A Post-Liberal Peace: Eirenism and the Everyday," 562.
45. Moore, *Peacebuilding in Practice: Local Experience in Two Bosnian Towns*. Also see Donais, *Peacebuilding and Local Ownership: Post-Conflict*

Consensus-Building, Michael Barnett and Christoph Zürcher, "The Peacebuilder's Contract: How External Statebuilding Reinforces Weak Statehood," in *The Dilemmas of Statebuilding: Confronting the Contradictions of Postwar Peace Operations*, ed. Roland Paris and Timothy D. Sisk (New York: Routledge, 2009).
46. Ole Jacob Sending, "The Effects of Peacebuilding: Sovereignty, Patronage and Power," in *A Liberal Peace? The Problems and Practices of Peacebuilding*, ed. Susanna Campbell, David Chandler, and Meera Sabaratnam (London: Zed Books, 2011), 71.
47. Mac Ginty, "No war, no peace: Why so many peace processes fail to deliver peace," 146.
48. See Campbell and Peterson, "Statebuilding," 339.
49. Mac Ginty, "Hybrid Peace: The Interaction Between Top-Down and Bottom-Up Peace," 394.
50. Campbell and Peterson, "Statebuilding," 343.
51. Yordán, "Towards Deliberative Peace: A Habermasian Critique of Contemporary Peace Operations," 60.
52. Donais, *Peacebuilding and Local Ownership: Post-Conflict Consensus-Building*, 5.
53. John Brewer, "Sociology and Peacebuilding," in *Routledge Handbook of Peacebuilding*, ed. Roger Mac Ginty (New York: Routledge, 2013).
54. Kora Andrieu, "Civilizing Peacebuilding: Transitional Justice, Civil Society and the Liberal Paradigm," *Security Dialogue* 41, no. 5 (2010): 549.
55. Mac Ginty, "No war, no peace: Why so many peace processes fail to deliver peace," 156.
56. Stefanie Kappler and Oliver Richmond, "Peacebuilding and Culture in Bosnia and Herzegovina: Resistance or Emancipation?," *Security Dialogue* 42, no. 3 (2011): 265.
57. Mac Ginty, "No war, no peace: Why so many peace processes fail to deliver peace," 156.
58. Oliver P. Richmond, "De-Romanticising the Local, De-Mystifying the International: Hybridity in Timor Leste and the Solomon Islands," *Pacific Review* 24, no. 1 (2011): 119.
59. Chandler, "Race, Culture and Civil Society: Peacebuilding Discourse and the Understanding of Difference," 379.
60. Richmond, "De-Romanticising the Local, De-Mystifying the International: Hybridity in Timor Leste and the Solomon Islands," 117.
61. Ibid.
62. Usman A. Tar, *The Politics of Neoliberal Democracy in Africa: State and Civil Society in Nigeria* (New York: Tauris Academic Studies, 2009), 5.

63. Andrieu, "Civilizing Peacebuilding: Transitional Justice, Civil Society and the Liberal Paradigm," 547–48.
64. As Benjamin Broom argues in "Managing Differences in Conflict Resolution: The Role of Relational Empathy," in *Conflict Resolution Theory and Practice: Integration and Application*, ed. Dennis Sandole and Hugo van der Merwe (Manchester: Manchester University Press, 1993), communicative action can establish a foundation of empathy in relation to the conflict parties, which he terms as a "third culture of relational empathy".
65. Donais, *Peacebuilding and Local Ownership: Post-Conflict Consensus-Building*, 153.
66. Oliver P. Richmond, "Resistance and the Post-Liberal Peace," in *A Liberal Peace? The Problems and Practices of Peacebuilding*, ed. Susanna Campbell, David Chandler, and Meera Sabaratnam (London: Zed Books, 2011), 228–29.
67. "Resistance and the Post-Liberal Peace," *Millennium-Journal of International Studies* 38, no. 3 (2010): 670.
68. "Resistance and the Post-Liberal Peace," 228–29.
69. Audra Mitchell, "Quality/Control: International Peace Interventions and 'the Everyday'," *Review of International Studies* 37, no. 4 (2011): 1627.
70. Thania Paffenholz, "Unpacking the Local Turn in Peacebuilding: A Critical Assessment Towards an Agenda for Future Research," *Third World Quarterly* 36, no. 5 (2015).
71. Richmond, "Resistance and the Post-Liberal Peace," 671.
72. "Resistance and the Post-Liberal Peace," 677.
73. Ibid.
74. De Certeau cited in ibid.
75. Ibid.
76. See "A Post-Liberal Peace: Eirenism and the Everyday," 577.
77. Ibid.
78. Anna M. Agathangelou and Lily H. M. Ling, "The House of IR: From Family Power Politics to the Poisies of Worldism," *International Studies Review* 6, no. 4 (2004): 42.
79. Richmond, "A Geneology of Peace and Conflict Theory," 31.
80. Richard Lappin, "Peacebuilding and the Promise of Transdisciplinarity," *International Journal on World Peace* 26, no. 3 (2009): 71.
81. Ibid.
82. Jonathan Spencer, *Anthropology, Politics and the State: Democracy and Violence in South Asia* (Cambridge: Cambridge University Press, 2007).
83. Richmond, "Resistance and the Post-Liberal Peace," 689.
84. Mac Ginty, "Hybrid Peace: The Interaction Between Top-Down and Bottom-Up Peace," 396.

85. Edward Said, *Culture and Imperialism* (London: Vintage, 1994), 230.
86. Richmond, "Resistance and the Post-Liberal Peace," 689.
87. Mac Ginty, "Hybrid Peace: The Interaction Between Top-Down and Bottom-Up Peace," 403.
88. Donais, *Peacebuilding and Local Ownership: Post-Conflict Consensus-Building*, 37.
89. Mac Ginty, *International Peacebuilding and Local Resistance: Hybrid Forms of Peace*, 9.
90. "Hybrid Peace: The Interaction Between Top-Down and Bottom-Up Peace," 402.
91. See *International Peacebuilding and Local Resistance: Hybrid Forms of Peace*, 85.
92. Stamnes, "Values, Context and Hybridity: How can the insights from the liberal peace critique literature be brought to bear on the practices of the UN Peacebuilding Architecture?," 15.
93. Mark R. Duffield, *Development, Security and Unending War: Governing the World of Peoples* (Cambridge: Polity, 2007), 234.
94. Richmond, "A Geneology of Peace and Conflict Theory," 31.
95. Sending, "The Effects of Peacebuilding: Sovereignty, Patronage and Power," 56.
96. Paffenholz, "Unpacking the Local Turn in Peacebuilding: A Critical Assessment Towards an Agenda for Future Research."

References

Agathangelou, Anna M., and Lily H. M. Ling. "The House of IR: From Family Power Politics to the Poisies of Worldism." *International Studies Review* 6, no. 4 (2004): 21–49.
Andrieu, Kora. "Civilizing Peacebuilding: Transitional Justice, Civil Society and the Liberal Paradigm." *Security Dialogue* 41, no. 5 (2010): 537–58.
Bain, William, ed. *The Empire of Security and the Safety of the People*. London: Routledge, 2006.
Baranyi, Stephen, ed. *The Paradoxes of Peacebuilding Post-9/11*. Stanford, CA: Stanford University Press, 2008.
Barnett, Michael, and Christoph Zürcher. "The Peacebuilder's Contract: How External Statebuilding Reinforces Weak Statehood." In *The Dilemmas of Statebuilding: Confronting the Contradictions of Postwar Peace Operations*, edited by Roland Paris and Timothy D. Sisk. New York: Routledge, 2009.
Boutros Ghali, Boutros. "An Agenda for Peace. Preventive Diplomacy, Peacemaking and Peace-Keeping. Report of the Secretary-General Pursuant to the Statement Adopted by the Summit Meeting of the Security Council on January 31, 1992." New York: United Nations, 1992.

Brewer, John. "Sociology and Peacebuilding." In *Routledge Handbook of Peacebuilding*, edited by Roger Mac Ginty, 159–70. New York: Routledge, 2013.

Broom, Benjamin. "Managing Differences in Conflict Resolution: The Role of Relational Empathy." In *Conflict Resolution Theory and Practice: Integration and Application*, edited by Dennis Sandole and Hugo van der Merwe, 97–111. Manchester: Manchester University Press, 1993.

Campbell, Susanna, and Jenny H. Peterson. "Statebuilding." In *Routledge Handbook of Peacebuilding*, edited by Roger Mac Ginty, 336–46. New York: Routledge, 2013.

Chandler, David, ed. *Peace Without Politics?: Ten Years of International State-Building in Bosnia*. Abingdon: Routledge, 2006.

Chandler, David. *International Statebuilding: The Rise of Post-Liberal Governance* [in English]. London and New York: Routledge, 2010.

———. "Race, Culture and Civil Society: Peacebuilding Discourse and the Understanding of Difference." *Security Dialogue* 41, no. 4 (2010): 369–90.

de Soto, Alvaro, and Graciana del Castillo. "Obstacles to Peacebuilding Revisited." *Global Governance* 22, no. 2 (2016): 209–27.

Donais, Timothy. *Peacebuilding and Local Ownership: Post-Conflict Consensus-Building*. New York: Routledge, 2012.

Duffield, Mark R. *Development, Security and Unending War: Governing the World of Peoples*. Cambridge: Polity, 2007.

Fisher, Markus. "The Liberal Peace: Ethical, Historical, and Philosophical Aspects." Discussion Paper 2000.07, Harvard Kennedy School, MA, 2000.

Franks, Jason, and Oliver P. Richmond. "Coopting Liberal Peace-Building." *Cooperation and Conflict* 43, no. 1 (2008): 81–103.

Hughes, Jenny, James Thompson, and Michael Balfour. *Performance in Place of War*. Calcutta: Seagull Press, 2009.

Jackson, Richard. "Post-Liberal Peacebuilding and the Pacifist State." *Peacebuilding* 6, no. 1 (2018): 1–16.

Jacoby, Tim. "Hegemony, Modernisation and Post-War Reconstruction." *Global Society* 21, no. 4 (2007): 521–37.

Jeong, Ho-Won, ed. *Approaches to Peacebuilding*. New York: Palgrave Macmillan, 2002.

Kappler, Stefanie, and Oliver Richmond. "Peacebuilding and Culture in Bosnia and Herzegovina: Resistance or Emancipation?" *Security Dialogue* 42, no. 3 (June 2011): 261–78.

Knaus, Gerhard, and Felix Martin. "Travails of the European Raj." *Journal of Democracy* 14, no. 3 (2003): 60–74.

Lappin, Richard. "Peacebuilding and the Promise of Transdisciplinarity." *International Journal on World Peace* 26, no. 3 (2009): 69–76.

Lederach, John P. *Building Peace: Sustainable Reconciliatin in Divided Societies*. Washington, DC: U.S. Institute of Peace, 1997.

Mac Ginty, Roger. "Hybrid Peace: The Interaction Between Top-Down and Bottom-Up Peace." *Security Dialogue* 41, no. 4 (August 2010): 391–412.

———. "Gliding the Lily? International Support for Indigenous and Traditional Peacemaking." In *Palgrave Advances in Peacebuilding: Critical Developments and Approaches*, edited by Oliver P. Richmond, 347–66. Basingstoke: Palgrave, 2010.

———. "No war, no peace: Why so many peace processes fail to deliver peace." *International Politics* 47, no. 2 (2010): 145–62.

———. *International Peacebuilding and Local Resistance: Hybrid Forms of Peace*. Basingstoke: Palgrave Macmillan, 2011.

Mac Ginty, Roger, and Oliver Richmond. "Myth or Reality: Opposing Views on the Liberal Peace and Post-War Reconstruction." *Global Society* 21, no. 4 (2007): 491–97.

Mayall, James. "Security and Self-Determination." In *The Empire of Security and the Safety of the People*, edited by William Bain. Abingdon: Routledge, 2006.

McCandless, Erin. "Lessons from Liberia: Integrated Approaches to Peacebuilding in Transitional Settings." Occasional paper 161, Institute for Security Studies, 2008: 1–20.

Mitchell, Audra. "Quality/Control: International Peace Interventions and 'the Everyday'." *Review of International Studies* 37, no. 4 (2011): 1623–45.

Moore, Adam. *Peacebuilding in Practice: Local Experience in Two Bosnian Towns*. Ithaca: Cornell University Press, 2013.

Newman, Edward. "The International Architecture of Peacebuilding." In *Routledge Handbook of Peacebuilding*, edited by Roger Mac Ginty, 311–24. New York: Routledge, 2013.

Notter, James, and Louise Diamond. *Building Peace and Transforming Conflict: Multi-Track Diplomacy in Practice*. Occassional Paper 7. Washington, DC: Institute for Multi-Track Diplomacy, 1996.

Paffenholz, Thania. "Unpacking the Local Turn in Peacebuilding: A Critical Assessment Towards an Agenda for Future Research." *Third World Quarterly* 36, no. 5 (2015): 857–74.

Paris, Roland. "International Peacebuilding and the '*Mission Civilisatrice*'." *Review of International Studies* 28, no. 4 (2002): 637–56.

Pugh, Michael. "The Political Economy of Peacebuilding: A Critical Theory Perspective." *International Journal of Peace Studies* 10, no. 2 (2005): 23–42.

———. "The Problem Solving and Critical Paradigms." In *Routledge Handbook of Peacebuilding*, edited by Roger Mac Ginty, 11–24. New York: Routledge, 2013.

Richmond, Oliver P. "A Post-Liberal Peace: Eirenism and the Everyday." *Review of International Studies* 35, no. 3 (July 2009): 557–80.

———. "A Geneology of Peace and Conflict Theory." In *Palgrave Advances in Peacebuilding: Critical Developments and Approaches*, edited by Oliver P. Richmond, 14–38. Basingstoke: Palgrave Macmillan, 2010.

———, ed. *Palgrave Advances in Peacebuilding: Critical Developments and Approaches*. Basingstoke: Palgrave Macmillan, 2010.

———. "Resistance and the Post-Liberal Peace." *Millennium-Journal of International Studies* 38, no. 3 (2010): 665–92.

———. "De-Romanticising the Local, De-Mystifying the International: Hybridity in Timor Leste and the Solomon Islands." *Pacific Review* 24, no. 1 (2011): 115–36.

———. "Resistance and the Post-Liberal Peace." In *A Liberal Peace? The Problems and Practices of Peacebuilding*, edited by Susanna Campbell, David Chandler, and Meera Sabaratnam, 226–44. London: Zed Books, 2011.

Said, Edward. *Culture and Imperialism*. London: Vintage, 1994.

Schellhaas, Constanze, and Annette Seegers. "Peacebuilding: Imperialism's New Disguise?" *African Security Review* 18, no. 2 (2009): 1–15.

Sen, Amartya Kumar. "Democracy as a Universal Value." *Journal of Democracy* 10, no. 3 (1999): 3–17.

Sending, Ole Jacob. "The Effects of Peacebuilding: Sovereignty, Patronage and Power." In *A Liberal Peace? The Problems and Practices of Peacebuilding*, edited by Susanna Campbell, David Chandler, and Meera Sabaratnam, 55–68. London: Zed Books, 2011.

Spencer, Jonathan. *Anthropology, Politics and the State: Democracy and Violence in South Asia*. Cambridge: Cambridge University Press, 2007.

Stamnes, Eli. "Values, Context and Hybridity: How can the insights from the liberal peace critique literature be brought to bear on the practices of the UN Peacebuilding Architecture?" Working paper, Norwegian Institute of International Affairs and Centre for International Policy Studies, University of Ottawa, 2010.

Tar, Usman A. *The Politics of Neoliberal Democracy in Africa: State and Civil Society in Nigeria*. New York: Tauris Academic Studies, 2009.

Yordán, Carlos L. "Towards Deliberative Peace: A Habermasian Critique of Contemporary Peace Operations." *Journal of International Relations and Development* 12, no. 1 (2009): 58–89.

CHAPTER 3

Theatre for Peacebuilding

This chapter explores the arts—specifically theatre—as a potential approach to address what remains unaddressed within prevalent approaches to peacebuilding. It looks at theatre along three levels: the first section examines the political relevance of theatre and how it has been used to engage with people and communities. Theatre's potential to contribute to peacebuilding comes out in these engagements.

The second section highlights *how* and *where* theatre contributes to the prevalent peacebuilding discourse. Theatre addresses gaps and adds to the existing approaches in two ways: it broadens peacebuilding beyond the parameters of existing approaches, and when appropriately applied, expresses local complexities and encourages context specific solutions. These are key factors in enhancing the sustainability of peacebuilding. Therein lies the contribution of theatre for peacebuilding.

Third section illustrates *how* theatre works for peacebuilding: multi-voiced and dialogic form of theatre plays a key role here. Exploring the potential of multivocality and the dialogic in relation to the nexus of theatre and peacebuilding offers new insights. Finally, the chapter comments on the challenges and concerns that arise in using theatre for peacebuilding.

© The Author(s) 2018
N. Premaratna, *Theatre for Peacebuilding*,
Rethinking Peace and Conflict Studies,
https://doi.org/10.1007/978-3-319-75720-9_3

Potential: Shaping People and Politics

Art forms engaging with issues of war and peace make up crucial elements in peacebuilding and anti-war movements: these include, but are not limited to, music, painting, fiction, performance, film, and photography. Take Picasso's *Guernica* painted in response to the Spanish Civil War or John Lennon's *Give Peace a Chance*. These are constantly referred to as points of inspiration, solidarity building, and in general, as a way of facilitating a shared vision when it comes to the practice of peacebuilding. Art also enables healing through facilitating self-expression and reflection. The contribution of different art forms and how they contribute can differ according to the context and cause.

Theatre as a form of art is constantly singled out for its political relevance among other forms of art by historical and contemporary thinkers alike. Plato perceives theatre to be highly disruptive. The stage, as he sees it, is a space where public activity and fantasies can take place simultaneously. Associated with this is a significant capacity to disrupt the separation of "identities, activities and spaces"[1]; or, the established hierarchies and social structures seen in the polis, and therefore, significant potential in shaping politics anew. Further emphasising this political potential of theatre, Derrida argues that theatre has the capacity to produce "meaning-effects" that go beyond the mere fictional values ascribed to the stage within the modern society.[2]

The crucial point here is the possibility of an effect through theatre that goes beyond its entertainment and aesthetic value. Theatre does not necessarily generate positive outcomes and it is not the only, or the most powerful, way of scripting politics. Yet, its potential for political significance stands out among other forms of art. Theatre presents a conduit that is connected to politics and everyday life: it provides a space that is both *influenced by* and *influences* the existing politics, while remaining outside the boundaries of complete subjectivity to the established hierarchies.

Theatre, as a performing art, draws from the symbolic and performative power invested in ceremony and rituals. When appropriately harnessed and presented, the performative power in rituals and the symbolic introduce fresh political spaces, discourses, and vocabularies that challenge the dominant and established modes of power.[3] Theatre, in turn, can utilize this capacity to replicate and at times, intentionally challenge existing politics. Indigenous theatrical performances for peacebuilding in

Kenya, that draw from ritual, dance, and symbolic performances at the ground level, are seen to have the capacity to demobilise the younger generation.[4] The Peruvian theatre group Yuyachkani's plays such as *Rosa Cuchillo* and *Antigona* successfully integrate ritualistic elements to problematize the way the state treats indigenous communities, and addresses a pressing need in these communities for grieving and healing.[5]

History of Political Scripture

Theatre's history of political scripture is a potent sign of the contribution theatre can make to peacebuilding. Theatre has a history of being used as a tool for shaping politics in different continents. The *Acting Together Anthology* documents a number of examples where theatre is used for reconciliation and conflict transformation spanning different parts of the world.[6] Particularly in the Global South, art and theatre are seen as imbued with meaning, passion and transformation—a blend of traditional practices that evolve along the needs of the community to suit contemporary requirements.[7] *Mapping South Asia through Contemporary Theatre* brings together several authors to discuss how theatre simultaneously plays a reflective and a constitutive role in contemporary politics of several South Asian countries.[8] Art and theatre were powerful modes of defining a sense of nation during the colonial period[9]: work of Rabindranath Tagore in India and the Buddhist monk S. Mahinda in Sri Lanka are cases in point. Their poetry is widely acknowledged for the impact these had in providing a vision, shape and drive to the political struggle in each country. The well-known Indian critic Sadanand Menon comments on the role theatre played in mobilising thousands of people to join the Indian freedom struggle in the late 1800's.[10] Amidst heavy state censorship during 1987 insurgency in Sri Lanka, theatre was one of the few remaining modes of expressing public dissent.[11] This space kept the public conscience alive and provided much needed courage and hope at that time, while also serving as a platform to build people's resistance to the government.

Theatre for peacebuilding bridges performance and politics. As such, it is on the one hand a form of art and thus aims to entertain, while on the other hand it carries forth a clear political agenda to constitute a peaceful society. Scholars even go so far as to recommend adopting a lens of performance to analyse politics and political institutions, recognising the salience of performance in scripting politics: for a lens of performance allows us to read the subtle shifts in the channels of power that performance can generate within political institutions.[12] Such a framework acknowledges the nuances in the shaping and making of power politics, not only at the highest levels of authority, but also at a broader public level.

The measures of control upon performances and the scholarly interest in the issue are further indicators of theatre's impact in the political sphere. Plato perceived that theatre is worth banishing from the polis, due to the extent to which its capacity to camouflage itself had the potential to reshape the polis and undermine the hierarchy of roles found therein.[13] *The censorship of British drama 1900–1968* engages with the policy relevant measures of censorship placed upon British theatre of the period, that engaged with topics such as the World Wars, international politics, religion and the monarchy.[14] Several attempts at legislative control on theatre in colonial India further indicate theatre's significance in constituting politics: for example, take the Dramatic Performances Control Bill of 1876 introducing censorship in India for the first time. Through their very existence, these measures of control acknowledge the power and potential of theatre.

Theatre has a history of effectively engaging with and transforming the political. The ability to generate political solidarity across differences is what we need to build peace within the inevitably political, divisive cultural narratives that develop in protracted conflict situations. Thus, the history of being used as a tool to communicate and unite communities for collective action enhances theatre's appropriateness as a peacebuilding approach.

Theatre Forms

There are numerous theatre forms intentionally developed and used for personal and social engagement. Two directions in which these theatre forms develop are of particular relevance to theatre for peacebuilding: theatre forms that stem from a therapeutic approach, aiming for healing or reconciliation, and theatre forms that adopt a broader social lens which are more overtly political in nature. These categories overlap and are more akin to a spectrum with clearer consolidations towards either end. The classification is not intended as a comprehensive overview of theatre forms relevant for peacebuilding. Instead, it merely seeks to establish that theatre can contribute to peacebuilding by looking at selected ways in which theatre has been used for healing or reconciliation, and empowerment and development.

Healing and Reconciliation

Healing and rituals are important elements in facilitating reconciliation and specific theatre forms focus particularly on these aspects of transformation. Psychodrama and its later development of drama therapy are cases in point. Both these theatre forms are intentionally developed for therapeutic purposes and focus on individual healing and transcending personal conflicts. Introduced by Jacob Levy Moreno in the late 1940's, psychodrama requires individuals to dramatize their past from different perspectives, and respond spontaneously in order to facilitate personal growth or healing through the act of re-enactment.[15] Drama therapy broadens psychodrama in its scope and practice, while keeping the primary aim of transformation or healing through therapeutic use of theatre at a small group or personal level intact. A ten-week pilot study carried out with twenty-two autistic children between the ages of seven and twelve, argues that drama therapy helps them overcome their internal obstacles by developing their imagination, as well as their communication and the ability to interact with each other.[16]

While both drama therapy and psychodrama are useful for reconciliation at a personal level, and are indeed used for psychosocial counselling in some post-conflict situations, feasibility of incorporating this at a broader level of peacebuilding is questionable. The overlap between the individual focus and the therapeutic approach calls for a well-trained practitioner, and requires a significant investment of time and energy on a case-by-case basis. The practical challenges, though, do not undermine the healing and reconciliation potential of theatre in general: it simply calls for different theatre forms that incorporate these potentials, and yet offer a broader scope of application.

Some therapeutic theatre forms for conflict transformation are apt for working at community level. Take playback theatre, developed by Jonathan Fox in 1975. Used at a group or community level, playback theatre emphasises symbolic representation and incorporates elements of storytelling, songs, rituals and dances. The playback theatre team is made up of a conductor, actors and a musician and is held in a workshop style that is often limited to the participants. After a facilitated initial phase, the conductor invites the participants to share a personal experience, often involving a challenging situation or conflicting emotions. Once the story is shared, the actors improvise and enact the story back to the teller and the group. This method opens up the story to a process of dialogue, and facilitates healing through listening by validating the personal narrative within the communal forum and empathising with the narrator through performance. Rowe discusses the healing and transformation facilitated through playback theatre in relation to social intervention[17] and Carlin and Park-Fuller comment on the social efficacy of playback theatre in performing disaster narratives with regard to 9/11, Hurricane Katrina and the Haiti earthquake.[18]

Playback theatre can contribute to reconciliation and conflict transformation. In working with people from conflicting ethnic groups, it can facilitate the construction of cohesive narratives and help form closer relationships.[19] The process of remembering/re-telling of individual narratives opens up the stories to new insights and interpretations. This can, in turn, result in the transformation of personal memories of anger, hatred and victimhood into a shared community exchange, facilitating personal or small group reconciliation. The expression and the resulting personal reconciliation with events is a necessary step in eventually being able to hear and see the humanity of the other side. Hence, playback theatre has the potential to initiate reconciliation through healing and re-articulating conflict memories. Given that it is at its most effective among a closed group who respect each other and agree to abide by the ethics of the theatre from, playback theatre often engages with small groups.

Playback theatre, like all other forms of theatre, is not necessarily positive. The outcome of the practice heavily depends on the skills and awareness of the team, and the structure and design of the activity. Rea Dennis questions the playback theatre form and the space it allows for power hierarchies to emerge in relation to a study within an Australian refugee context.[20] The design of the playback theatre form automatically assumes that a democratic citizenship exists at the context. The requirement for the personal story telling in that particular context, as Dennis argues, plays into the existing hierarchies and runs the risks of colluding with the existing negative stereotypes. Other authors also problematize the personal story telling requirement of playback theatre.[21] While telling a personal story can bring out the therapeutic elements of theatre, the practitioners of playback theatre are not necessarily trained psychotherapists. Given that the workshops are often conceptualised as isolated one-off events, the question remains whether playback theatre is equipped to adequately deal with the deeper issues it elicits from the participants.

Empowerment and Development

Theatre of the Oppressed and applied theatre are two noteworthy theatre forms with a broader lens that are intended to be political in nature. These are arguably the best known and most influential theatre forms used for social change at present. The notion of empowerment in Theatre of the Oppressed and applied theatre often extends from the individual to the communal. The notion of empowerment here involves cultivating power within the individual and encourages solidarity, that involves moving to collective action that can in turn, initiate change. Thus, unlike drama therapy or psychodrama, both these theatre forms integrate the personal, small-group and communal levels in their work.

These theatre forms overlap and are at times loosely gathered within the broader categorisation of applied theatre. However, each theatre form has distinctive characteristics and is used in its own right by practitioners. Each is also an umbrella term drawing together a number of related theatre forms. Together, these theatre forms indicate theatre's ability to contribute to peacebuilding.

Theatre of the Oppressed

Theatre of the Oppressed (TO) is also referred to as theatre for empowerment. Developed by Augusto Boal, this marks a key development in theatre.[22] A number of theatre forms such as legislative theatre, invisible theatre and forum theatre fall within the umbrella term Theatre of the Oppressed. Each of these theatre forms has personal empowerment directed at social action at its core, and voices the perspectives of the marginalised or oppressed. The theatre format promotes dialogue and discussion within the individual and among the audience through the very structure of the play. TO, thus, challenges oppression by using theatre to build power within and power with, respectively, among the individuals and communities from marginalised or silenced positions. Theatre works here as a platform that bridges the personal with the political. Personal empowerment leading to social change emerges through this bridging. While this transformation and the space to speak up are crucial aspects for conflict transformation, TO is largely used and discussed within a framework of development and empowerment.

Forum Theatre (FT) is the primary theatre form within the TO repertoire. In FT, a play resembling a real life situation of oppression or injustice is performed onstage. A facilitator called Joker comes onstage at the end of the play, asks for a re-enactment, and invites the audience to intervene by replacing a character and striving to rewrite the story at any point to make the narrative fairer. From then on, it is impromptu. The Joker facilitates the process and discussions. The audience is called spect-actors, as they are both the audience and the actors.

TO provides a space not only for personal reflection, discussion, and debate, but also for practicing speaking up and taking action at everyday situations of oppression. By introducing the "spect-actor", TO blurs the barrier between spectator and actor. The action of coming onstage to rewrite the play itself becomes a conscious act of resistance to the exclusionary narratives. The facilitated onstage space for dialogue and disagreement on issues relevant for the community nurtures critical thinking and creativity.[23] This specific approach towards the spectators—drawing them into the play with an active role of reconstituting the story—is a unique characteristic of the varied theatre forms developed under TO.

The concept of the spect-actor is intimately connected to the process of change effected through FT, and TO: by enacting interventions in the play to change its narrative, TO encourages intervening in similar real life situations the community experiences at a daily level. Such actions bridge the personal and political by combining both the "therapeutic and pedagogical-political imperative," making TO one of the most influential theatre forms of the post-war period.[24]

Several studies confirm the salience of TO and FT. Nick Hammond reports one such study conducted to explore the effectiveness of FT in eliciting and promoting children's views, with the participation of twenty six students and three teachers.[25] Participants indicate significant improvements in "empowerment" and "social justice and equality" by the end of the research. For example, the data reported that as a result of bringing together the adults (power-holders) and children (powerless) in the FT space, the children feel more confident to share their opinions.

A primary challenge facing TO, especially with its popularity among theatre practitioners, is the implementation of the FT model across different cultural and socio-political contexts. The relevant issues, their manifestation, and the ways in which these can be addressed, differ at each context. FT needs to take each aspect into account and adapt accordingly. For example, a neighbour intercepting and admonishing an alcoholic husband is probably not an apt example of an intervention for the US. Yet, this is a viable and an effective intervention for rural Bengal.

A weak adaptation process negatively affects FT. Take the FT event organised by the Beyond Borders theatre group in 2006 in Sri Lanka, on bullying. Despite its relevance for students from a western context, bullying was not a theme that an average Sri Lankan student in the audience related to, at the time. Consequently, the play failed to elicit audience interventions or generate a meaningful discussion. To optimally utilise the FT form, the play has to resonate with the genuine issues of the community. Thus, unless carefully adapted thematically and structurally, the unconventional format and overt references to power hierarchies can render FT redundant.

Though scholars have hardly examined FT and TO from a peacebuilding perspective, both these hold much potential for conflict transformation. Given the plurality and facilitated dialogue embedded in its structure, TO can accommodate diverse voices within its form, initiating dialogue between and across their varied positions. It opens up the theatre space to the infinite possibilities that are rooted in the local context, and are flexible and responsive to different locations. Given its focus on empowerment and development, TO is especially apt for addressing issues of structural discrimination and violence, such as cast, class, gender, or economic exploitation.

Applied Theatre
Applied theatre is an umbrella term introduced in the early 2000's. It gathers a number of theatre forms developed with an underlying social consciousness. TO inspired and played a noteworthy role here.[26] Developments of theatre that are separate from the TO repertoire—such as theatre in/for education, community theatre, Drama for Conflict Transformation and prison theatre—are categorised under the title of applied theatre.[27]

Applied theatre can be broadly defined as theatre for a specific purpose that actively engages with the audience. Ackroyd perceives applied theatre as a continuum and proceeds to identify two key distinguishing aspects of an applied theatre project: the "intention to generate change" and the "participation of the audience."[28] The theatre practice is carried out to serve a purpose and the practitioners and scholars of the theatre form are interested in the power of theatrical tools and concepts, and how these can contribute towards the broader purpose.[29] Thus, unlike TO, applied theatre can maintain a close association with the mainstream theatre studies while enjoying a high degree of autonomy and flexibility at the same time.[30] Whereas TO has a clear empowerment focus in its conception and functions within a prearranged structural framework, applied theatre focuses on exploring issues connected to the community, self or the society, demonstrating a flexibility that extends to structure, form, content, and context. These factors make applied theatre a significant development in using theatre for social change.

The performance spaces of applied theatre often take it away from mainstream theatre. Similar to some forms under Theatre of the Oppressed, applied theatre often takes place with marginalised or disadvantaged groups in non-mainstream settings.[31] Going beyond the hierarchy of the stage in this manner is also a factor that enables participant's voices to be heard and included. This too adds to applied theatre's potential in peacebuilding.

Applied theatre aims to ground itself in the lived experiences of people. It takes the perspective that fiction and reality (or the imagination and the real) are both narrative constructions and as such, are always interrelated and embedded in each other: thus Nicholson argues that understanding the malleability of narratives—both in fiction and in reality—is central to the practice of applied drama.[32] This emphasised plurality and dialogic nature of applied theatre is highly conducive to peacebuilding: it offers the possibility of bringing different and contradictory voices together through a shared everyday reality. Hence scholars term it as a discursive practice driven by the desire to make a contribution to others' lives[33]; a space where "new possibilities for mankind can be imagined"[34] or where theatre can be employed to strengthen communities.[35] Further, such practices are seen to be capable of embracing emotions, "empathic dialogue and mutual exchange."[36] These observations on applied theatre show the potential depth of theatre's engagement. The theatre form is also noted for its effectiveness in "initiating dialogue and transforming social relations."[37] As such, applied theatre adopts a broader social lens and has significant potential for peacebuilding.

There have been concerns regarding the development of applied theatre discourse. Despite its broad scope, the term is justifiably contested for leaving out certain branches of socially engaged theatre. Ackroyd notes that there is an increasing tendency to idealise applied theatre; a refusal to acknowledge that as a powerful medium, applied theatre can serve questionable causes, as well as those that are humanitarian.[38] Drawing from a number of authors, she further challenges the emerging "exclusionary" trends: What can be termed as applied theatre has existed among many cultures and traditions before the introduction of the term, and as such it has varied roots and cannot be restricted to a handful of specific theatre forms.

Nicholson's analogy of applied theatre as a gift is also problematic: the concept of a gift and the act of gifting here is seen as a one-way process. There is a clear giver and a beneficiary. It encourages the reader to understand the theatre practice in terms of implied power hierarchies and the discourse of charity. This perception jeopardises the participatory approach of applied theatre, making it somewhat distinct from the take of Boal's Theatre of the Oppressed.

Given its broader spectrum, applied theatre is increasingly used to refer to theatre activities for conflict transformation. Centres for Applied Theatre Research, established at the Griffith University in Australia and the University of Manchester in England, are indicative of the increasing attention on using theatre for conflict transformation. With these numerous theatre forms originating from different disciplines and contexts, it is evident that theatre forms for conflict transformation are many and varied, having gradually developed bridging several disciplines in its process.

Accordingly, theatre has a marked potential for contributing to peacebuilding. Theatre has an established history of political scripture and a number of theatre forms are developed for various aspects of individual and systemic transformation. The efficacy of these forms suggests theatre's potential to contribute to peacebuilding. Despite this established history, theatre still remains at the fringes of peacebuilding discourse.

Filling the Gaps: Theatre and the Prevalent Peacebuilding Discourse

As discussed, theatre can contribute to peacebuilding. But how exactly can theatre advance prevailing approaches to peacebuilding? What are the specific areas and ways in which theatre contributes to the discourse? This section identifies and discusses two predominant and overlapping themes under which theatre contributes to peacebuilding: Firstly, theatre has the capacity to broaden peacebuilding beyond the parameters of existing approaches. Secondly, theatre can offer a context-specific approach rooted within and driven by the local community that is particularly suited to express local complexities. As discussed in the previous chapter, these are key in articulating sustainable peacebuilding. Theatre has the capacity to approach peacebuilding through these significant but little discussed avenues within prevalent approaches.

Expanding Parameters

Theatre can expand the parameters of existing approaches to peacebuilding. Theatre's approach can broaden the conventional boundaries of regular discourse, and can effectively tackle the emotional legacies of conflict.

Beyond Regular Communication

Art in general, and specifically theatre, has the potential to broaden the conventional boundaries of regular discourse—or in other words, the day-today ways in which we articulate ourselves. It is important to go beyond boundaries of regular discourse in building peace in intractable conflicts. The discourse of each community's regular conversations become insinuated with conflict dynamics and embedded with stereotypes that fuel the conflict and perpetuate dehumanisation.[39] The phrases, idioms, jokes and gestures all contribute to the creation and perpetuation of dichotomies. Participants in co-existence activities at times sense this, and as a result, restrict themselves to a rigid, polite conversational level that prevents a deeper connection.[40] Theatre has the potential to avoid being trapped at this level with its broader repertoire in communication that goes beyond the scope of regular interaction.

Theatre has two advantages here: embodying different forms of art enables theatre to facilitate a broader expression, and the imagination of theatre offers innovative peacebuilding potential. These features of theatre are interrelated, and together, open up multiple avenues of expression conducive to a deeper level of peacebuilding that is difficult to achieve within the conventional peacebuilding approaches.

Different Forms of Art, a Broader Expression

Theatre embodies a number of art forms, encompassing a broad spectrum of communication that surpasses the capabilities of regular, rational discourse upon which peacebuilding relies on. When used for peacebuilding, this plurality and fluidity enhances the accessibility of theatre as a medium and succeeds in reaching different individuals at multiple levels. Specific art forms such as literature and music are noted as particularly suited to capture the emotional dimensions of terrorism.[41] Theatre provides a space where not only these, but also a number of other conventional art forms such as dance, poetry, painting and varied fusions of these forms can be put forth simultaneously. Due to this fluidity and plurality inherent in its form, theatre has the capacity to command the varied expressions facilitated through each individual art form. As a result, peacebuilding through theatre can reach beyond the parameters of verbal communication.

The multiple avenues of reach are particularly apt given the essential public nature of theatre. A theatre audience that shares the same activity at a given point in time is often a random crowd that comes from different backgrounds and levels, bringing different expectations and narratives with them. The production onstage combines a range of avenues—be this in the art forms, characterisation, or mode of delivery—to address such an audience consisting of diverse individuals. The flexibility and plurality this offers is a significant asset in peacebuilding, especially when taking into account the need for peacebuilding to reach across a broad range of individuals with varying perspectives about the conflict.

The diversity in expression and communication within theatre is an important factor with much potential for peacebuilding. Scholars agree. Shank observes that the "arts have the capacity to communicate in an elicitive, culturally ambidextrous, and nonverbal way."[42] Mani argues that unlike the detached, reduced form of representation that is offered through news and policy reports, representing the impact of the conflict through arts equally humanises the conflict parties despite the dehumanisation of war.[43] The arts essentially take place through accessible human narratives of expression in one form or other, and that, she claims, has a cathartic effect. With its space for non-verbal expression, theatre has the potential to express what might be difficult to put into words. Indeed, for most of those affected by war, "[n]ondiscursive modes of expression" might be the only available way to make meaning out of the violations they have experienced.[44] Theatre, in such cases, has the potential to bring out narratives that often remain silenced within the dominant and the regular discourse of conflict contexts. Encompassing both verbal and non-verbal modes of expression, theatre facilitates articulating experience within its sphere to be less subjective to the authoritarian discourse and more multivocal and pluralistic. Theatre, thus, offers much potential for sustainable peacebuilding.

Space of the Imagination
The imagination of theatre contributes to peacebuilding by enabling creativity and distancing that in turn, can transcend the boundaries of real and imagined. The distancing that occurs between the real and the imagined through theatre offers an opportunity to take part in conflict narratives outside the risks and restrictions of real life. This imagined space is safer for expression than the outside, which is often threatening and retributive towards free expression. Also the notion of playing a role has the capacity to suspend preconceptions. This too is an effective mechanism in addressing sensitive issues in a conflict situation.

The space of theatre is also a communal space, and the imagination of theatre makes it further so. Taking part in theatre is hardly an isolated experience and necessitates an interactive form of engagement. Thus, the staged experiences can be or become group experiences that are shared and expressed with relative safety. Theatre's imagination allows individuals to take on roles that might often be denied to them in real life, facilitating the expansion of perceptive and expressive possibilities.[45] The insights and empathy this offers is often unattainable within the day-to-day communication and is imperative for sustainable peacebuilding.

The room for imagination enables theatre to transcend the boundaries of regular discourse and frame contentious issues in ways that are more acceptable. This includes conflict issues and narratives that may bring prevalent peacebuilding methods to an impasse. Often, people in protracted conflicts find it difficult to visualise a time when everyone coexisted, for our imagination and thinking are limited by what we witness around us.[46] Creativity and imagination permits going beyond the observable in real life to tell alternative stories. Applied theatre, using the space of theatre's imagination, attempts to redress the balance in situations by telling alternative stories from multiple perspectives.[47] Theatre can either sidestep or overcome the inconsistencies in the existing conflict discourses, while presenting new ways of looking at things: these new perspectives can invite people to respond and engage in relationships with each other.[48] Novelty or creativity therefore is key to initiate conflict transformation, for conflict transformation attempts are more likely to succeed when they break out of the established conflict patterns.[49] Art in general and specifically the imagination of theatre presents an opportunity for breaking out of the established patterns. Thus, the transformative re-articulation theatre offers is crucial for a sustainable peacebuilding process. Creative rearticulation is crucial to present a vision of cohesion and harmony for sustainable peacebuilding. Theatre embodies the creativity and flexibility to facilitate such inclusive re-articulation in the place of existing divisive narratives.

Take origin myths for example: a reinterpretation of the origin myths of conflicting groups need to lose their totalitarian grip[50] so that the narratives of authoritarian discourse, constructed and backed up by emotion and culture, can create an inclusive and understanding society. Myths and legends are fundamental in constituting our identities as individuals and members of groups. During conflict, the divisive aspects of these take prominence as communities collect data that confirm the myths of the respective groups. As long as these myths stay coherent, they strengthen the divisive narratives. Reinterpreting the divisive narratives, and unearthing those that are inclusive and cohesive can considerably further peacebuilding's agenda.

Challenging such foundational elements of culture can be a daring act even at times of peace. Nevertheless, the creativity and flexibility permitted within the imagination of theatre renders these origin myths malleable, opening them up for new information, new themes and new roles. It is seen as the one forum within which these "narratives can (and must be) embodied and re-represented," thus enabling aspects of history and communal narratives to be explored, dismantled and reconstructed through a collective process; by rewriting these, we rewrite ourselves.[51] Hence the creativity and flexibility within theatre is pivotal to facilitate the transformation of narratives within an authoritative discourse. It leads to the construction of newer, inclusive identities and shared historical narratives between groups.

Tackling Emotional Cultures of Conflict

Yet another potential of theatre that transcends the boundaries of prevalent peacebuilding is its ability to engage with emotion. The emotions of fear and anger prevail after conflict, contributing on the one hand to the identity and community formation, and on the other hand to the perpetuation of conflict.[52] Grief and despair also leave strong emotional legacies that need to be addressed for post-conflict transformation. Providing an inclusive space where all concerned parties, including victims and perpetrators, can come together and witness each other's emotional pain is crucial to reach emotional understanding.[53] The prevailing approaches to peacebuilding have repeatedly been critiqued for their failure to do so.

Theatre for peacebuilding can be particularly effective here: it provides a space to express and engage with personal and communal emotions, triggering a transformation of emotional cultures of conflict.

Scholars increasingly note the need for peacebuilding to broaden its scope from the rational and analytical approaches, to incorporate the emotional and psychological aspects. Roland Bleiker sees emotions playing an important social and political role, particularly in the process of constituting identity and community attachments.[54] Emotions are a "socio-political force"[55] or a form of "insight and judgement"[56] that can be harnessed for transformation once it is acknowledged as such. When it comes to mediating ethnic conflicts, Kaufman observes that the "emotion-laden symbolic politics" that emerge in the discussions prove to be more challenging than the interests at stake. Martha Nussbaum also argues in *Political Emotion* that cultivating public emotions oriented towards the nation and national goals can succeed in encouraging people to think broader and commit to projects for the common good.[57] Focusing on justice alone while neglecting emotions, as it is often the case with prevailing peacebuilding approaches, is simply not enough. Addressing the emotional aspects of a conflict is imperative for its sustainable transformation.

Theatre as a form of art engages with emotions: an emotionally driven pattern drawing from and engaging with the psychology of local communities can transform the heated emotions of conflict into empathy and connection. Access to emotions is a key contribution art-based approaches offer. The "emotive nature" of art and especially theatre given its immediate, embodied presentation, encourages people to feel the grief of war at a personal level, incurring a resulting desire to put an end to the misery.[58] A "more productive approach" to peacebuilding would acknowledge a group's perception of threats to their identity, and would seek to reduce the intensity of the threats through working within a group's narrative to make them more cooperative, forge new links or rearrange the old in ways that are culturally acceptable.[59]

Empathising with the emotions of the other—as all good art and theatre encourage us to do—humanises the conflict dynamics. Bringing conflict dynamics to the personal level facilitates speaking directly to the emotions of the participants, be they victims or perpetrators of violence. Personalisation in this manner transforms the overwhelming generic masses of people represented in conflict statistics to individual beings who deserve empathy.[60] Based on empirical research, Gallagher and

Service argue that performance evokes feeling, and that the responses of participants in this go beyond rational cognition[61]: seeing things from the perspective of another invites the audience to feel empathy and engage in a deeper reflection.

The personal expression and constitution of emotion that takes place within theatre can be taken towards a broader collective consciousness. It is an ideal local—the only, according to some—that permitted the expression of emotion, preparing for and leading towards a radical change in national politics in a number of countries spanning different time periods.[62] Post-conflict transformation is indeed a radical sociopolitical change from the conditions of war. Theatre as a peacebuilding approach can constitute notions of inclusive and cohesive social relations and personal and communal identities by working through the existing destructive emotions in search of healing.

The resulting emotional transformation through art provides a deterrent to return to the conflict. It has the capacity to transform human intentions for war: one person at a time while growing in momentum to encompass communities, societies and nations. The change brought through emotions goes beyond the regular discourse and seeps inside us to evoke a deeper response, a conviction that lasts. When used as an integral component of a broader conflict resolution process, theatre for peacebuilding can make a significant contribution towards transforming emotional legacies of conflict.

Failure to address the emotional and psychological dynamics of a conflict often results in further complicating the conflict resolution process, and also enhances the likelihood of falling back into violence.[63] The prevailing approaches to peacebuilding are not sufficiently equipped to deal with the "emotional dangers that accompany communities of fear and anger" and lasting sustainable peace is unlikely to be achieved unless these emotional residues beyond and beneath the institutional approaches to peacebuilding are satisfactorily dealt with.[64] While these still remain at the margins of the existing social-political-economic landscape, tapping into the resources offered within the cultural, emotional and psychological spheres are vital to ensure the sustainability of peace.

Theatre for peacebuilding has the potential to broaden peacebuilding beyond the parameters of existing approaches. It broadens the disciplinary boundaries of peacebuilding and opens up alternative channels of communication. The different forms of expression and emotions facilitated through theatre have the potential to reach people where conventional peacebuilding approaches cannot. The changes enacted within theatre's imagination have the potential to be integrated into the real life. Such integration can have a significant impact upon the subsequent action of people and communities.[65] Both qualitative and quantitative studies suggest that performances motivated by social change effectively changes the attitudes and perceptions of audiences.[66] Theatre can initiate shifts in and open up new ways of forming identities that are more conducive to peacebuilding.

A Context Specific Approach

Theatre is not always context specific or local. But when it is, it holds significant potential as a peacebuilding approach. This is the second overarching theme under which theatre's potential in building peace is discussed here. The first chapter outlined the need for local, context specific approaches to peacebuilding. The process of peacebuilding through theatre addresses this gap in a number of ways.

We see theatre's potential along two interrelated themes: theatre takes peacebuilding beyond the layer of civil society to engage with the life and culture of the context. This, in turn, opens up the possibility of transforming the residual conflict memories and narratives through theatre.

Engaging with Local Life and Culture

Unlike the prevalent peacebuilding approaches where a pre-constructed, elite-driven civil society automatically becomes the focus, art based approaches like theatre for peacebuilding have the capacity to reach further and draw from the local, everyday experiences of people. Art exists in almost all communities, even at the most difficult of times, in one form or another. It is intimately bound with the life and culture of the community and thus, goes beyond the civil society to work within the lifeworlds of individuals. Mani claims that even today art is an essential part of the everyday lives for a vast majority of the people in Global South.[67] She further notes that art holds meaning beyond aesthetic pleasure. As a "fundamental component of culture," art inevitably becomes a "primary vehicle of cultural expression and transmission."[68] Thus, theatre as a form of art can deeply embed itself in the local from which it emerges. When effective, theatre initiatives for peacebuilding are essentially linked to and relates to those very conditions that produced it. It invariably has to have this communal engagement, and has to reach beyond the civil society to the local everyday lives in order to be accepted and sustain as a theatre production. Since the agency to accept or reject a theatre project rests with the public, a production that fails to speak to the life and culture of the community would automatically fail. When effectively implemented, theatre for peacebuilding can penetrate the façade of civil society, to provide an authentic engagement with the life and culture of the local community.

As a collaborative community activity that brings people together within a shared spatio-temporal span, theatre has the potential to heal conflict memories and repair broken relationships. The invariably public nature of theatre sets it apart from most art forms, giving theatre an added advantage in being used for peacebuilding. Theatre includes both the actors onstage and the audience, allowing politics to emerge in the relationship between the two.[69] The "heart of the 'aesthetic process' in theatre is found not in the 'action on stage' but in the *'realization created by the audience'*."[70] Audience engagement is a crucial part of the theatre process, considerably broadening its reach for peacebuilding. The physical process through which theatre initiatives bring people to work together is also salient. It is seen as "one of the most powerful mediums" through which we can initiate live, in-person contact between individuals from different conflict sides.[71] Theatre can add to prevailing peacebuilding approaches by encouraging collective behaviours such as gathering, working, and acting together, while repairing conflict memories and relationships in the process.

The participatory nature of theatre is of special relevance here: the actors and audience in theatre for peacebuilding approaches are often interrelated in some way. They could belong to conflicting groups or a third party, or to the same community as an audience. Irrespective of these differences, the audience and actors often come from the larger socio-political context, as individuals relating to the conflict and its transformation process from their unique standpoints. Shared, plural environment of the performance facilitates an interrelated and interactive approach in engaging with the conflict.[72] Theatre also allows re-enactments of the larger political scene within its space facilitated by the presence of recognisable features, accents and local knowledge of the actors. Participation in theatre has the potential to initiate shifts in identity that result in more pluralistic and inclusive behaviour patterns conducive to peacebuilding.[73]

The communal nature of theatre, combined with the flexibility and resilience of the form, contributes to peacebuilding as an approach applicable throughout the different phases of conflict. Theatre works within the everyday and is easily integrated into the everyday life and culture of the context. It initiates the process of peacebuilding by challenging the way we think and represent the political conditions at an everyday level, and has the potential to encourage reflection that opens up insights that are both political and ethical.[74] As such, peacebuilding through theatre can start at any point in the conflict cycle, from the initial kindling of animosity to the post-conflict reconciliation and conflict prevention in the end.

Transforming Conflict Memories and Narratives

Theatre's capacity to transform conflict memories and narratives enhances its potential as a context specific approach. Each conflict is different and the respective conflict memories and narratives also differ. Transforming these requires engagement at a genuinely local level, and becomes an initial step in grasping local complexities of conflict. Theatre offers a place where personal as well as collective memories can take place live on stage. The act of expression within the theatre space allows these diverse, and at times conflicting conflict memories, to engage in conversation with each other, converge, and rearticulate. The conscious act of remembering/forgetting occurring in this rearticulation becomes an "instrument of dialogue and inclusion."[75] The resulting process enables personal and collective reconciliation through redefining the past and present relationships between the conflict memories and narratives, while opening up new pathways for the present and future narratives. This transformation can extend to conflict memories and narratives at personal, collective, and cultural spheres.

Theatre can transform personal narratives of conflict through utilising the public space of theatre. Literature on the healing and therapeutic application of theatre, discusses in detail the symbolic potential of transformation in the process of performing on the public sphere of the stage. The stage offers a space where the silenced individual narratives and suppressed perspectives can be voiced and made a part of the social discourse; an opportunity to "restore through re-enactment" the fragmented meaning and lives in post-conflict contexts.[76] Theatre provides an opportunity to reconstitute reality to present a reconciliatory and cohesive vision within its imagination in a shared communal forum. When effective, individuals and communities can create and reflect upon a collective pro-peace experience that is ultimately locally owned. Such shared envisioning holds significant potential for transforming narratives and identities at both a community and personal level.[77] Thus, theatre as a context specific approach can access the personal narratives of conflict residing within individuals, effect healing within these, and initiate the rearticulation of cohesive narratives.

Theatre has the potential to rearticulate collective memories of conflict. Collective memories are formed around the emotionally invested events and people in the past, that are particularly relevant in shaping a group's understanding of itself and the issues it faces.[78] Narratives, ritual expressions and enactments, and symbolic landscapes are important conceptual tools in mobilising collective memories in contexts with strong memories of deep-rooted trauma or hostility.[79] The direct engagement of participants and their emotions required by each one of these three aspects can significantly affect the creation and reinforcement of both individual and group memory. Theatre has the capacity to encompass and expand into all four aspects, thus enhancing its potential in addressing collective memory in a conflict context. For example, drawing from the work of Madis Koiv and Merie Karusoo, Kruuspere argues that Estonian memory theatre, tapping into the emotions of anger and laughter in performing events from the past from the Soviet and Nazi occupation, is capable of initiating an alternative process of remembrance.[80] Theatre thus has the potential to express and rearticulate collective memories, contributing to a peacebuilding process through creating a shared future.

Similarly, theatre can play a central role in rearticulating cultural memory. History is a form of cultural memory, for the dominant discourses functioning within culture heavily affect the narrative of history.[81] Thus the cycle of conflict is reproduced through history: the enemy is remembered as a receptacle for all our negative characteristics.[82] They are portrayed as wholly other, culturally despicable and inferior. The conflict dynamics being played out through the culture actively silence the shared characteristics and at the same time, highlight the differences. Theatre can draw from counter-memories that exist in the context and tell the stories that are suppressed, censored or altered by the dominant narratives and authorities. It can creatively intervene in the selective process of cultural memorisation by bringing people together and effecting connections between and among the conflict sides. Bridging narratives in this manner results in a personal and communal rearticulation of cultural memory. Once these memories are articulated and fully integrated into the communal narratives, they are carried on as part of the everyday processes of cultural expression and transmission. Thus, using theatre results in making peacebuilding a locally driven, context-specific process that does not require external monitoring or interventions to ensure its continuation. It is an ideal local discourse founder that can generate local consensus and make peacebuilding a more authentic, locally led process. Theatre, therefore, can potentially address a pressing need in prevalent approaches to peacebuilding.

Rearticulation of memory and narratives through theatre can bridge the past with present and future in a positive manner. It is the responsibility of the practitioner to use theatre to remember the past, in ways that will support the society to overcome present challenges.[83] Art, be it theatre or any other, becomes invested with power when it transcends the trajectory of the past and present: Homi Bhabha argues that such art, rendering the past into a "contingent 'in-between' space", can delve into and bring forth a renewal or a rearticulation of the past that "innovates and interrupts the performance of the present".[84] What is brought out of this in-between space and what is sent back there, ultimately has to be regulated by the ethics and principles of the practitioner, and when it comes to theatre for peacebuilding, those ethics and principles must be conducive to building peace within a given context. Theatre for peacebuilding, thus, has the potential to reorient collective memories of conflict towards reconciliation, contributing positively to the peacebuilding process.

Despite still being relegated to the fringes, theatre for peacebuilding is an important area in peacebuilding. Lederach observes that a successful peace process is defined by the willingness of the actors to embrace complexities, and the creativity and flexibility of the process that facilitates moving away from polarising simplistic narratives.[85] Theatre has both. It can significantly add to the prevalent approaches as a context specific approach that can express local complexities and open up communication between parties and narratives in conflict. It can broaden peacebuilding beyond the parameters of existing approaches, articulating new and alternative pathways through which reconciliation can take place.

How: The Way in Which Theatre Works for Peacebuilding

Having established that theatre can contribute to peacebuilding and identified where exactly and how it contributes to address the gaps in prevalent approaches, this chapter proceeds to understand *how* theatre works for peacebuilding. In exploring theatre as a peacebuilding approach, the discussion up to this point highlighted the *potential* of theatre. Unless properly utilised, this potential itself does not contribute to peace, and indeed, can do the reverse in some cases. To understand how to effectively *use* theatre for peacebuilding, we first need to explore *how* theatre works: the avenues through which theatre opens up possibilities of conversation between parties and narratives in conflict and initiate peacebuilding.

Scholars have taken different approaches to theorise how theatre works for peacebuilding: the *Acting Together* anthology argues that theatre works as a permeable membrane that sits between the real and the imagined. According to this approach, what takes place in the real world filters into theatre, shaping what takes place there: what takes place in the creative realms of theatre, in turn, filters into the everyday world shaping our thought and behaviours patterns. Thus, theatre is likened to a permeable membrane that regulates this filtering process between the imagined and the real.

Apart from this, commentators also identify noteworthy contributions of theatre in relation to aspects such as healing and reconciliation. Cohen identifies three general direction of change effected through the arts that is particularly relevant[86]: silenced words and suppressed actions are expressed; capacities that were impaired or underdeveloped are nourished and restored; and previously straightforward imperatives—such as those toward justice, memory, identity, and resistance—become animated by the disciplines of the moral imagination, generally resulting in more complex and nuanced understandings and manifestations. Being broadly encompassing, these shed some light on the process of peacebuilding through theatre. The focus here is on the end result and not particularly on identifying features within theatre that is central for theatre's potential for peacebuilding.

What are the key elements in theatre or the theatrical form that is ideally suited to bring out these aspects conducive to peacebuilding? What is it that is seen in theatre that makes it applicable across varied conflicts and forms an underlying link across all the different theatre forms? Understanding these elements ingrained in the theatre form gives us the points we need to focus on, in using theatre as a peacebuilding approach. Thus, exploring the elements of theatre that are fundamental to its peacebuilding approach addresses a strategic gap in establishing theatre as an important but often overlooked area in peacebuilding.

The multivocal and dialogic nature of theatre warrants further study from this peacebuilding perspective. Plurality and dialogue built into and effected through theatre—in other words, the multivocal and dialogic form of theatre—enhances theatre's adaptability and is developed in a myriad of ways in theatre approaches for peacebuilding. The notions of multivocality and dialogic have been separately discussed in performance studies and conflict resolution as central elements pertinent to the study and practice of each discipline. An empirical exploration of the nexus between these, as seen within theatre's multivocal and dialogic form for peacebuilding, is a novel contribution this book proceeds to offer.

Multivocality: Including Diverse Voices

Multivocality features high in conflict resolution and performance studies. Being products of a complex web of traditions, norms, practices and worldviews that constitute our societies, the diversity and contradictions inherent in these shapes our political meaning making.[87] To comprehend and rearticulate such a world, we need lenses that can capture this multiplicity. Mainstream social science research methods are challenged for being incapable of capturing this plurality.[88] The resulting call to acknowledge multiple ways of relating is especially relevant in peacebuilding. Bringing conflicting parties together requires the bringing together of multiple worlds that have their own ways of seeing, being and relating to. This is what peacebuilding at the local level calls for. And eliciting this particular quality is key for building sustainable peace.

Art in general is uniquely suited to express multiple voices. Art forms such as fiction and poetry allow tensions within the linear, central narratives to emerge.[89] Art, thus, is a medium that can embrace and bring together multiple, contradictory voices within its space.

Scholars especially highlight the multivocality of theatre. Edith Hall notes that the fictional representatives of the marginal characters that are often silenced in the public political discourse appear and address the public through tragic theatre.[90] Mark Chou, also with reference to Greek Tragedy, speaks of a form of multivocality that has a deep democratic potential in its ability to make visible multiple versions of reality, actions, and actors in such a way to challenge the existing political order.[91] Here multivocality includes a diverse range of "narratives, individuals, and issues", often giving voice to those who were silenced or stripped of a voice.[92]

While the term has been widely discussed in relation to tragedy, multivocality is not limited to this specific dramatic form. Theatre in general can actively work to incorporate different voices, and voices that are less heard within the mainstream politics. The multiple avenues of expression facilitated within theatre are key in enabling this multivocality. Analysis of multivocality in tragedy revolves around the representations onstage. With the development of theatre forms such as Theatre of the Oppressed, the scope of multivocality becomes further inclusive and plural through incorporating the audience into the theatre process. The spectrum of voices that are expressed go beyond those of the actors to incorporate voices from the community, their experiences and lifeworlds. The impact of such expression is also not limited to the stage. Once elicited onstage, these multiple voices go beyond the theatre space and materialise in other spheres of everyday life.

Multivocality holds an important place within peacebuilding. War discourse often actively works to reduce multivocality in a number of ways. Conflict results in a weakening of democratic processes, and this in turn leads to a suppression of plurality. Quite often public information sources and media are co-opted during war times to promote the norms and values of the ruling elite,[93] honing and promoting homogenous, monovocal narratives on the one hand and curbing dissent on the other. Thus, dualistic interpretations characterise conflict and post-conflict situations. The plurality existing at the ground level is no longer visible and is often silenced or ignored to facilitate the war narratives. Encouraging multivocality is crucial to move beyond such exclusionary war or conflict discourse and to open up the local context for the spectrum of voices existing within it. Reconciliation and peacebuilding become possible once these multiple narratives of conflict are brought forth and opened up for discussion.

Theatre as an important but neglected area in peacebuilding warrants further exploration. Peacebuilding needs to identify approaches that facilitate multivocality. Such approaches can satisfactory represent local complexities and through bringing marginalised narratives into the mainstream social politics, support peacebuilding to find sustainable solutions to the complicated issues at stake. The multivocality of theatre has the potential to facilitate the expression of different and contradictory points of view in a manner that is safe and acceptable. Expression of diverse voices is important for arriving at sustainable solutions during conflict, and for healing and reconciliation in a post conflict situation. Given the little space alternative narratives of conflict would have within mainstream politics, platforms like theatre that are difficult to regulate can become especially powerful modes for peacebuilding during the changing phases of conflict. The multivocal form of theatre is a key feature warranting further inquiry on how it contributes to peacebuilding.

Dialogue to the Dialogic: A Constant Process of Interaction

Theatre has significant potential to create a space for dialogue. Participatory and community theatre for conflict resolution emphasise verbal dialogue between the parties. Commentators argue that such interactive dialogue taking place among and between the participants is crucial for transformation.

Theatre can reach beyond dialogue, to the dialogic. Bakhtin defines dialogic (or dialogism) as engaging in a constant process of dialogue with the text, which, in turn, makes meaning out of the present as well as the past. Making meaning, here, is a process of open-ended negotiation that is constantly in flux.[94] Theatre with its multiple forms of communication and the fluidity embedded in the theatre form itself, presents a potent vehicle for such a dialogic discourse. Thus the dialogue that takes place among the participants, as it is often the focus of theatre for conflict transformation practitioners, makes up only for a part of theatre's dialogic potential. The dialogic form of theatre can utilise the entirety of the performance and can emerge in creative methods. The dialogism of theatre, in this approach, reaches beyond the stage and the performance. It takes place between and among the multitude of voices expressed during theatre and continues beyond the time and space of the performance. Theatre offers a rich lens to work through in exploring how the arts script peace and the particular issues at stake in this process.

The dialogic form of theatre, when intentionally used for peacebuilding, has the possibility of bringing together transformation and meaning making. Both Freire and Bakhtin agree that human nature is dialogic and that we exist in a state of dialogue with each other. It is seen as a crucial element in our meaning-making processes. While Bakhtin argues that the dialogic is a feature of social discourse that is particularly applicable to the arts, for Friere it is at the foundation of empowerment and transformation. Theatre, intentionally performed to address an issue, brings together these two aspects of the dialogic: meaning making and transformation. However, the transformatory potential of theatre needs to be empirically explored in order to fully understand and utilise it for peacebuilding.

Dialogic engagement holds a central position in understanding and resolving conflict. Monologues and exclusionary propaganda rhetoric, prevalent within war discourse, deter a dialogic process. Thus, reinstitution of the dialogic paves way for opening up to an exchange between multiple narratives that exist at a local level. Discussions on a dialogic framework for interpreting inter-group processes,[95] and significance of dialogic relations in governance initiatives for conflict resolution with particular emphasis on the importance of positive dialogical relations between varying actors involved in the conflict resolution process[96] show the centrality of dialogue in conflict resolution and peacebuilding.

The multivocal and dialogic form of theatre enhances theatre's capacity for peacebuilding. The expression of multiple voices and the consequent dialogue among and between these, can result in forming new connections and offering alternative pathways through a stalemate of conflict. An approach that embodies both multivocality and the dialogic has the potential to facilitate transformation of conflict parties and narratives to be inclusive and empathetic. Some scholars see the possibilities offered for transformative relationships to be the ultimate guideline when it comes to assessing contemporary peacebuilding.[97] Therefore, multivocal and the dialogic form of theatre holds great potential for peacebuilding.

While the role of the dialogic and multivocality has been extensively discussed and their significance recognised within conflict resolution and art separately, the nexus of theatre's dialogic and multivocal form and peacebuilding is yet to be explored. The empirical exploration offered through the Part II of this book tackles this issue.

Challenges and Concerns

Theatre for peacebuilding is not an all-encompassing answer to the issues with prevalent approaches to peacebuilding. Two key concerns are discussed here.

Art and theatre are simply tools. The interests of this book essentially limit the discussion to theatre, for when it is specifically used for peacebuilding. But this is not the case at all times. Like any other art form or a tool, theatre too can be used to promote any ideology, including war. Evidence comes from different corners of the world: one such example is Sri Lanka. In order to rally public support for the last phases of war, the government extensively used art and culture. State media stations produced and promoted songs and soap operas that promoted nationalistic rhetoric, portrayed soldiers as heroes, and valorised the war. The government specifically sponsored a chain of cinematic productions on victorious Sinhalese kings who fought to protect or unify the island. Leni Riefenstahl used her films to support the Nazi ideology. James Thompson in *Performance In Place of War* documents a number of instances when performance was used to promote war in different places. As such, aesthetics are neither "good nor bad," but are malleable, adding a "different dimension to our understanding of the political."[98] Thus theatre and art in general is simply a medium that can be used to promote any ideology. Theatre by itself is not positive or conducive to peace. It becomes so as a result of intentional production or interpretation.

Yet, adopted as a lens, theatre can provide deeper insights into politics and access to the community. Aesthetics as a method can enact the multiplicities of the world, enabling a fairer representation of existing political issues.[99] Theatre, drawing from the many resources aesthetics offer, can reach into and bring out the recesses of community consciousness and everyday life that is difficult for other, mainstream peacebuilding approaches to reach. As argued earlier in this chapter, when specifically used for the purpose of peacebuilding, theatre holds much potential.

The second pertinent concern is the possible appropriation of theatre or art produced *for* peacebuilding by contradictory discourses. Theatre for peacebuilding projects can be co-opted in their interpretation even after their production. Art forms, once they are produced, can no longer be contained within a single narrative. Art's political significance heavily relies on how it is understood or interpreted by the audience. The audience interpretation—intentional or unintentional—can vary from the intentions of the production team. Such reinterpretation can replace or distort the original reading of the play. Take *Pongu Thamil*, a cultural festival held in the LTTE controlled area initiated during the cease-fire period as an alternative nonviolent form of expression for the moderate Tamils. The LTTE, as a founding member of the *Pongu Thamil* movement shared, appropriated the movement for its own political propaganda and used the events as thinly veiled recruitment platforms. Theatre productions and art forms can therefore be used to serve conflicting ideologies either by appropriation or by removing them from the contexts from which they originate. The fluidity and plurality of art—and specifically theatre—is both its strength as well as weakness. Simply put, it is a malleable tool, neither good nor bad.

Conclusion

Theatre as an art form is a medium that potentially broadens the reach and breadth of contemporary peacebuilding. The gaps in the prevalent approaches to peacebuilding are gradually yet insistently becoming apparent. Post-conflict situations that heavily and exclusively relied on the prescribed methods of institution building, abstract rights, and democratic procedures, face constant challenges as a result of failing to resonate with the ground level. As the previous chapter concluded, peacebuilding needs to develop strategies that can bridge the gap between political decision-making and the everyday lifeworlds of people living in conflict contexts.

This chapter explored the nexus of theatre and peacebuilding, looking at the ways in which theatre can contribute to peacebuilding. Firstly, it drew from theatre's history of political scripture and the repertoire of theatre forms with potential for social change to establish that theatre can contribute to peacebuilding. Secondly, it explored how theatre could help to address the existing gaps in prevalent peacebuilding, examining the ways in which theatre broadens the parameters of conventional approaches and offers a context specific approach. Theatre's ability to tap into and engage with emotions is central here. As the third stage, it looked at how theatre works for peacebuilding. Multivocality and dialogism as overlapping elements in theatre and peacebuilding holds much promise in responding to this question.

The empirical exploration that follows in Part II of the book starts from this foundation established in Part I. As Roland Bleiker notes, this is a time when "political dilemmas require new and innovative responses" and aesthetics are of particular relevance here as they offer us a "more nuanced understanding of the political."[100] Instead of offering instant definitive solutions to a conflict, theatre encourages a pluralistic take: it opens up the "single-voiced and single-minded" approaches, stories, narratives and politics that often are at the root of conflicts to "multiple voices and the possibility of multiple truths."[101] In the process of engaging with these multiple narratives, theatre for peacebuilding can draw from and reconstitute the lifeworlds of people, taking peacebuilding deeper into the heart of communities. Theatre can, therefore, facilitate peacebuilding to engage with the ground level and consequently, with public opinion. However, theatre itself is not sufficient in taking this process forward: neither does it provide an overarching framework to replace the existing approaches to peacebuilding. Theatre for peacebuilding simply offers a complementary process to initiate or support a peace process; it provides an alternative way of looking at conflict that can be adapted and integrated as an approach to positively enhance the depth and sustainability of the peacebuilding process. The empirical exploration into different case studies in the next part of the book facilitates a deeper understanding.

Notes

1. Cited in Jacques Ranciere, *The Politics of Aesthetics*, trans. Gabriel Rockhill (New York: Continuum, 2004), 13.
2. Cited in Alison Ross, "Derrida's Writing-Theatre: From the Theatrical Allegory to Political Commitment," *Derrida Today* 5, no. 1 (2008): 89.
3. Shirin M. Rai, "Analysing Ceremony and Ritual in Parliament," *The Journal of Legislative Studies* 16, no. 3 (2010): 292.
4. Kitche Magak, Susan Mbula Kilonzo, and Judith Miguda-Attyang, "The Place and Prospects of Indigenous Theatrical Performances in Peacebuilding in Kenya," *African Conflict and Peace building Review* 5, no. 1 (2015).
5. See Diana Taylor and Sarah J. Townsend, *Stages of Conflict: A Critical Anthology of Latin American Theater and Performance* (Ann Arbour, MI: University of Michigan Press, 2008); Cynthia E. Cohen, Roberto Gutiérrez Varea, and Polly O. Walker, eds., *Acting Together: Performance and the Creative Transformation of Conflict: Volume 1: Resistance and Reconciliation in Regions of Violence* (Oakland, CA: New Village Press, 2011).
6. *Acting Together: Performance and the Creative Transformation of Conflict: Volume 1: Resistance and Reconciliation in Regions of Violence*, 11.
7. Rama Mani, "Women, Art and Post-Conflict Justice," *International Criminal Law Review* 11, no. 3 (2011): 550.
8. Ashis Sengupta, ed., *Mapping South Asia Through Contemporary Theatre: Essays on the Theatres of India, Pakistan, Bangladesh, Nepal and Sri Lanka* (Basingstoke: Palgrave Macmillan, 2014).

9. Dia Da Costa, *Development Dramas: Reimagining Rural Political Action in Eastern India* (New Delhi: Routledge, 2010), 45.
10. Shalini Umachandran, "The Freedom Struggle Performers Staged," *The Times of India*, August 15, 2010.
11. See Rajini Obeyesekere, *Sri Lankan Theatre at a Time of Terror* (New Delhi: Sage, 1999); Madhawa Palihapitiya, "The Created Space: Peacebuilding and Performance in Sri Lanka," in *Acting Together: Volume I*, ed. Cynthia E. Cohen, Roberto Gtierrez Varea, and Polly O. Walker (Oakland, CA: New Village Press, 2011).
12. Rai, "*Analysing Ceremony and Ritual in Parliament*," 292.
13. Ross, "Derrida's Writing-Theatre: From the Theatrical Allegory to Political Commitment."
14. Steve Nicholson, *The Censorship of British Drama, 1900–1968*, 4 vols. (Exeter, UK: University of Exeter Press, 2003).
15. Jacob Levy Moreno, *Psychodrama, First Volume* (New York: Beacon House, 1946).
16. See Julie Beadle-Brown et al., "Imagining Autism: Feasibility of a Drama-Based Intervention on the Social, Communicative and Imaginative Behaviour of Children with Autism," *Autism* (Published online ahead of print, 13 September 2017). Available at: https://doi.org/10.1177/1362361317710797.
17. Nick Rowe, *Playing the Other: Dramatizing Personal Narratives in Playback Theatre* (London: Jessica Kingsley Publishers, 2007).
18. Phyllis Scott Carlin and Linda M. Park-Fuller, "Disaster Narrative Emergent/Cies: Performing Loss, Identity and Resistance," *Text and Performance Quarterly* 32, no. 1 (2011).
19. Cynthia Cohen, "Creative Approaches to Reconciliation," in *The Psychology of Resolving Global Conflicts: From War to Peace*, ed. Mari Fitzduff and Chris E. Stout, Vol. 3 (Westport, CT: Praeger Security International, 2006).
20. Rea Dennis, "Inclusive Democracy: A Consideration of Playback Theatre with Refugee and Asylum Seekers in Australia," *Research in Drama Education: The Journal of Applied Theatre and Performance* 12, no. 3 (2007).
21. See Steve Nash and Nick Rowe, "Safety, Danger and Playback Theatre," *Dramatherapy* 22, no. 3 (2000).
22. See Augusto Boal, *The Aesthetics of the Oppressed* (London: Routledge, 2006).
23. Da Costa, *Development Dramas: Reimagining Rural Political Action in Eastern India*, 63.
24. Christopher B. Balme, *The Cambridge Introduction to Theatre Studies* (Cambridge: Cambridge University Press, 2008), 185.
25. Nick Hammond, "Introducing Forum Theatre to Elicit and Advocate Children's Views," *Educational Psychology in Practice* 29, no. 1 (2012): 2.

26. See Helen Nicholson, *Applied Drama: The Gift of Theatre* (Basingstoke: Palgrave Macmillan, 2005); Balme, *The Cambridge Introduction to Theatre Studies*.
27. See Monica Prendergast and Juliana Saxton, *Applied Theatre: International Case Studies and Challenges for Practice* (Bristol: Intellect, 2009) for a detailed discussion.
28. Judith Ackroyd, "Applied Theatre: Problems and Possibilities," *Applied Theatre Researcher* 1 (2000).
29. Balme, *The Cambridge Introduction to Theatre Studies*, 181–182.
30. See *The Cambridge Introduction to Theatre Studies*.
31. James Thompson and Tony Jackson, "Applied Theatre/Drama: An E-Debate in 2004: Viewpoints," *RIDE-Research in Drama and Education* 11, no. 1 (2006): 92.
32. Nicholson, *Applied Drama: The Gift of Theatre*.
33. *Applied Drama: The Gift of Theatre*, 16.
34. Phillip Taylor, *Applied Theatre: Creating Transformative Encounters in the Community* (Ann Arbor, MI: The University of Michigan, 2003), xxx.
35. *Applied Theatre: Creating Transformative Encounters in the Community* (Ann Arbor, MI: The University of Michigan, 2003), xxi.
36. Kennedy Chinyowa, "Emerging Paradigms for Applied Drama and Theatre Practice in African Contexts," *Research in Drama Education* 14, no. 3 (2009): 330.
37. Kathleen Gallagher and Ivan Service, "Applied Theatre at the Heart of Educational Reform: An Impact and Sustain Ability Analysis," *Research in Drama Education—The Journal of Applied Theatre and Performance* 15, no. 2 (2010): 251.
38. Judith Ackroyd, "Applied Theatre: An Exclusionary Discourse?" *Applied Theatre Researcher* 8 (2007): 6.
39. Cynthia Cohen, "Engaging with the Arts to Promote Coexistence," in *Imagine Coexistence: Restoring Humanity After Violent Ethnic Conflict*, ed. Martha Minow and Antonia Chaves (Hoboken, NJ: Jossey-Bass, 2003), 270.
40. "Engaging with the Arts to Promote Coexistence," in *Imagine Coexistence: Restoring Humanity After Violent Ethnic Conflict*, ed. Martha Minow and Antonia Chaves (Hoboken, NJ: Jossey-Bass, 2003), 2–3.
41. Roland Bleiker, *Aesthetics and World Politics* (Basingstoke: Palgrave Macmillan, 2009), 60.
42. Michael Shank and Lisa Schirch, "Strategic Arts-Based Peacebuilding," *Peace & Change* 33, no. 2 (2008): 237.
43. Mani, "Women, Art and Post-Conflict Justice," 551–552.
44. Cohen, "Engaging with the Arts to Promote Coexistence," 2.
45. Boal, *The Aesthetics of the Oppressed*.

46. See Cohen, "Engaging with the Arts to Promote Coexistence."
47. Nicholson, *Applied Drama: The Gift of Theatre*, 63.
48. Cohen, "Engaging with the Arts to Promote Coexistence," 3.
49. William J. Long and Peter Brecke, *War and Reconciliation: Reason and Emotion in Conflict Resolution* (Cambridge: MIT Press, 2003).
50. See Sara Cobb, "Fostering Coexistence in Identity-Based Conflicts: Towards a Narrative Approach," in *Imagine Coexistence*, ed. Antonia Chayes and Martha Minow (San Francisco: Jossey Bass, 2003).
51. David Williams, "'Remembering the Others That Are Us': Transculturalism and myth in the theatre of Peter Brook," in *The Intercultural Performance Reader*, ed. Patrice Pavis (London: Routledge, 1996), 68.
52. Emma Hutchison and Roland Bleiker, "Reconciliation," in *Routledge Handbook of Peacebuilding*, ed. Roger Mac Ginty (New York: Routledge, 2013), 82.
53. Roland Bleiker and Emma Hutchison, "Fear No More: Emotions and World Politics," *Review of International Studies* 34, no. 1 (2008).
54. Bleiker, *Aesthetics and World Politics*, 62.
55. Hutchison and Bleiker, "Reconciliation," 82.
56. Bleiker, *Aesthetics and World Politics*, 62.
57. Martha C. Nussbaum, *Political Emotions* (Cambridge: Harvard University Press, 2013), 3.
58. Carol Rank, "Promoting Peace Through the Arts" (Paper Presented at the International Peace Research Association, Leuven, Belgium, July 2008), 1.
59. Marc Howard Ross, "Psychocultural Interpretations and Dramas: Identity Dynamics in Ethnic Conflict," *Political Psychology* 22, no. 1 (2001): 174.
60. Mani, "Women, Art and Post-Conflict Justice," 551–552.
61. Gallagher and Service, "Applied Theatre at the Heart of Educational Reform: An Impact and Sustain Ability Analysis."
62. Anette Storli Andersen and Jon Nygaard, "Narod Sobie—Theatre as the Nation in Itself: Three Case Studies of Theatre and National Emotions," *Nordic Theatre Studies* 21(2009).
63. Robert L. Rothstein, *After the Peace: Resistance and Reconciliation* (Boulder, CO: L. Rienner Publishers, 1999), 17.
64. Hutchison and Bleiker, "Reconciliation," 85.
65. See Baz Kershaw, "Performance, Community, Culture," in *The Routledge Reader in Politics and Performance*, ed. Lizbeth Goodman and Jane De Gay (London: Routledge, 2000).
66. Dena L. Hawes, "Crucial Narratives: Performance Art and Peace Building," *International Journal of Peace Studies* 12, no. 2 (2007).

67. Mani, "Women, Art and Post-Conflict Justice," 550.
68. "Women, Art and Post-Conflict Justice," 549.
69. See Ranciere, *The Politics of Aesthetics*, 17.
70. Anthony Jackson, "The Dialogic and the Aesthetic: Some Reflections on Theatre as a Learning Medium," *Journal of Aesthetic Education* 39, no. 4 (2005): 109.
71. Cohen, Varea, and Walker, *Acting Together: Performance and the Creative Transformation of Conflict: Volume 1: Resistance and Reconciliation in Regions of Violence*, 42.
72. Shank and Schirch, "Strategic Arts-Based Peacebuilding," 235.
73. See Jenny Hughes, James Thompson, and Michael Balfour, *Performance in Place of War* (Calcutta: Seagull Press, 2009), 138.
74. Hans Magnus Enzensberger, Poesie und Politik (Frankfurt: Suhrkamp, 1987/1962), 135 cited in Roland Bleiker, *Aesthetics and World Politics*, 8.
75. "Forget IR Theory," *Alternatives* 22, no. 1 (1997): 59.
76. Cynthia E. Cohen, Roberto Gutiérrez Varea, and Polly O. Walker, eds., *Acting Together: Performance and the Creative Transformation of Conflict: Volume 2: Building Just and Inclusive Communities* (Oakland, CA: New Village Press, 2011), x.
77. See *Acting Together: Performance and the Creative Transformation of Conflict: Volume 2: Building Just and Inclusive Communities* (Oakland, CA: New Village Press, 2011), 174.
78. Marc Howard Ross, "The Politics of Memory and Peacebuilding," in *Routledge Handbook of Peacebuilding*, ed. R. Mac Ginty (New York: Routledge, 2013), 92.
79. "The Politics of Memory and Peacebuilding," in *Routledge Handbook of Peacebuilding*, ed. R. Mac Ginty (New York: Routledge, 2013), 96.
80. Piret Kruuspere, "Estonian Memory Theatre of the 1990s: Emotional Scale from Fear to Laughter," *Nordic Theatre Studies* 21 (2009).
81. Kansteiner (2002).
82. Cohen, "Engaging with the Arts to Promote Coexistence."
83. Clarke E. Cochran, "Joseph and the Politics of Memory," *The Review of Politics* 64, no. 3 (2002).
84. Homi K. Bhabha, *The Location of Culture* (London: Routledge, 1994), 7.
85. John P. Lederach, *Building Peace: Sustainable Reconciliatin in Divided Societies* (Washington, DC: U.S. Institute of Peace, 1997).
86. Cohen, Varea, and Walker, *Acting Together: Performance and the Creative Transformation of Conflict: Volume 2: Building Just and Inclusive Communities*, 172.
87. Boyu Chen, Ching-Chane Hwang, and Lily H. M. Ling, "Lust/Caution in IR: Democratising World Politics with Culture as a Method," *Millennium—Journal of International Studies* 37, no. 3 (2009).

88. Anna Agathangelou and Lily H. M. Ling, "Fiction as Method/Method as Fiction: Stories and Storytelling in the Social Sciences," (Working Paper, Graduate Program in International Affairs (GPIA), Centre for Security Studies, ETH Zurich, 2017), 2.
89. Ibid.
90. Edith, Hall, "The Sociology of Athenian Tragedy," in *The Cambridge Companion to Greek Tragedy*, ed. Patricia E. Easterling (Cambridge: Cambridge University Press, 1997), 93.
91. Mark Chou, *Greek Tragedy and Contemporary Democracy* (New York: Bloomsbury Academic, 2012).
92. *Greek Tragedy and Contemporary Democracy* (New York: Bloomsbury Academic, 2012), 52.
93. Teun A. Van Dijk, "Discourse and Manipulation," *Discourse and Society* 17, no. 3 (2006).
94. This notion is extensively discussed in relation to Literature. See Mikhail Mikhailovich Bakhtin, Michael Holquist, and Caryl Emerson, *The Dialogic Imagination: Four Essays* (Austin: University of Texas Press, 1981).
95. Seamus A. Power, "Towards a Dialogical Model of Conflict Resolution," *Psychology & Society* 4, no. 1 (2011).
96. Anna Bernhard and Janel B. Balvanek, "The Importance of Dialogical Relations and Local Agency in Governance Initiatives for Conflict Resolution" in *CORE Policy Brief* (Oslo: PRIO, 2013).
97. Ho-Won Jeong, ed. *Approaches to Peacebuilding* (New York: Palgrave Macmillan, 2002), 7.
98. Bleiker, *Aesthetics and World Politics*, 11.
99. Anna M. Agathangelou and Lily H. M. Ling, *Transforming World Politics: From Empire to Multiple Worlds* (New York: Routledge, 2009), 99.
100. Bleiker, *Aesthetics and World Politics*, 82.
101. *Aesthetics and World Politics*, 188.

References

Ackroyd, Judith. "Applied Theatre: Problems and Possibilities." *Applied Theatre Researcher* 1 (2000).

———. "Applied Theatre: An Exclusionary Discourse?" *Applied Theatre Researcher* 8 (2007).

Agathangelou, Anna, and Lily H. M. Ling. "Fiction as Method/Method as Fiction: Stories and Storytelling in the Social Sciences." GPIA Working Papers Graduate Program in International Affairs (GPIA), Centre for Security Studies, ETH Zurich, 2017.

Agathangelou, Anna M., and Lily H. M. Ling. *Transforming World Politics: From Empire to Multiple Worlds*. New York: Routledge, 2009.
Andersen, Anette Storli, and Jon Nygaard. "Narod Sobie—Theatre as the Nation in Itself: Three Case Studies of Theatre and National Emotions." *Nordic Theatre Studies* 21 (2009): 40–50.
Bakhtin, Mikhail Mikhailovich, Michael Holquist, and Caryl Emerson. *The Dialogic Imagination: Four Essays*. Austin: University of Texas Press, 1981.
Balme, Christopher B. *The Cambridge Introduction to Theatre Studies*. Cambridge: Cambridge University Press, 2008.
Beadle-Brown, Julie, David Wilkinson, Lisa Richardson, Nicola Shaughnessy, Melissa Trimingham, Jennifer Leigh, Beckie Whelton, and Julian Himmerich. "Imagining Autism: Feasibility of a Drama-Based Intervention on the Social, Communicative and Imaginative Behaviour of Children with Autism." *Autism* (Published online ahead of print, 13 September 2017). Available at: https://doi.org/10.1177/1362361317710797.
Bernhard, Anna, and Janel B. Balvanek. "The Importance of Dialogical Relations and Local Agency in Governance Initiatives for Conflict Resolution." In *CORE Policy Brief*. Oslo: PRIO, 2013.
Bhabha, Homi K. *The Location of Culture*. London: Routledge, 1994.
Bleiker, Roland. "Forget IR Theory." *Alternatives* 22, no. 1 (1997): 57–85.
———. *Aesthetics and World Politics*. Basingstoke: Palgrave Macmillan, 2009.
Bleiker, Roland, and Emma Hutchison, "Fear No More: Emotions and World Politics." *Review of International Studies* 34, no. 1 (2008): 115–135.
Boal, Augusto. *The Aesthetics of the Oppressed*. London: Routledge, 2006.
Carlin, Phyllis Scott, and Linda M. Park-Fuller. "Disaster Narrative Emergent/Cies: Performing Loss, Identity and Resistance." *Text and Performance Quarterly* 32, no. 1 (2011): 20–37.
Chen, Boyu, Ching-Chane Hwang, and Lily H. M. Ling. "Lust/Caution in Ir: Democratising World Politics with Culture as a Method." *Millennium—Journal of International Studies* 37, no. 3 (2009): 743–66.
Chinyowa, Kennedy. "Emerging Paradigms for Applied Drama and Theatre Practice in African Contexts." *Research in Drama Education* 14, no. 3 (2009): 329–46.
Chou, Mark. *Greek Tragedy and Contemporary Democracy*. New York: Bloomsbury Academic, 2012.
Cobb, Sara. "Fostering Coexistence in Identity-Based Conflicts: Towards a Narrative Approach." In *Imagine Coexistence*, edited by Antonia Chayes and Martha Minow, 294–310. San Francisco: Jossey Bass, 2003.
Cochran, Clarke E. "Joseph and the Politics of Memory." *The Review of Politics* 64, no. 3 (2002): 421–44.
Cohen, Cynthia. "Engaging with the Arts to Promote Coexistence." In *Imagine Coexistence: Restoring Humanity after Violent Ethnic Conflict*, edited by Martha Minow and Antonia Chaves. Hoboken, NJ: Jossey-Bass, 2003.

———. "Creative Approaches to Reconciliation." In *The Psychology of Resolving Global Conflicts: From War to Peace*, edited by Mari Fitzduff and Chris E. Stout. Vol. 3 Interventions. 69-102. Westport, CT: Praeger Security International, 2006.

———, Roberto Gutiérrez Varea, and Polly O. Walker, eds. *Acting Together: Performance and the Creative Transformation of Conflict: Volume 1: Resistance and Reconciliation in Regions of Violence*. Oakland, CA: New Village Press, 2011.

———, eds. *Acting Together: Performance and the Creative Transformation of Conflict: Volume 2: Building Just and Inclusive Communities*. Oakland, CA: New Village Press, 2011.

Da Costa, Dia. *Development Dramas: Reimagining Rural Political Action in Eastern India*. New Delhi: Routledge, 2010.

Dennis, Rea. "Inclusive Democracy: A Consideration of Playback Theatre with Refugee and Asylum Seekers in Australia." *Research in Drama Education: The Journal of Applied Theatre and Performance* 12, no. 3 (2007): 355–70.

Gallagher, Kathleen, and Ivan Service. "Applied Theatre at the Heart of Educational Reform: An Impact and Sustain Ability Analysis." *Research in Drama Education—The Journal of Applied Theatre and Performance* 15, no. 2 (2010): 235–53.

Hall, Edith. "The Sociology of Athenian Tragedy." In *The Cambridge Companion to Greek Tragedy*, edited by Patricia E. Easterling, 93–126. Cambridge: Cambridge University Press, 1997.

Hammond, Nick. "Introducing Forum Theatre to Elicit and Advocate Children's Views." *Educational Psychology in Practice* 29, no. 1 (2012): 1–18.

Hawes, Dena L. "Crucial Narratives: Performance Art and Peace Building." *International Journal of Peace Studies* 12, no. 2 (2007): 17–29.

Hughes, Jenny, James Thompson, and Michael Balfour. *Performance in Place of War*. Calcutta: Seagull Press, 2009.

Hutchison, Emma, and Roland Bleiker. "Reconciliation." In *Routledge Handbook of Peacebuilding*, edited by Roger Mac Ginty, 81–90. New York: Routledge, 2013.

Jackson, Anthony. "The Dialogic and the Aesthetic: Some Reflections on Theatre as a Learning Medium." *Journal of Aesthetic Education* 39, no. 4 (2005): 104–18.

Jeong, Ho-Won, ed. *Approaches to Peacebuilding*. New York: Palgrave Macmillan, 2002.

Kershaw, Baz. "Performance, Community, Culture." In *The Routledge Reader in Politics and Performance*, edited by Lizbeth Goodman and Jane De Gay, 136–42. London: Routledge, 2000.

Kruuspere, Piret. "Estonian Memory Theatre of the 1990s: Emotional Scale from Fear to Laughter." *Nordic Theatre Studies* 21 (2009): 89–97.

Lederach, John P. *Building Peace: Sustainable Reconciliatin in Divided Societies.* Washington, DC: U.S. Institute of Peace, 1997.
Long, William J. and Peter Brecke. *War and Reconciliation: Reason and Emotion in Conflict Resolution.* Cambridge: MIT Press, 2003.
Magak, Kitche, Susan Mbula Kilonzo, and Judith Miguda-Attyang. "The Place and Prospects of Indigenous Theatrical Performances in Peacebuilding in Kenya." *African Conflict and Peace Building Review* 5, no. 1 (2015): 18–40.
Mani, Rama. "Women, Art and Post-Conflict Justice." *International Criminal Law Review* 11, no. 3 (2011): 543–60.
Moreno, Jacob Levy. *Psychodrama, First Volume.* New York: Beacon House, 1946.
Nash, Steve, and Nick Rowe. "Safety, Danger and Playback Theatre." *Dramatherapy* 22, no. 3 (2000): 18–20.
Nicholson, Helen. *Applied Drama: The Gift of Theatre.* Basingstoke: Palgrave Macmillan, 2005.
Nicholson, Steve. *The Censorship of British Drama, 1900–1968.* 4 vols. Exeter, UK: University of Exeter Press, 2003.
Nussbaum, Martha C. *Political Emotions.* Cambridge: Harvard University Press, 2013.
Obeyesekere, Rajini. *Sri Lankan Theatre at a Time of Terror.* New Delhi: Sage, 1999.
Palihapitiya, Madhawa. "The Created Space: Peacebuilding and Performance in Sri Lanka. In *Acting Together: Volume I*, edited by Cynthia E. Cohen, Roberto Gtierrez Varea, and Polly O. Walker, 73–95. Oakland, CA: New Village Press, 2011.
Power, Seamus A. "Towards a Dialogical Model of Conflict Resolution." *Psychology & Society* 4, no. 1 (2011): 53–66.
Prendergast, Monica, and Juliana Saxton. *Applied Theatre: International Case Studies and Challenges for Practice.* Bristol: Intellect, 2009.
Rai, Shirin M. "Analysing Ceremony and Ritual in Parliament." *The Journal of Legislative Studies* 16, no. 3 (2010): 284–97.
Ranciere, Jacques. *The Politics of Aesthetics.* Translated by Gabriel Rockhill. New York: Continuum, 2004.
Rank, Carol. "Promoting Peace Through the Arts." Paper Presented at the International Peace Research Association, Leuven, Belgium, July 2008.
Ross, Alison. "Derrida's Writing-Theatre: From the Theatrical Allegory to Political Commitment." *Derrida Today* 5, no. 1 (2008): 76–94.
Ross, Marc Howard. "Psychocultural Interpretations and Dramas: Identity Dynamics in Ethnic Conflict." *Political Psychology* 22, no. 1 (2001): 157–78.
Ross, Marc Howard. "The Politics of Memory and Peacebuilding." In *Routledge Handbook of Peacebuilding*, edited by R. Mac Ginty. New York: Routledge, 2013.

Rothstein, Robert L. *After the Peace: Resistance and Reconciliation.* Boulder, CO: L. Rienner Publishers, 1999.
Rowe, Nick. *Playing the Other: Dramatizing Personal Narratives in Playback Theatre.* London: Jessica Kingsley Publishers, 2007.
Sengupta, Ashis, ed. *Mapping South Asia Through Contemporary Theatre: Essays on the Theatres of India, Pakistan, Bangladesh, Nepal and Sri Lanka.* Basingstoke: Palgrave Macmillan, 2014.
Shank, Michael, and Lisa Schirch. "Strategic Arts-Based Peacebuilding." *Peace & Change* 33, no. 2 (2008): 217–42.
Taylor, Diana, and Sarah J. Townsend. *Stages of Conflict: A Critical Anthology of Latin American Theater and Performance.* Ann Arbour: University of Michigan Press, 2008.
Taylor, Phillip. *Applied Theatre: Creating Transformative Encounters in the Community.* Ann Arbour, MI: The University of Michigan, 2003.
Thompson, James, and Tony Jackson. "Applied Theatre/Drama: An E-Debate in 2004: Viewpoints." *RIDE-Research in Drama and Education* 11, no. 1 (2006): 90–95.
Umachandran, Shalini. "The Freedom Struggle Performers Staged." *The Times of India*, August 15, 2010.
Van Dijk, Tuen A. "Discourse and Manipulation." *Discourse and Society* 17, no. 3 (2006): 356–83.
Williams, David. "'Remembering the Others That Are Us': Transculturalism and myth in the theatre of Peter Brook." In *The Intercultural Performance Reader*, edited by Patrice Pavis, 67–78. London: Routledge, 1996.

PART II

Exploring Theatre in Local Peacebuilding Processes

CHAPTER 4

Jana Karaliya: Inviting a Shared Future

Jana Karaliya is a theatre group from Sri Lanka. Being an ethnic separatist conflict between the minority Tamils and majority Sinhalese-led government, and known as the longest lasting conflict in South Asia,[1] the Sri Lankan conflict presents challenging dynamics for peacebuilding. The key parties in conflict are the Government of Sri Lanka (GoSL) and the Liberation Tigers of Tamil Eelam (LTTE). Jana Karaliya started in 2002 during a ceasefire between the parties, and continued its peacebuilding activities throughout the resumption of conflict; a fully-fledged war followed by a military defeat of the LTTE and the ensuing post-war period. Consequently, the protracted violence and the unique dynamics of the ethnic conflict shape Jana Karaliya's approach to using theatre for peacebuilding.

The multivocal and dialogic form of theatre in Jana Karaliya creates a space where parties and narratives in the Sri Lankan ethnic conflict can come together. The group uses theatre's multivocal and dialogic form in unique ways to facilitate a safe, shared, resilient turf amidst the prevalent ethnic tensions.

The group is called Jana Karaliya, Makkal Kalari and Theatre of the People respectively in Sinhalese, Tamil and English. I use Jana Karaliya here as it is the primarily used version by the group.

The chapter explores the work of Jana Karaliya, grounding it in the context of Sri Lanka. Background information on the Sri Lankan conflict elicits challenges for peacebuilding at ground level that Jana Karaliya proceeds to address. The discussion also situates the theatre group within its particular working context by illustrating Jana Karaliya's approach to peacebuilding in the Sri Lankan conflict.

A close study of the theatre practice of Jana Karaliya reveals how theatre opens up possibilities of conversation between parties and narratives in conflict. Three key spheres come to the fore here: personal, emotional and societal. The multivocal and dialogic form of theatre opens up and brings together the attitudes and narratives in conflict in these three spheres to initiate peacebuilding among and between these.

The chapter briefly outlines the challenges and the limitations the organisation faces in relation to its particular theatre style and practice. The challenges in safely navigating aesthetics and politics in fragile volatile conflict contexts arise as a key theme here.

CONFLICT BACKGROUND[2]

Sri Lanka is an island nation with a diverse ethno-religious population going back over 2500 years. A former colony of the Portuguese, Dutch, and finally, the British empires, Sri Lanka received independence in 1948 through a largely political process. Today, the country is a democracy with an Executive President as the head of the State.

According to the 2012 Census Report, the current population stands at a 20.2 million.[3] The major ethnicities in the country are Sinhalese, Tamils, and Moors, respectively accounting for a 74.9, 15.3, and 9.3% of the total population[4]. There is also a small Burgher community that is located mainly in Colombo and the Eastern Province. The three major languages spoken in the country are Sinhala, Tamil, and English. While the first two languages are often exclusively associated with the respective ethnicities, the Moor population in the country uses both. English is recognised as a link language. Religious demarcations are also primarily seen along ethnic lines, with 70% of the population—almost all Sinhalese—being Buddhist, a 12.6% Hindus who are almost all Tamils and a 9.7% Muslims who are mostly Moors. Catholics and Christians are largely from the Sinhala, Tamil, and Burgher ethnicities and make up a total of 7.4% of the total population. Literacy rates in Sri Lanka are high compared with the other nations in the region, standing at a 92.6% for males and a 90% for females.[5]

The ethnic conflict is not the first or the only conflict Sri Lanka faced after independence. The two suppressed insurgencies from the Southern youth in 1971 and 1988–1989 are noteworthy for their scale and duration of violence.

A Brief Overview

The key conflict is between the GoSL and the LTTE, respectively seen to represent the interests of Sinhalese and Tamils. Ethnic grievances leading to the violent turn of the conflict and the undeniable ethno-politicisation of central parties frame the Sri Lankan conflict as an ethnic conflict. As in most protracted conflicts, the roots of the conflict in Sri Lanka are disputed. Some focus on the colonial legacy while others place more emphasis on the political dynamics since independence from Britain in 1948.[6] Others again trace the conflict back through centuries to the periodic invasions of the island kingdom from the Indian subcontinent, especially from Tamil speaking entities in Southern India.

Civilian riots in 1983 marked a violent turn in the conflict. There were several violent outbursts leading up to this event such as the 1958 and 1977 ethnic riots targeted at the Tamil minority, and the 1981 burning of the Jaffna library. However, the most visible—and horrifying—set of attacks and retaliation took place in 1983 following the killing of 13 soldiers deployed in Jaffna on the 23rd of July. This attack triggered an anti-Tamil pogrom in the capital and a few other cities led by organised mobs. The government at the time failed to provide protection and indeed is justly accused of aiding the mobs. These incidents resulted in consolidating the key parties of the conflict as the LTTE and the armed forces of the Sri Lankan government.

The original points of contention in the conflict emerged with the implementation of the so-called "anti-Tamil legislation" soon after independence,[7] and continued to revolve around access to government decision making pertaining to resource distribution, language use, development, and power devolution. The policies focused on clamping down on the privileges the minorities enjoyed during the colonial period. The Sinhala Only act of 1956 made Sinhala the official language of Sri Lanka, effectively curtailing the non-Sinhala speakers—largely the Tamil minority—from accessing state facilities[8] and rendered those who were already within the administrative structure incapable of functioning. This is the first of a series of actions Sinhalese political leaders made to reclaim opportunities and power that were unequally distributed during the colonial period in a bid to secure the majority's vote. Continued ethnocentric politics of the successive Sri Lankan governments—particularly the constitutional amendments in the 1970[9]—were instrumental in institutionalizing the Sinhalese ethnic dominance, and further alienating the Tamil community.

Policies aimed at redressing the situation failed due to a lack of political goodwill. The 13th amendment to the 1978 constitution introduced in 1987 is a case in point: the amendment recognized Tamil as an official language and instituted provincial councils for increased power devolution. These measures failed in implementation because of an absence of political goodwill, and partly due to the existing political system of the country. The Westminster model of democracy left behind from the colonial period favoured a centralized, majoritarian political system[10] instead of a participatory system capable of incorporating the nuances of minorities. Thus, the heterogeneity in the country gave rise to a "culture of ethnic outbidding" where the majority wielded power in its favour.[11] The limitations of the existing political system and the apparent lack of political goodwill of the Sinhalese political leaders contributed to the LTTE's consolidation over the years. The group demanded a separate state—a Tamil homeland—in the North and East, provinces with a strong Tamil speaking denomination. Consequently the Sri Lankan ethnic conflict is also seen as an ethnic separatist conflict.

Peace Process, Final Phase of War and the Post-conflict Period

The peace process failed due to the absence of a ground level movement for peace and a sincere commitment to peace by the conflict parties. In 2000, the government and the LTTE invited Norway to facilitate a peace process. The parties sign a Memorandum of Understanding (MoU) and soon after in 2002, a Cease Fire Agreement (CFA). Relief was only temporary as multiple varieties of spoiler violence surfaced within a short period.[12] A new government formed with the support of nationalistic parties renewed intense military operations in 2005. In response, LTTE carried out a series of suicide bombings and targeted assassinations. Both the parties used the cease-fire to strengthen their firepower and establish strongholds. By 2006 the situation deteriorated to the point that the conflict was in the open again. Following a last attempt at resuming talks in 2007, GoSL officially withdrew from the CFA in January 2008.[13] Guided by external agents, the entire peace process relied on economic recovery as its primary and possibly the sole motivation. In pushing the liberal agendas and expectations forward hoping to bring about an immediate change within the country, the international community failed to take into account the sincerity of either the government or the LTTE and their preparedness for peace.[14] Thus, the Sri Lankan peace process overlooked ground level preparation within either community. As a result, six years after signing the CFA war resumed in full scale.

With that, the Sri Lankan government aimed for a military solution to the conflict with renewed military zeal, increasing recruitment and fostering an unprecedented military budget. A sweeping cultural campaign for war accompanying these changes succeeded in garnering public support as never before. Consequently, the LTTE was militarily defeated on May 19, 2009. State troops found its leader Velupillei Prabhakaran dead in the attack and the government firmly re-established its authority over the former LTTE controlled areas. A victor's peace emerging from the elimination of its adversary reigned the post-war period in Sri Lanka.

In order to facilitate the post-conflict transition of Sri Lanka, the government promised a political solution and appointed a Lessons Learnt and Reconciliation Commission (LLRC) to investigate into the alleged war crimes. Rehabilitation camps were established for the surrendered LTTE soldiers. Nevertheless, in accordance with empirical research where violent political transformation is shown to produce societies characterised by violence,[15] a pervading suppression of dissent and an absence of genuine political will prevented reconciliation or satisfactory integration of the communities in Sri Lanka. Left largely unaddressed the conflict dynamics continued, and allowed to flourish unchecked, the Sinhala-Buddhist nationalistic groups and sentiments that endorsed the war created further division and violence.

A regime change in 2015 brought about some positive changes in the situation. The newly elected government took some steps to contain militarisation and reduce the excessive military presence in the North and East. In October 2015, Sri Lanka co-sponsored a UN Human Rights Council resolution that calls for a judicial process to look into war crimes and disappeared people.

These changes, though positive, are insufficient. While there is some progress on the commitments made to the UN Human Rights Council, implementation at the ground level is yet to take place. President

Maithripala Sirisena intervened to stall operations of the Office on Missing persons, which was approved by the Parliament in August 2016. Despite pre-election promises, a new constitution incorporating mechanisms for a less centralised, more inclusive system of governance shows limited signs of materialising. The current government has failed to construct a congruent narrative of neither reconciliation nor coexistence. As a result, it is constantly pushed to a defensive position while the Sinhala-Buddhist nationalist elements prevalent during the former regime are increasingly gaining more power.

Challenges at Community Level

Legacies of the ethnopolitical conflict shape the social topography of Sri Lanka, posing challenges for sustainable peacebuilding at a community level. Key here are the human impact of the conflict, the continuing ambiguity associated with peace activism, and limited interaction between different ethnicities.

Human Impact

The conflict had a significant human impact that is yet to be satisfactorily addressed. An accurate calculation of the civilian deaths during the conflict is not available due to the absence of impartial observers on the ground during the last phase of the conflict. The report of the Secretary General's Panel of Experts appointed for Sri Lanka quotes from credible sources that the death toll could be around 40,000[16] during the last few months of the conflict, but assumes that the actual number could be as high as 75,000.[17] The loss of lives before the last phase of the conflict is estimated to be between 64,000 and 75,000, while the number of those who have migrated due to the conflict is over a million.[18] Human Rights Watch reports that nearly 300,000 civilians were confined in detention centres[19] while 350,000 were displaced during the final days. Thus, the human cost of the conflict alone made a significant impact upon the Sri Lankan community, both the Tamils and Sinhalese.

Human rights violations from the government's side as well as from the LTTE are other factors that add to the human impact of the conflict. The UN investigative panel identifies some key violations by the government: these include the killing of civilians through shelling, shelling humanitarian objects such as hospitals, denying humanitarian assistance to and inflicting human rights violations upon LTTE suspects and Internally Displaced People.[20] The final phase of the war saw a large number of civilians trapped between the government's advancing forces and the LTTE's final stand. The government is accused of knowingly shelling all the hospitals in Vanni, the United Nations hub and own-designated no fire zones where civilians were encouraged to gather for safety.[21] Also, the government actively prevented supplying food, water and medicine to those who were trapped in-between and unable to escape.[22] There are plausible accusations of those who surrendered to the army being executed[23] and those who were arrested—even on the suspicion of being LTTE supporters or simply to be questioned—being detained indefinitely, raped, tortured and disappeared[24]; and state forces using paramilitary groups for these tasks where necessary.[25] Sri Lanka is consistently ranked as having one of the highest numbers of disappearances in the world over the years, according to the UN Working Group on Enforced or Involuntary Disappearances.[26] Disappearances, arbitrary arrest and detention, assassinations and reports of similar activities come not only from the Tamil community, but also from the Sinhalese and Muslims.[27]

LTTE's actions were hardly any better: banned as a terrorist organisation in over thirty countries, they were frequently charged with extortion of money,[28] abduction and execution of civilians for dissent/punishment and forced child recruitment among many other allegations. During the final stage of war LTTE used civilians as hostages and shot those who attempted escape. Going even further, they used these hostages as a strategic human buffer in the face of GoSL's attack.[29] Scholars observe that LTTE's rule during the cease-fire also failed to benefit the Tamil civilians.[30] These actions considerably impaired LTTE's image among the Tamils community itself. Thus, while the conflict might have started with strong "identitarian motives", factors such as "[i]ntragroup rivalry, forced taxation, prestige, wealth, electoral advantage and anticipated Statehood" became the motivating factors that prolonged and shaped the conflict.[31]

Though the state as well as international agents initiated procedures for addressing war related grievances, the impact of these is dubious. The government appointed the LLRC in 2010 in a response to local and international concerns on the atrocities committed during the last phase of conflict. The LLRC held sessions at national and district level with little actual impact upon the population. The international community continue to challenge it as a deeply flawed, inadequate accountability mechanism that is "neither independent nor impartial in composition",[32] and as a result, unable to meet international standards as an accountability process.[33] Consequently, the UN Human Rights Council passed three resolutions in 2012, 2013 and 2014, gradually increasing in their intensity in the face of Sri Lankan government's noncompliance. Considerable resistance from the then regime diluted the potential impact these could have had within the country. The resolution in 2014 authorised an international war crimes probe from 2002 to the end of war in 2009. The new government elected in January 2015 took a less defensive position than the former regime, and co-sponsored a UN Human Rights Council resolution in October 2015. The resolution aims to promote reconciliation, accountability, and human rights in Sri Lanka, and proposes a judicial process that looks into war crimes and disappeared people to this end. The progress is slow and consequently the government received a two-year extension to implement the proposals at the 34th UN Human Rights Council held in March 2017. Both the post-war governments have made little progress towards conflict transformation when it comes to concrete actions at the ground level.

The resulting impunity for the human rights abuses during and after the conflict is a serious obstacle to reconciliation at the ground level. Authorities often ignore abuses and are slack in investigations. Amnesty International questions their credibility and impartiality even when these are conducted, since there is hardly any "effort to prosecute alleged violators."[34] The few cases that do get to the courts stand the risk of being dismissed. Amnesty International points out that this deplorable state of impunity is primarily due to the lack of political will of the authorities and draws attention to the government's consistent refusal to allow the international to play a role ensuring an impartial process for the victims.[35] Despite the government change in 2015, the situation has not improved. The proposed hybrid judiciary through the UN resolution is yet to be implemented. The feasibility of a hybrid mechanism is questionable given the predominantly Sinhala Nationalist sentiments among a majority of the population. Therefore, even at nearly half a decade after the end of war, a genuine effort at formal reconciliation—an initial step of the larger peacebuilding process—is yet to take place in Sri Lanka.

Peace and Dissent Made Ambiguous

Yet another challenge for sustainable peacebuilding is the ambiguity with which peace activism and dissent has been regarded within the country. Due to the strong nationalist discourses and patriotic rhetoric prevalent within both Sinhala and Tamil communities, "peace activism" as well as any form of dissent has come to occupy a delicate position that is often regarded as treacherous. The liberal values pushed through the peace process strongly painted it as a "western", "capitalist" enterprise, alienating the process from the nationalist, Sinhalese-led South. During the resumption of the war, the state took ample advantage of this situation by grouping all civil resistance against the war into this "western", "capitalist" unpatriotic category and thereby effectively clamping down on all forms of local dissent with near impunity. Consequently, the NGOs have come to be commonly referred to and perceived as "anti-governmental"[36] and "anti-Sri Lankan traitors"[37] through state media,[38] isolating these from the mainstream discourse. All forms of dissent among civil society such as journalism and political activism underwent this labelling. Tactics for civilian repression in the interest of the state or/and politicians' actions often took the form of smear campaigns, intimidation, attack, abduction, persecution and killings[39] Despite sustained local and international agitation, as argued above, we are yet to see a "credible investigation of these claims" or an "effort to prosecute alleged violators."[40] This made genuinely working for peace a dangerous activity in Sri Lanka: speaking out or deviating from the state's version or perspective has become a risky endeavour.

The situation has not undergone a significant change even after the regime change in 2015. While the civilian repression has lessened and there is more freedom for media, activists, and dissent, there is minimal improvement at policy level and judiciary actions that address issues of justice and grievances. Peacebuilding in the Sri Lankan post-conflict conditions needs to be sufficiently creative and unorthodox to escape state or ethno-nationalistic scrutiny, while still being effective.

Lack of Interaction Between Ethnicities

One of the key challenges for sustainable peacebuilding is to overcome ethnic polarisation. The violent conflict is only one factor in this division. Two other significant factors that take the ethnic polarisation beyond the actual history of violent conflict are the geographical separation and the divide and rule policy of the British. Linguistic and religious differences also create a divide, exceedingly limiting the spaces where the conflict parties can come together. Altogether, these allow mistrust and stereotypes to prevail within a highly militarised nationalistic context.

From history, Sinhalese and Tamils generally had separate geographical concentrations that limited interethnic interaction at an everyday level. Tamils are predominant in the North and East of the country while the South was predominantly Sinhalese.[41] Language policies of the independent Sri Lanka[42] and ethnic cleansing carried out by LTTE[43] furthered this divide. Deteriorating security conditions due to conflict obstructed overland connection between the North and the South. First with the closure of the A9 highway connecting the North with Central Province in 1984, and secondly with the termination of the Jaffna—Colombo railway line in 1990. Thus, commuting between the two areas was almost impossible for the majority of the last thirty years.

The end of violent conflict brought changes in this situation. Travelling between the North and South resumed with the reopening of the A9 in 2009. The possibility for increased interaction between ethnicities this offers could be a positive turn.[44] It is hard to say the same for some of the post-conflict reconstruction and resettlement plans launched thereafter. Efforts at imposing a Sinhala-Buddhist identity upon the cultural and geographical spaces are evident. Consider the widespread practices of renaming Tamil villages and roads with Sinhala names—at times with those of the soldiers—and marking the land with newly erected Buddhist statues and temples.[45] Combined with the absence of a proper overarching peacebuilding process at the ground level, such actions invariably breed resentment[46] and further alienation. Thus, the post-war accessibility between the North and the South, despite increased space for interethnic interaction, is fraught with tensions.

Language is another key factor that hinders conflict parties and narratives from coming together and as such, is a key element to be addressed for sustainable peacebuilding. While Tamil was also recognized as an official language in 1987, there is little evidence that this is fully implemented.[47] Minority language speakers are marginalised within the public sphere, which indicates a lack of consideration and respect from the policy makers. The breakdown in communications, alienation and the construction of stereotypes between Sinhalese and Tamils are long-term consequences of this language separation.

The resulting mistrust and fear from lack of interaction creates the space for ethnic stereotypes to emerge and continue in the Sri Lankan context. Given the absence of a common ground where the parties and narratives in conflict can come together, each ethnicity often operates from very different frames of reference: it is difficult to reach a holistic agreement about exactly what the conflict is about, when it started or who it involves. As a result, external events carry multiple and preferred interpretations and these in turn reconstitute the internal frameworks and perceptions of each group, which then again shapes subsequent behaviour.

Later developments also contributed to the emergence of a religious tension within Sri Lankan conflict dynamics. Sinhala Buddhist groups are becoming alarmingly pervasive in recent years, demanding a dominant Sinhala-Buddhist ethno-religious identity associated with the entire island.[48] The anti-Muslim riots triggered in 2014 and 2018, indicate the increasing tendency to relapse into violence. This adds a religious element to the ethnopolitical divisions within the country.

Intense militarization in the post-war context of Sri Lanka poses a significant challenge to sustain peacebuilding at the community level. The post-war regime integrated the military into key governmental positions and agencies: consider the fusion of civic and military spheres in forming *The Ministry of Defence and Urban Development*. With compulsory military training for the university entrants and the Administrative Service recruits, it further encroached the civilian spheres. Violence permeated the society at all levels. Consequently, there were frequent majority attacks on minorities during the regime.[49] Accountable governance, thus, was halted for military ends in the immediate post-war phase.[50]

There were limited spaces where parties and narratives in conflict can safely interact during and after the conflict. Factors such as physical separation and linguistic and cultural differences hindered cooperation while unresolved human rights abuses, intimidation of voices for peace and intense militarization discouraged communities from moving forward. These issues, while less intense after 2015, are still present to varying degrees and remain among the key challenges for sustainable peacebuilding in Sri Lanka.

It is evident that the post-war regime—if it is to move towards peacebuilding—is greatly in need of pluralistic and inclusive spaces where the parties and narratives in conflict can be brought together. The commentators speak of so-called intractable conflicts: situations where antagonisms have persisted for so long that they have created a vicious cycle of violence.[51] This aptly captures the post-conflict situation of Sri Lanka. Apart from political reforms and structural violence resulting from a populist take to governance, peacebuilding in Sri Lanka needs efforts targeted at increasing peaceful interactions between the ethnic communities. In fact, as the regime change in 2015 indicates, a top-level political change is insufficient to bring about changes at the ground level. Creating a pluralistic and an inclusive ground is the first step of sustainable peacebuilding in order to ensure that the political and structural reforms are accepted by the masses. Creative peace initiatives that are flexible and resilient that engage with the communities can do much here. These initiatives have to be capable of providing a space where not only the Sinhalese and Tamils but also the unique narratives of each group can come together within a united platform to create a shared narrative.

Theatre in Sri Lanka

Sri Lankan theatre has been a site of political struggle and expression during the conflict in Sri Lanka. Artistes from different ethnic and social backgrounds took to the stage as individuals and groups to showcase the futility the war, drawing inspiration from local and international theatre traditions. The shifting political realties and the resulting inaccessibility of public spaces including theatres forced the artistes to seek alternative performance spaces and innovative theatre approaches.[52]

A notable theatre production is Euripides's *The Trojan Women*, produced by Dharmasiri Bandaranayake. A veteran Sinhalese artist who took a political stand against the war from a beginning, Bandaranayake worked with a large crew made up of some of the best artists in the industry in 2000 to bring the play to the Sri Lankan stage for the first time. Produced in Sinhalese and initially performed in Colombo, *The Trojan Women* garnered extensive media attention. It also faced significant backlash from extremist factions for its anti-war sentiments. The play had to be discontinued for a while as a result, but resumed performances during the ceasefire period and toured the North and East as well.

Some other plays draw from local theatre traditions and legends to counter the war narratives. *Ravanesan*, initially by Vidyanandan and subsequently by Sinnaiah Maunaguru are examples from the Tamil theatre. A Tamil theatre practitioner and academic from the East, Maunaguru revived *Ravanesan* in 2010. The play reinterpreted the legend of Ravana and his defeat at the hand of Rama, using Tamil Kooththu drama tradition. The story is well known in the Indian subcontinent as a part of *Ramayana*. Instead of valorising war as the narrative usually does, Maunaguru's version highlighted the needless suffering of the bystanders. *Rathnawalli* by Sunil Abeysiriwardene is a parallel example from the Sinhalese theatre. *Rathnawalli* reinterpreted the legend of Dutugemunu, the first Sinhalese king to defeat the Tamil kingdom in the North and unite the island. The story draws attention to the conscious utilisation of Sinhala Buddhist nationalism for state-expansion, and the doubts and remorse Dutugemunu felt regarding the process. Both these plays are remarkable in that they engage with popular, mainstream, pro-war versions of deep-rooted myths of each community, and open these up for alternative interpretations that are completely new and more humanistic.

Apart from individual artistes, there are many theatre groups and organisations that work for peacebuilding. Theatre Action Group in the North is an example of a theatre group that works in Tamil and focuses on the healing and expression of the Tamil communities. Centre for Performing Arts in Colombo and Jaffna produces plays in both Sinhalese and Tamil languages depending on the group they work with. Inter-Act Art, Act4, Abhina, and Stages Theatre are some other groups that primarily work in Sinhalese and English and engage with the conflict and related issues through their performances.

Despite the number of groups and activists using theatre for peacebuilding in Sri Lanka, not many succeed in continuing a sustained, focused, and an intentionally designed approach that tackle the changing dynamics of the Sri Lankan conflict. While some of the plays are powerful, their impact is limited by the restrictions of the traditional stage, language and/or the transient nature of isolated performances. In Sinhalese or Tamil, these cater to a relatively monolingual audience. While these open up the space for personal reflection and engagement within a given ethno-linguistic group, a sustained effort through theatre that initiates and continues with the transformation is absent.

Jana Karaliya

Jana Karaliya operates in the context of Sri Lanka's deeply entrenched conflict as a mobile, multi-ethnic and multi-religious theatre group. The group stands out among the other theatre groups in the country due to their novel approach to peacebuilding. Its name in local vernacular stands for "Theatre of the People." As per its name, Jana Karaliya has succeeded in attracting the support of both the conflict parties in Sri Lanka, a feat achieved by only a very few peacebuilding organizations. Parakrama Niriella and H. A. Perera founded the theatre group in 2002 and the group has been active since 2003. A seven-person management team is there for support as needed and regular reporting purposes, while the Jana Karaliya artiste team shares the responsibility for everyday management and group activities. Most of the participants join Jana Karaliya with prior experience in performing arts and receive more training within the group. Members have their living costs covered and also receive a monthly allowance. Jana Karaliya receives occasional financial support from external bodies and also generates income from public performances. The group's external sponsors include various non-governmental organisations as well as governmental bodies,[53] depending on specific programmes. Over the years, Jana Karaliya has developed strategies, networks, and resources that make the group remarkably resilient (Fig. 4.1).

The physical set-up of the Jana Karaliya theatre is designed to facilitate a multitude of voices that broaden our individual boundaries.

Fig. 4.1 People gather and stand in line outside the mobile theatre, waiting to attend the evening performance

The performance takes place in what is called a "new arena theatre." The stage is located in the middle of a tent. Seating for the audience consists of simple ascending platforms that surround the performance space. In order to reach the seating, the audience has to pass through or around the theatre space. The entry into theatrical space thus takes place through a vivid physical experience that clearly separates the theatrical realm from the conflict bound personal reality that exists outside the tent. The setup of the stage creates a marked enclosure, a separate space where the actors and the audience form a shared community that blurs their respective ethno-political boundaries and roles.

The group formation facilitates a space where the parties and narratives in conflict can be brought together in multiple ways. Inclusion of ethnic diversity and collaboration is mandatory in all the work they undertake. The dialogic and multivocality embedded in the group structure, focus, and preferred theatre form of Jana Karaliya works to create a space where parties and narratives in conflict can come together.

Theatre Approach

The theatre approach of Jana Karaliya demonstrates how dialogic and multivocality bring together parties and narratives in the Sri Lankan conflict. This is evident through four aspects: the group structure and focus, the process of theatre production, the preferred theatre type of the group, and the script.

The objective of peacebuilding is built into the structure and focus of Jana Karaliya. The group aims to take high quality theatre productions to distant areas of the country and to promote peacebuilding among different ethnicities. Such a focus also emerges through the group structure. Jana Karaliya's structure is highly multivocal. It has up to twenty-five members from different ethno-religious and regional backgrounds at any given time. A majority of members are from Sinhala speaking communities, but there is also a significant number of Tamil speaking members. Given this structure—a multi-ethnic team, living, working and touring together—the objective of peacebuilding comes through as a powerful message. When performing, the group stays in one location for about three months, but the time could be shorter or longer depending on the situation. They live and travel together except for brief periods when the members return home. In touring, Jana Karaliya performs in a mobile theatre tent that can house five hundred people at a time and carries two mini theatres that can provide shade for up to three hundred children. Apart from performing within the tent, Jana Karaliya goes into rural schools and conducts education and social change oriented theatre trainings and workshops with the students and teachers. Members of the theatre group carry out activities involved in setting up the theatre, production and performance as well as workshops. Hence mutual understanding, tolerance and trust within and among themselves and the communities where they travel become essential for the group's overall survival. The focus on peacebuilding and reaching out to the less-travelled areas of the country with this message are features built into the very structure of the group. As such, the structure of Jana Karaliya embodies strategies that facilitate multivocality and dialogue. It provides a space where the two ethnicities and their cultures interact with and merge within and beyond the group boundaries.

Jana Karaliya productions also reflect its space for multiple voices and dialogue. These include plays based on original scripts, reproductions and adaptations, some of which are translations of world literature. Parakrama Niriella—a founder—wrote most of the initial scripts. Now, the group members are increasingly taking a proactive role in the writing, translation, and direction of plays. At present, Jana Karaliya repertoire carries several plays produced by its team members. Almost all of these are co-directions of the Tamil and Sinhalese members and won awards at consecutive National Drama Festivals.

The preferred theatre type of the group also facilitates multiple voices and dialogue. Jana Karaliya uses applied theatre. Applied theatre is an umbrella term that incorporates a broad spectrum of dramatic genres performed for social change. The intentional use of drama for social change is the definitive factor here. This flexibility allows Jana Karaliya to draw from and experiment with a broad spectrum of theatre, ranging from traditional theatre forms to the classical and street theatre and at times, forum theatre.[54] Thus, the group is not limited to a given theatre framework and has the freedom to shape its own theatre practice.

Jana Karaliya scripts also emphasise multivocality: they work to bring out the less heard and marginalised voices. The group engages with issues of social justice and discrimination, and consequently problematizes the existing system. The plays invite the audience to think that notions of "good" and "bad" have their rationale in the interests of the dominant social group and are at best, only one narrative of the many that exist. Hence, the plays invite viewers to be critical about their own attitudes and thinking patterns. On purpose, they do not directly engage with the Sri Lankan conflict through their scripts. Doing so, they believe, would alienate the audience and further entrench divisive ethnic narratives by reiteration. Scripts about justice and unity that are equally relevant at a different socio-political level address the conflict indirectly. They draw from Sinhala and Tamil theatre and cultural traditions and perform the plays in both the languages. Adding to this is the politically significant fact that the plays are organised and performed by a multi-ethnic cast who work, travel and live together. Jana Karaliya through its theatre approach creates a shared ideological platform at an everyday level that encourages people to come together, transcending their divisive ethno-political boundaries.

Creating Space for Parties and Narratives in Conflict

Peacebuilding takes place through Jana Karaliya's theatre practice. Inoka, a team member observes that the transformation is something "so subtle" that she cannot express it in words: as she says, it happens through the drama, the touring, in the mobile theatre, and in the interaction with the community through the drama.[55] In closer examination, we can identify three levels at which the multivocality and dialogic of Jana Karaliya changes attitudes at to create a space where parties and narratives in conflict can come together: personal, emotional and societal. This is to say that the dialogic and multivocality of Jana Karaliya's theatre form (1) provides a forum through which individuals can come to terms with their personal experiences of conflict and become more attuned to understanding and appreciating the former enemies; (2) facilitates ways in which individuals and groups can come to terms with the deep emotional wounds inflicted by conflict; and (3) makes the surrounding societal discourses more attuned to accommodating parties that were once in conflict and create more inclusive and pluralist historical narratives. These three methods, spanning the personal, emotional, and societal spheres, facilitate bringing the parties and narratives in conflict together through the space of theatre.

Transforming Personal Experiences of Conflict

The first step towards creating a space where parties and narratives in conflict can come together is the transformation of individual experiences of conflict. This is a feature that almost all Jana Karaliya members identified as essential for their participation: the hope that transforming their own personal experiences with conflict can eventually create a more inclusive and harmonious societal order. Transforming personal experience with conflict is particularly crucial in Sri Lanka, where communication between the groups in conflict was stalled for nearly thirty years and there is little authentic cross-ethnic interaction. Additionally, each of the two major conflict parties has come to constitute their identity around efforts to demonize the other. Within each ethnic group, the stereotyped other is perceived as undesirable and a threat: Tamils associate the Sinhalese with an oppressive state and a brutal military apparatus. The Sinhalese, by contrast, see the Tamils as a disruptive and dangerous terrorist group.[56]

These antagonistic attitudes become insinuated into the day-to-day ways in which people articulate their views, sense of self and interactions with others. The resulting stereotypes continuously fuel conflict and dehumanize the perceived enemy.[57] Stereotypes are found in all realms of Sri Lankan society. Even highly educated people often propagate the myth of ancient hatreds, alleging some sort of irremovable natural differences that inevitably breed conflict. Consider a statement by a former Dean of the Faculty of Human and Social Sciences, University of Ruhuna: "I have met with Tamil students and teachers. But I am not in favour of any close association or forming ties with Tamils … I think the differences we see among the races are natural. I think that forming ties with people of another culture is something dishonourable."[58] This is a widely shared belief even during the post-war period: Take the comment from a Sinhala Buddhist mother in Colombo: "I know that the Tamil medium teachers are training the Tamil kids to become "Kotiyas" [Tigers]."[59] Thus, opening up these stereotypes and humanising each other is a key step in the path to sustainable ground level peacebuilding.

Breaking down stereotypes and deep-seated antagonism, as Jana Karaliya tries to do in performances across Sri Lanka for several years now, is a long and arduous task. In fact, the very premise of Jana Karaliya is highly controversial: a multi-ethnic cast performing in a country devastated by ethnic conflict. Consider the reaction of Sokkalingam Krishanthan, a Tamil theatre group member from Trincomalee, a city particularly affected by ethnic violence. In "FLICT Super Stars," a report prepared for Facilitating Local Initiatives for Conflict Transformation (FLICT) in 2006, Marissa Fernado records Krishanthan's recollection of his initail fear of the multi-ethnic cast of Jana Karaliya: "I was seated on a chair in that corner over there and I looked at those around me with great suspicion and mistrust. I was actually quite convinced that one of the guys [Sinhalese] was a member of the CID [Criminal Investigation Division]." The artistes often arrive at the team as representatives of their respective ethnic group, bearing all its fears, hatred and perceptions.

Almost all the group members comment that engaging in theatre gradually changed their sentiments. Fernando's report documents comments from several others: "[T]hrough the exercises of drama, singing, music and other activities we were able to forge a strong bond. We were able to overcome many of our preconceived ideas about each other and work together towards a common goal." And here a similar example from Sumudu Mallawarachchi, another Sinhalese Jana Karaliya member: "Before I joined Jana Karaliya I used to judge people by looking at them but after I joined, I've learned to respect them, their culture, and their ideas." The theatre group creates a space where individuals from different ethnic groups in the country come together, enabling each one to get to know the other ethnicity. Through this process of facilitating dialogue with and among the cast that brings out different viewpoints, their personal experience and narratives on conflict undergo a transformation.

The same kind of initial suspicion—and often hostility—occurred in the communities where Jana Karaliya performed. Consider the case of Padaviya, a predominantly Sinhalese village situated between the fault-lines of ethnic conflict. As a result of its location and violent history, the village had a population with strong anti-Tamil sentiments. Not surprisingly, the multi-ethnic theatre group was not well received initially. But after a few performances and theatre workshops, the situation gradually became less tense. Children who first reacted to the performance with hostility came to adore Kopika, a Tamil member of the cast. They took to following her around wherever she went. Such a change of attitude—and the resulting ability to form relationships where before there was only hostility—is possible after personal conflict experiences are transformed into narratives that are less vengeful and more accepting of others. Jana Karaliya achieves this through facilitating interaction between ethnicities at a personal level, in a space that is usually not associated with the conflict.

Niriella and the Jana Karaliya members note that while this initial suspicion is the norm for all their first visits, second visits to the same location invariably prove to be very different. It is often a warm welcome stemming from the first encounter. In the second visit to Jaffna, they were inundated with invitations for house visits. In the second visit to Anuradhapura, they had to extend their stay and cram in extra performances to cater to the crowd. In the second visit to Galle, people protested so much about the group's leaving that the team was forced to dismantle the mobile theatre at night and leave early in the morning to avoid the pleas. Thus Jana Karaliya facilitates and nurtures bringing out multiple voices and dialogue through its theatre space. They provide a space where parties and narratives in conflict can come together in each community they visit, initiating transformation.

Transforming Individual Experiences with Conflict

There are three key elements in the personal transformation process initiated by Jana Karaliya: encouraging expression, challenging stereotypes and initiating dialogue. These exemplify the ways in which multivocality and dialogic become integral for transforming personal experiences of conflict. The discussion shows how multivocality and the dialogic emerge through the process, creating a space where parties and narratives in conflict can come together at a personal level.

Encourage Expression

Expressing experiences with conflict—whether they are first hand or learned through others in the community—is frequently regarded as a key step in transformation. Jana Karaliya embraces this multivocal element by presenting a public forum where people can voice their feelings. Doing so allows individuals who experienced conflict a chance to come to terms with past events and perhaps even heal some of the related trauma. In an ideal scenario, sharing testimonies of conflict also gives members of the audience—and perhaps members of the hostile parts of the community—the chance to see how the conflict was experienced from the other side.

Theatre's multivocality that comes from encouraging different forms of communication—including non-verbal ones—is central in this. The inability to speak each other's language substantially hinders communication between Sinhalese and Tamils in Sri Lanka. Such difficulty is surpassed in the theatre space, since here, the expression is an embodied experience that surpasses the limits of rational discourse. It can take different forms such as music, dance and other activities. Not even the different members of Jana Karaliya could talk to each other initially.

Their inability to communicate linguistically promoted other, non-verbal forms of communication. Such interactions may actually suit the Sri Lankan context well, since language is a key issue that aggravate the ethnic divisions. Thus, Jana Karaliya integrates multivocality and the resulting potential of dialogic into its theatre process.

Challenge Stereotypes

The second component in the personal transformation process is challenging stereotypes. It is intimately related to how theatre creates a distance between a fictional performance and the often-brutal reality experienced by the performer or spectator in the real world. The multivocal and dialogic form of theatre is integral to the process. Through its space where multiple voices can coexist without significant repercussions, theatre provides the opportunity to take part in conflict narratives outside the risks of real life. The performance is a safe space, so to speak—a space that enables individuals enmeshed in conflict to express themselves in a manner they may not be able to do otherwise. In Sri Lanka, the spheres outside art are far more hostile and would not necessarily tolerate the type of ideology represented through Jana Karaliya. Thus, the distance created between the performance space and real life is crucial in transforming stereotypes through theatre. It allows space—inside and outside us—for characters to break out of their stereotypes, opening possibilities for the third step in the individual transformation process: initiating an internal dialogue between the existing and the ideal.

The distancing that occurs in theatre facilitates multivocality. The notion of playing a fictional role, rather than living real life, challenges preconceived perceptions and makes room for multiple voices and views to be heard. Doing so is essential if one is to address key issues that account for the cycles of violence: hatred, deep-seated antagonisms, even unwillingness to hear the archenemy. Jana Karaliya creates the space not only for the group, but also for the audience to take on roles that might often be denied to them in real life, thus providing the chance to explore new ways of knowing the conflict and expressing its grievances.[60] Leela Selvarajan, a member of Jana Karaliya, notes that many people come to the stage to speak at the end of the performance: they come there to voice their opinions, to share how they felt with others and often they display vulnerability and an openness that is rarely seen in life outside.[61] Thus, through its theatre practice, Jana Karaliya facilitates multivocality within the individuals in the audience and the team alike.

Jana Karaliya's absence of specific ethno-religious or linguistic affiliation is another factor that facilitates moving away from stereotypes. When participating in the performances of Jana Karaliya the actors do not represent particular ethnic, religious, or political groups. They are there as actors. They perform as members of humanity at large. Theatre thus provides individuals with access to—and even ways of acting out—roles that they otherwise would never be able to experience. Consider a youth who attended a performance of Jana Karaliya in Kebithigollewa, another border village that suffered many massacres due to the conflict. He stresses "this was one of the most unforgettable moments in my life. I never thought that I would ever speak so freely with a young Tamil woman."[62] Thus, Jana Karaliya has created a space where the different ethnicities can come together to initiate shared narratives that are more pluralistic and inclusive.

Enhancing theatre's capacity for multivocality and the dialogic, Jana Karaliya offers participants a chance to slip in and out of different roles, perhaps even to try on the personae of the enemy. Doing so inevitably challenges the stereotypical perceptions that fuel the conflict in Sri Lanka—the idea, for instance, that Tamils are a certain type of people or that Sinhalese behave in a given way. These attitudes often change after performances. Numerous members stress this point in their interviews. Take Manjula Ramasinghe, a Jana Karaliya member from the strongly Sinhala community in Hambanthota. He believed that all the Tamils are terrorists and credited the theatre in helping him overcome the fear of interacting with them. Having engaged through the medium of theatre with other Tamil youths, he is now convinced that he has a lot of things in common with them despite the ethnic, cultural and religious differences that differentiate them. These barriers, he stresses, exist mostly in our minds and were established through hostile ways of constructing notions of identity and community.[63] This is but one example where Jana Karaliya was imperative in generating inclusive and pluralistic individual narratives on the ethnicities in conflict, where there was previously only alienation and antagonism.

Jana Karaliya enhances the multivocality and dialogic of its theatre form through challenging common language stereotypes. The group's plays are bilingual, with separate Tamil and Sinhala versions of the same play. Each performance features a multi-ethnic cast. When the Tamil actors speak with a Sinhala accent, and vice versa, the performance challenges the stereotypes each group believes in, rendering this very stereotype no longer valid to explain their experiences. Hence Jana Karaliya creates a space where separation between the two languages blurs, and standard ethnic monolingualism is renounced: challenging the language stereotypes creates shared, inclusive narratives that address a primary grievance related to the conflict.

A striking example for the potential impact of these role-play reversals is seen in the way Jana Karaliya was received by both the GoSL Army and the LTTE. This is an example highly stressed by Parakrama Niriella, a co-founder of Jana Karaliya. When performing in Anuradhapura in a ground close to the Army Hospital, the injured soldiers got so close to the group that they came regularly for performances and often provided food and snacks for the entire group. Similarly, the LTTE took responsibility for organising Jana Karaliya performances in Muthur when Jana Karaliya performed in the Eastern Province of the country, which was then under the LTTE control. They promised to ensure the safety of the entire group, and the LTTE Eastern Commander inviting the group for tea, voiced that "this is how we want to live in this country."[64] Thus, the group has effectively created a space where each ethnicity—even the militants—can stand together.

In an ideal scenario, then, role-plays and role reversals help people to reach some sort of common humanity in formerly opposed individuals. Embodying multivocality through theatre leads to a disintegration of stereotypes that each side has about the other and creates the space for inclusive personal narratives and communal relations.

Initiate Dialogue

The third element in how theatre transforms personal narratives is through initiating dialogue. Doing so improves communication and understanding between groups. Performing and touring together is a process that requires communication between performers as well as between performers and the audience. Jana Karaliya promotes dialogue by structural and psychological means. Unlike a proscenium stage, seating the audience in ascending platforms circling the stage as they do in

Jana Karaliya allows the audience to face each other, facilitating interaction and connection. Manjula, a member of the cast, believes that this is a key feature that encourages community dialogue.[65] The smiles and tears brought on by the performance become part of the dialogue among the audience members. These can convey subtle messages that are hard to be satisfactorily captured with words. For a politically charged society like Sri Lanka, this is an important element. Kalidas, Leela and other commentators do in fact stress that theatre—and the arts in general—is the key instrument through which dialogue can be reintroduced into communities that no longer talk to each other.[66] Therefore, Jana Karaliya actively generates spaces where individuals and personal narratives of conflict are brought together engage in dialogue (Fig. 4.2).

Encouraging expression, challenging stereotypes, and initiating dialogue are all key elements of Jana Karaliya's approach to transform individual experiences with conflict. Addressing the emotional impacts of the conflict is also a necessary task in transforming personal experiences of conflict.

Fig. 4.2 A scene from inside the mobile theatre

Addressing Emotional Impact of Conflict

The second theme through the chapter explores Jana Karaliya's process of creating a space where parties and narratives in conflict can come together, is its potential in creating more inclusive and less violence-prone emotional narratives. Doing so requires engaging with the types of collective emotions that fuel the conflict cycle.

The multivocal and dialogic form of theatre is particularly suited to the task. It calls for an embodied expression going beyond the boundaries of regular communication. Thus, engaging with emotions as Jana Karaliya does in its work indicates the embodiment of theatre's multivocal and dialogic form in their theatre practice.

Emotions are central in determining how we feel and behave as members of a collective and as individuals. They are even more central when dealing with the aftermath of conflict—a time when fear and hatred dominate the political landscape. A number of studies have demonstrated that the human mind is more likely to remember incidents with strong emotional associations, for all emotional memories receive preferential processing in registering, storing and retrieval in comparison to cognitive memories.[67] This privileged position in memory enables emotions to identify specific issues and establish priorities in the general reasoning mechanisms of the mind: hence emotions play a key role in devising strategies to achieve their preferred choices.[68] Through the process of influencing our remembering and decision-making, emotions become critical in deciding where we place ourselves and with whom we form alliances.

In post-conflict societies, feelings of anger and revenge are often so strong that they generate, contribute to and perpetuate highly dangerous cycles of violence. Ethnic contexts are particularly noted for being emotion-laden, rendering a shared future further obtuse.[69] Consider the stereotypical perceptions that each of the conflict groups in Sri Lanka has of the other. These stereotypes, which continually fuel conflict, are mostly based on anger and fear. They have been formed through the memory of violence and death.

Any peacebuilding effort needs to deal with the role of collective emotions in order to be successful in the long-term. Engaging with collective emotions requires space for the multivocal and dialogic. The challenge in engaging with emotions is two-fold: firstly it consists of recognizing how fear and anger create ever more conflict. Secondly it requires finding a way through which a sense of community can be created around feelings that do not incite hatred: these can be empathy or compassion for the former enemies or a mutual sense of grief, or, indeed, hope for a shared future. Establishing such an emotional transformation of community attachments and interactions is connected with a dialogic process and is of course, a long-term and difficult task. This is why it has to start at the local level and gradually work its way through society.

Local theatre groups, such as Jana Karaliya, are ideally placed to initiate and spread such processes of emotional transformation. The capacity to engage with emotions is, indeed, one of the key features of theatre as a peacebuilding method. The role of emotion within theatre can be explored under two main categories.

The first emotional feature of Jana Karaliya's work is its ability to provide actors and the audience the opportunity to re-live emotions. Re-living emotions allows them to come to terms with their grief and anger, thus taking an important step towards coming together. Consider the strong visual impact of theatre in creating shared images, which many commentators associate with the potential of replacing old (conflict prone) memories with new, different ones.[70] Kalidas[71] astutely picked up on this aspect of theatre in saying that "people see theatre like pictures. If we do a workshop for theatre, it will end with the day. But because theatre creates pictures it is different. We are remembered." He further explains his point with an example: "we stayed in Anuradhapura for about three months, and the people there tell us that when they see the ground, it is always Jana Karaliya they remember. This stays inside people's minds because it is pictures. That is what theatre is." Anuradhapura is an area that is deeply woven into the divisive conflict narratives. It is a centre of several Sinhala-Buddhist kingdoms and has witnessed severe LTTE attacks. It also has a strong military presence. Thus, the story holds much significance. The ability of theatre to bring out the emotional perspectives is key in this transformation. Jana Karaliya succeeds in creating a space where parties and narratives in conflict come together to form a shared emotional narrative through experiencing and reliving emotions as a community.

The second aspect has to do with how theatre can contribute to the establishment of more inclusive emotional attachments to communities. Facilitating inclusive emotions illustrates the dialogic process that results from re-living emotion as discussed earlier. In the process of re-living emotion, Jana Karaliya might help to attenuate often-divisive emotions, such as anger, fear and hatred. These emotions often become key rallying points after conflict. Grief and loss, by contrast, are often silenced and so are attempts to show empathy to the opposing side. Selective suppression of emotions actively limits multivocality and dialogue. To continue with the previous example of Anuradhapura, a land that held a strong anti-Tamil and militarised Sinhalese identity, now also holds parallel memories of a harmonious multiethnic theatre group. Consequently, more inclusive emotions have gradually entered the spaces so far held by anger and fear. The resulting shift in the community enables the expression of emotions like grief, loss and empathy that contribute to reconciliation. Jana Karaliya, accordingly, creates a space where emotional narratives of parties in conflict can come together.

Jana Karaliya brings together communities and enables them to deal with these issues at their own pace, in their own ways. Given that the group stays in one location for a period of three months performing as often as requested, the community engagement is prolonged. In doing so, it potentially creates new and less divisive emotional narratives among communities, through a multivocal and a dialogic process. At the end of each performance, the cast introduces themselves, saying their name and hometown, using the language they are most comfortable with. This routine often becomes an emotional moment for the audience. As a group member observes: "when we talk to them some of them start to cry, there's always a reason behind why they cry and most of the time it's because they feel silly about the grudge they've been holding against the Tamil people."[72]

As this section illustrated, theatre can make space for transforming emotions so that anger, fear, and hatred are no longer dominant, but make room for sadness and grief that in turn, become sources of commonness and a space where both the communities can come together. Reconciliation might come about when certain emotions, such as hatred and anger, are superseded by different ways of engaging with past traumatic events.[73] Focusing on loss and grief, for instance, is much more likely to bring about a shared sense of community. Consider how a member of Jana Karaliya observes that "[i]f we've made a change within the people then I feel that this is what we've achieved."[74] Hence theatre in Jana Karaliya actively engages with emotion, thus facilitating a space where parties and narratives in conflict can come together creating inclusive emotional narratives in the place of divisive narratives of hatred and fear through utilising the multivocal and dialogic form provided therein.

Creating Inclusive and Pluralistic Societal Narratives

Jana Karaliya presents much potential for creating a space where parties and narratives in conflict can come together at the societal level. The ways in which Jana Karaliya initiates inclusive and pluralistic societal narratives is closely related to dialogic process and multivocality encouraged through the group. The personal and emotional transformations discussed earlier are part of a larger peacebuilding process that involves transformation of societal attitudes among parties to the conflict. Questions of identity, historical memory and cultural belonging are essential to the process of overcoming conflict. As previously discussed, in the Sri Lankan context, each party to the conflict rehearses a different understanding of the past and upholds a different notion of what it means to be a member of society. Often these forms of identity are highly politicized and involve constituting the other party to the conflict as alien and/or inferior.

Jana Karaliya creates a space where multiple societal narratives are brought together to be more inclusive and pluralistic in this milieu in three noteworthy methods: the group through its structure and productions, draws from and merges the different drama traditions of the Sinhalese and Tamils, giving rise to new societal narratives; it triggers pluralistic societal narratives among the audience members by representing a possible ideal microcosm of ethnic collaboration; finally, it presents an alternative ideological platform where the parties and narratives in conflict can come together as allies.

Merging Traditions

Jana Karaliya draws from and merges the Tamil and Sinhalese drama traditions and in turn, cultures. This process initiates a dialogue between the respective groups and thereby gives rise to inclusive and pluralistic narratives. While there are some similarities between artistic and cultural traditions in the Sinhalese and Tamil communities, there are notable differences. For Jana Karaliya's director Parakrama Niriella, the very space of theatre is a forum where different cultural and aesthetic traditions can come together and produce a new and more positive attitude.[75] Jana Karaliya draws from both the traditions in producing its plays. Take *Charandas* for an example: the Sinhala production of *Charandas* uses drums and other music instruments along with costumes and steps used in Tamil theatre styles while the Tamil production does vice versa. Niriella cites the local language adaptations of the Sanskrit drama *Mrichchhakatika*, *Meti Karattaya* (Sinhala) and *Mruchchakateeham* (Tamil), as cases in point where plurality in the Sri Lankan society come together to promote cooperation and inclusiveness.[76] He notes this to be a different turn in Sri Lankan theatre since this transition of cultural aspects to both ethnicities at the same time has not happened before. In the process of effecting this transition, Jana Karaliya bridges the relationships between Tamil and Sinhala artistes, initiating a process of dialogue between them.

Jana Karaliya also encourages the transfer of traditional stories from one culture to the other: translation of *Enthayum Thayum* by the renowned Tamildramatist Kulanthei Shanmugalingam into a Jana Karaliya Sinhala production and the production of *Nalapana Jathakaya* from Buddhist mythology by a Tamil youth group are examples.

Jana Karaliya also plays a critical role in claiming a place for Tamil theatre at a national level, thereby highlighting the potential and diversity it offers. Such visibility is important for creating inclusive and pluralistic societal narratives. While theatre is a highly valued form of art in both the communities, we see Tamil theatre only in small pockets, limited to specific areas. It is difficult to fully appreciate or utilise the wealth of resource available within Tamil theatre and the artists engaging in it. Jana Karaliya Tamil language productions are robust and high quality, wining several national drama festival awards and representing Sri Lanka in international drama festivals. The group contributes to enriching Tamil theatre through producing young talents as well. Take Loganathan, who honed his language and translation skills through Jana Karaliya and has produced work that draws much local and international appreciation.[77] Similarly, Jana Karaliya has produced accomplished actors, production managers, lighting and sound directors. The vice versa is true for Jana Karaliya as well. As Leela personally testifies, the group takes Sinhala plays to communities where Sinhala theatre has not reached before: being a Tamil from a peripheral area, she saw a Sinhala play for the first time after she joined Jana Karaliya.[78] Enhancing visibility and empowerment of both the theatre forms contributes to pluralistic and inclusive societal narratives.

The personal development that takes place in this process also results in creating inclusive and pluralistic social narratives. It opens up new paths for communities where there were none, bringing in the voice of communities hitherto neglected. Take the example of Kalidas,[79] who comes from an estate Tamil community in the upcountry. The impact of Jana Karaliya has been immense upon him and his community. Recipient of the Best Actor Award in the State Drama Festival in 2006, he perceives the momentum of Jana Karaliya and his role in it as a turning point for his entire community. It enables him to open a new avenue for his community to belong to the larger society and make themselves heard. This is the case for Ajanthan as well[80]: as the lighting director for the team and also the winner of a Best Actor-Tamil Award at the State Drama Festival, he sees himself as a path-breaker for his school, community, and the Tamil cultural sphere in general. There are many other similar stories. These stories mark the beginning of different, new cultural narratives for people who were marginalised and traditionally limited to a set of given designations that all too often created tension and friction. Jana Karaliya, therefore, draws from and merges the drama traditions in the island, giving voice to where there was none or very little, initiating a process of dialogue between the cultures and creatinginclusive and pluralistic societal narratives in the process.

A Microcosm of Ethnic Cohesion

Another way in which Jana Karaliya triggers pluralistic societal narratives is by emulating a model microcosm that exemplifies ethnic cohesion of an ideal Sri Lanka. The primary way in which Jana Karaliya engages with the conflict is through its group theatre process. The team is bilingual, reconciling the language issue that is a primary grievance of the larger conflict. The different ethnicities work together in the group, living and travelling as a family for the better part of a year. The process of producing the drama and the actual production itself is a demonstration of ethnic cooperation. The group, with time, becomes an exemplary ideal of reconciliation and cohabitation, existing within the widespread conflict narratives outside. The alternative contemporary narrative Jana Karaliya represents in the larger conflict context, challenges the predominant stereotypes by its very existence and smooth functioning (Fig. 4.3).

Through its travels, the group presents a unique microcosm of ethnic cooperation that has the potential to initiate inclusive and pluralistic social narratives within the communities they encounter. Jana Karaliya's practice of living and working for an extended period within a given community supports this process. It facilitates the time and social engagement required for the gradual formation of new cultural narratives in the place

Fig. 4.3 A scene from Jana Karaliya play *Charandas*, featuring two long-term actors of the group: Logananthan Suman (right) plays the lead role, while Sumudu Mallawarachchi plays the lead supporting role (left)

of existing ones. Manjula[81] explains that after about a month of performances, the villagers start coming every evening to the theatre, not only to see the same performances over and over, but also to be in an environment that allows them to interact with each other. This involves meeting and engaging with various people they would otherwise not interact with, including people from other ethnic groups. An audience member observes that "engaging in creative activities together like this can be more effective than simply producing or watching a drama."[82] This goes hand in hand with Jana Karaliya's belief that the process is stronger than any message conveyed through a drama. The persons actively engaged in such processes deeply understand the values of inclusiveness and the strength in unity. The group focuses on the process through which it works. Within the larger social context, Jana Karaliya functions as a model microcosm that travel, live and learn together: a group that promotes multivocality and initiate dialogic processes of interethnic relationships. This harmonious multi-ethnic gathering epitomizes an ideal existence between Sinhalese and Tamils—as a potential manifestation of the end result of conflict transformation and reconciliation.

An Alternative Ideological Platform

The final way in which Jana Karaliya encourages pluralistic and inclusive societal narratives is through presenting an alternative ideological platform where the parties and narratives in conflict can come together as allies to express themselves and forge relationships. The group does not discuss peace, or explicitly use peace as a theme in its dramas.[83] Instead, Jana Karaliya focuses on the shared issues the ethnicities face as a strategy for finding common ground.

As a shared ideological platform for all ethnicities, Jana Karaliya's dramas often bring up a critique against the ruling elite classes and portray the oppression of working classes. Several group dramas are evidence of these critiques, such as *Charandas, Andara Mal* and *Sekkuwa*. Parakrama Niriella explains that the group has also actively supported and "constantly joined hands with progressive labour movements through creative activities."[84] Take the collaboration between Jana Karaliya and the Ceylon Workers' Red Flag Union in February 2011 in promoting awareness on the rights of labour communities in Hatton. Here, the organisation conducted street drama, and produced and performed four dramas on the issues estate sector women face. Afterwards, the group also facilitated forum discussions on behalf of the Red Flag Women's Movement. The political standpoints of the labour movements resonate within Jana Karaliya plays, presenting a neutral, alternative yet politically significant platform for the conflicting parties to rally together despite their differences.

Hence the theatre practice of Jana Karaliya creates a space where parties and narratives in conflict can come together at personal, emotional and societal levels to form inclusive and pluralistic narratives in the place of existing divisive and antagonistic narratives. Bleiker notes that the most effective way of challenging the prevalent stories is by telling new stories instead of the old[85]—and it is this that comes through the theatre process of Jana Karaliya. The group tells and embodies new stories of ethnic collaboration by its very existence and in the connections they make with the communities they travel through.

The multivocality in theatre that is integrated into the very structure of the group operates in different ways to bring out the different voices in the country, such as acknowledging, facilitating healing, and telling new stories of ethnic collaboration. The dialogic works through the space of theatre to initiate conversations that are more accommodating of the other, within and between the different ethnic groups and conflict narratives. It actively generates stories of ethnic collaboration within and beyond the group parameters. At a personal and communal level, these stories reorient the divisive narratives to be more accommodative and incorporative of the perceived enemy. Jana Karaliya prepares the ground for a larger reconciliation process to take place in Sri Lanka, by creating the space where shared relationships emerge between the Sinhalese and Tamils. This is crucial for building sustaining peace, where peace does not mean the mere absence of armed violence, but also an absence of the overarching attitudes that maintain and perpetuate conflict dynamics.

Challenges

A key limitation with Jana Karaliya's peacebuilding is its self-imposed restrictions on thematic engagement through scripts. At times, this runs the risk of misrepresenting the group as being intentionally and/or unintentionally complicit with the state ideology, despite the alternative ideological platform just discussed.

Jana Karaliya's self-imposed restrictions on thematic engagement with the conflict extend in two directions: firstly, the group intentionally refrains from performing or submitting scripts that run the risk of being banned by the Public Performance Board (PPB) of Sri Lanka. It is mandatory for any public performance to obtain PPB's approval for its script in advance. The group policy to abide by the rules appears sensible from certain perspectives. It is indeed unlikely that any scripts dissenting with the prevailing view of the government will be approved through this state apparatus. However, theatre is more than the script: there is clearly room to permeate the barrier of censorship while remaining within the mandatory framework. When there are high censorship regulations in place, pushing through even the tiny loopholes takes on an enormous significance.

Nevertheless, Jana Karaliya's intentional withholding of utilizing the full potential of theatre curtails the group's reach in building peace to a certain extent. Jana Karaliya's passive acceptance in this issue can imply a voluntary subjection to the state views. It can be further interpreted as a silent endorsement or an agreement. Parakrama Niriella acknowledges this in saying that the group intentionally does not produce dramas that the PPB is "compelled to ban." He justifies this approach on the grounds of group interests: "If we continue to do dramas subjected to regular bans we won't be able to carry out our mission."[86] Thus, while the group's choice in performing only the plays that are approved by the PPB is open to challenge, a vision of surviving as a theatre for peacebuilding group in the long-term drives this decision rather than an actual desire to comply.

Jana Karaliya's second restriction on thematic engagement is its reluctance to directly engage with conflict issues.[87] Until recently, the group purposely did not discuss the conflict through its plays. The decision to focus on social justice issues provides an alternative ideological platform that accommodates the ethnicities. However, this can leave Jana Karaliya's plays open to interpretations that are not always conducive to peacebuilding. Movements for social justice also operate within nationalistic stances. These groups can appropriate Jana Karaliya plays to serve their own ends. One such example is the staging of *Charandas* in 2007 at Pannala. *Janatha Vimukthi Peramuna* (Peoples Liberation Front), a leftist political party that supported the war from a Sinhala-nationalist standpoint organised the event in support of a cause that was rather partisan in the conflict, and hence problematic from a peacebuilding point of view. This incident generated an internal discussion that made the group more vigilant in choosing their external performances. The conscious decision to avoid thematic discussion on conflict, therefore, leaves Jana Karaliya plays open for external appropriation. The dominant conflict discourse can use them to fulfil its political agendas.

One can even go so far as to argue that it is this thematic neutrality that facilitates Jana Karaliya's acceptance among the conflict groups; that it is this neutrality that mitigates political repression and community resistance through its non-confrontational manner. Here, the community acceptance Jana Karaliya enjoys can be won at the risk of ignoring or glossing over core issues behind the conflict. Instead of proactively facilitating a shared understanding, it could allow the bridge between the two ethnicities to be conceptualised in their own respective terms. Such a relationship may be fragile and easily unsettled as a result of external influences.

In the absence of direct thematic engagement with conflict, the question arises whether being portrayed as a microcosm of ethnic harmony makes Jana Karaliya inadvertently serve the requirements of the prevalent system. Looking at Jana Karaliya as a harmonious microcosm of interethnic cooperation makes the group an exception to the ordinary. The uniqueness of the group sets itself apart from the ground level society, as well as the realities and practical difficulties that go along with it. In this case, acceptance among the hardliners is easy to come: being a microcosm unto themselves, Jana Karaliya is a separate entity with no visible political associations. The resulting neutrality, bred in isolation, causes a possible distancing between the theatre group and its performance from the ground level, where conflict narratives exist and are applicable. While it is clear that Jana Karaliya holds much potential for peacebuilding, the idealisation and potential separation of being seen as an ideal microcosm and the thematic neutrality, can impair the group's political significance to some extent.

Nevertheless, given the nature of the group's work and the significance of its multi-ethnic bilingual existence, it is inconceivable that Jana Karaliya can indeed survive if not for these particular approaches in the script and the structure. Niriella justifies the non-engagement with conflict narratives on the grounds that it helps avoid alienation of audience and ensure the group's safety. At times, the thematic non-engagement has become the only means to ensure a measure of safety for the group. In each new location they travel to, Jana Karaliya is often reported to the police as a "suspicious group": the community as well as the local authorities look at them with hostility and subject them to informal—and at times formal—questioning. During the conflict period, members had to undergo rigorous security checks at the checkpoints they passed while travelling. Tamil members had to report to the police stations in certain areas and at times were detained for questioning. The founders, making use of their established reputation in the country, had to personally intervene in order to ensure the team's safety. Maintaining the very presence of Jana Karaliya itself is a challenging task due to the external pressures, not to mention the internal challenges that arise within a multi-ethnic group.

In abiding by the state rules, Jana Karaliya draws from and plays on the mainstream tendency to see theatre as a seemingly inconsequential medium to intervene in political affairs. Rai argues that performative acts in political ceremonies and rituals render the audience susceptible in two ways: "either by suggesting that what is performed is what politics is or by suggesting that the performance is of no consequence and therefore neither is the politics that it represents."[88] Jana Karaliya, in scripting politics, works along similar lines: with its scripts focusing on issues other than the conflict, Jana Karaliya thwarts possible objections from its audience. The group consciously cultivates the trait of presenting itself as seemingly inconsequential in terms of mainstream conflict issues, in the interests of the group's acceptance, survival, and continuation.

The very strength of its local and extended engagement also demonstrates the limits of the contribution that Jana Karaliya and other theatre groups can make to processes of peacebuilding. Healing the wounds of conflict takes time—often generations. It has to happen at the local level and it inevitably involves compromises and setbacks. Jana Karaliya shies away from directly engaging with contentious issues since doing so could lead to political repression. It could alienate the audience and thus defeat the very idea of promoting peacebuilding processes.

As a result of its chosen approach, Jana Karaliya has remained resilient throughout the changing phases of the conflict. With the different dynamics of the post-conflict situation, the group is gradually moving into discussing themes that are more relevant. Its recent plays discuss post-conflict resettlement issues and the language difficulties that the Tamil community faces. Also, the solidarity that is generated through living, working and travelling together, and in some ways through becoming a microcosm of ethnic harmony, enables the group to stand together on a daily basis against the entrenched ethnic divisions they encounter at each location. Therefore, presenting an alternative unifying ideological platform of social change through the group themes and the self-imposed restrictions of the group are slow but necessary, steady strategies for building peace in the particular conflict dynamics at play in Sri Lanka.

Conclusion

Jana Karaliya, as a multi-ethnic organisation working in Sri Lanka, has been politically active in a highly fragile context with changing phases of conflict. The peacebuilding approach of the group is inevitably shaped by this context. The group addresses a significant issue at the heart of the Sri Lankan conflict that continues to characterise the post-conflict scenario of Sri Lanka: the entrenched alienation of the Sinhala and Tamil ethnicities from each other, in part driven by exclusive narratives. As numerous accounts of the Sri Lankan conflict testify, the protracted conflict led to increasing ethnic separation and alienation along with intense militarisation of the island, culminating in peace activism itself being regarded as ambiguous and unpatriotic within the mainstream conflict narratives. Jana Karaliya, suitably adapted to survive in this divisive and repressive context existing even at this late post-conflict period, creates a space where these parties and narratives in conflict can safely come together. It is here that we can locate Jana Karaliya's significance as a local theatre group using theatre for peacebuilding.

This chapter explored three themes under which Jana Karaliya utilised the multivocal and dialogic form of theatre to create a space where parties and narratives in conflict can come together: changing conflict attitudes at the personal, emotional and societal levels. Transforming the personal narratives of conflict happens through expressing the experience of conflict, transcending stereotypes and initiation of dialogue between the different ethnicities at an individual level. Jana Karaliya engaged with the emotional residues of the conflict by using theatre as a space for remembering and reliving the feelings triggered by conflict, leading to the initiation of more inclusive emotional narratives among communities. The group uses theatre's dialogic and multivocal form, thirdly, to initiate pluralistic and inclusive societal narratives through bridging the theatre traditions of the conflict parties, by presenting a model microcosm of ethnic harmony and by presenting an alternative ideological platform where the ethnic adversaries can become allies.

The group's self-censorship presents certain limitations. Jana Karaliya seeks state approval for the scripts and refrains from thematically engaging with conflict issues. This creates a possibility of the group being co-opted into the system as an ideal but nationalist model of ethnic harmony. However, this limitation is also key in ensuring the group's safety and continuation. Self-censorship facilitates the group's extended, in-depth engagement in the fragile and repressive context of Sri Lanka where many others have failed to continue as impartial local peacebuilding organisations. These elements, initially seen as limiting, indeed form part of the group's resilience strategy.

It becomes apparent, therefore, that Jana Karaliya utilises the multivocal and dialogic form of theatre to create a space where parties and narratives can come together within the particular situation of Sri Lankan conflict: this flexibility through theatre helps the group navigate a fine line between aiming for legitimisation and vocalising political objectives associated with peacebuilding. Recognizing these limits, and acknowledging that transformation takes time, does not negate the power of theatre to create spaces that contribute in important ways to peacebuilding processes. Indeed, Jana Karaliya's role assumes further relevance given its subtle yet sustained activism that evolves in response to changing political conditions. Such artistic engagements are crucial for two reasons: they create the necessary local preconditions for peace, and they persistently generate hope and insights that political leaders can use to promote reconciliation at the national level. This unique way of approaching theatre for peacebuilding sets Jana Karaliya apart from the other two case studies discussed in this book.

Notes

1. Michael Walzer, *Arguing about War* (New Haven, CT: Yale University Press, 2004); Mona Fixdal, *Just Peace: How Wars Should End* (Palgrave Macmillan, 2012), 66.
2. This overview offers a generalised version and does not purport to encompass the complexities seen on the ground. It is solely meant for the outsider to gain a general understanding of the context for the purposes of relating to the way in which Jana Karaliya uses theatre as a peacebuilding method, and as such, is not comprehensive by any means.
3. Department of Census and Statistics - Sri Lanka, "Sri Lanka Census of Population and Housing - 2011" (Department of Census and Statistics - Sri Lanka, 2012).
4. This includes both the Sri Lankan and Indian Tamils, respectively making up 11.2% and 4.1% of the total population of the country.
5. While the literacy rate in Sri Lanka is high in comparison to the region, it is debatable whether it is as high as the statistics indicate. Several pertinent factors, such as accuracy of the data collection process and the criteria for assessing literacy, render the statistics questionable.
6. See Fixdal, *Just Peace: How Wars Should End*; Neloufer de Mel, Kumudini Samuel, and Champika K. Soysa, "Ethnopolitical Conflict in Sri Lanka: Trajectories and Transformations," in *Handbook of Ethnic Conflict: International Perspectives*, ed. Dan Landis and Rosita D. Albert (New York: Springer, 2012); and N. DeVotta, "Ethnolinguistic Nationalism and Ethnic Conflict in Sri Lanka," in *Fighting Words: Language Policy and Ethnic Relations in Asia*, ed. Michael E. Brown and Sumit Ganguly (Cambridge, MA: MIT Press, 2003).
7. Sarah Holt, *Aid, Peacebuilding and the Resurgence of War: Buying Time in Sri Lanka* (Basingstoke: Palgrave Macmillan, 2011), 5.
8. Due to widespread protests from the Tamil-speaking minority, a Special Provisions Act in 1958 amended The Sinhala Only Act to permit Tamil to be used in the North and East for administrative purposes, and as a medium of instruction in schools, universities, as well as in public examinations. Also, see *Aid, Peacebuilding and the Resurgence of War: Buying*

Time in Sri Lanka (2011); de Mel, Samuel, and Soysa, "Ethnopolitical Conflict in Sri Lanka: Trajectories and Transformations"; and R. A. L. H. Gunawardana, "Roots of the Conflict and the Peace Process," in *Buddhism, Conflict and Violence in Modern Sri Lanka*, ed. Mahinda Deegalle (New York: Routledge, 2006) for a detailed discussion on the correlation between the language policy and conflict.

9. Fixdal, *Just Peace: How Wars Should End*, 68.
10. Sumantra Bose, *Contested Lands: Israel-Palestine, Kashmir, Bosnia, Cyprus, and Sri Lanka* (Cambridge: Harvard University Press, 2007), 12.
11. Fixdal, *Just Peace: How Wars Should End*, 67.
12. See Alan Bullion, "The Peace Process in Sri Lanka," in *Conflict and Peace in South Asia*, ed. Manas Chatterji and B. M. Jain (Bingley, UK: Emerald, 2008); de Mel, Samuel, and Soysa, "Ethnopolitical Conflict in Sri Lanka: Trajectories and Transformations."
13. See Jonathan Goodhand, Jonathan Spencer, and Benedikt Korf, ed., *Conflict and Peacebuilding in Sri Lanka: Caught in the peace trap?* (London: Routledge, 2011) for a detailed analysis of the dynamics involved in the peace negotiations in Sri Lanka.
14. Oliver P. Richmond and Ioannis Tellidis, "The Complex Relationship between Peacebuilding and Terrorism Approaches: Towards Post-Terrorism and a Post-Liberal Peace?," *Terrorism and Political Violence* 24, no. 1 (2011): 126.
15. Richard Jackson, "Post-Liberal Peacebuilding and the Pacifist State," *Peacebuilding* 6, no. 1 (2018).
16. Marzuki Darusman, Steven Ratner, and Yasmin Sooka, "Report of the Secretary-General's Panel of Experts on Accountability in Sri Lanka" (The United Nations, March 31, 2011), 41.
17. "Report of the Secretary-General's Panel of Experts on Accountability in Sri Lanka" (The United Nations, March 31, 2011), 40.
18. Holt, *Aid, Peacebuilding and the Resurgence of War: Buying Time in Sri Lanka*.
19. Human Rights Watch, "World Report 2012: Sri Lanka" (Human Rights Watch, 2012).
20. Darusman, Ratner, and Sooka, "Report of the Secretary-General's Panel of Experts on Accountability in Sri Lanka," iii.
21. "Report of the Secretary-General's Panel of Experts on Accountability in Sri Lanka," 23–35.
22. Amnesty International Report 2012: The State of the World's Human Rights (Amnesty International, 2012), 3.
23. Two credible allegations against the government are the White Flag incident where Pulidevan and Nadesan—two prominent leaders of LTTE—were invited to surrender carrying white flags and subsequently

executed, and the case of Balachandran, the 12 year old son of the LTTE leader Prabhakaran who was executed at close range. See Amnesty International, "Sri Lanka: Reconciliation at a Crossroads: Continuing Impunity, Arbitrary Detentions, Torture and Enforced Disappearances" (Amnesty International, 2012), 4; Darusman, Ratner, and Sooka, "Report of the Secretary-General's Panel of Experts on Accountability in Sri Lanka," 43; and Frances Harrison, "Witnesses Support Claim That Sri Lanka Army Shot Prisoners," *The Independent*, February 24, 2013 for a detailed discussion.

24. Fixdal, *Just Peace: How Wars Should End*, 82; Darusman, Ratner, and Sooka, "Report of the Secretary-General's Panel of Experts on Accountability in Sri Lanka," 46–48.
25. Neil DeVotta, "Sri Lanka: From Turmoil to Dynasty," *Journal of Democracy* 22, no. 2 (2011): 133; see Darusman, Ratner, and Sooka, "Report of the Secretary-General's Panel of Experts on Accountability in Sri Lanka," 55.
26. See Human Rights Watch, "Recurring Nightmare: State Responsibility for 'Disappearances' and Abductions in Sri Lanka" (Human Rights Watch, March 6, 2008); Working Group on Enforced or Involuntary Disappearances, "Civil and Political Rights, Including the Questions of: Disappearances and Summary Executions: Question of Enforced or Involuntary Disappearances" (United Nations, January 18, 2002).
27. Amnesty International, "Sri Lanka: Reconciliation at a Crossroads: Continuing Impunity, Arbitrary Detentions, Torture and Enforced Disappearances," 4; DeVotta, "Sri Lanka: From Turmoil to Dynasty," 133.
28. "Sri Lanka: From Turmoil to Dynasty," 132.
29. Darusman, Ratner, and Sooka, "Report of the Secretary-General's Panel of Experts on Accountability in Sri Lanka," iii–iv, 64–66.
30. Fixdal, *Just Peace: How Wars Should End*, 82.
31. de Mel, Samuel, and Soysa, "Ethnopolitical Conflict in Sri Lanka: Trajectories and Transformations," 100.
32. Amnesty International, "Sri Lanka: Reconciliation at a Crossroads: Continuing Impunity, Arbitrary Detentions, Torture and Enforced Disappearances," 5.
33. Human Rights Watch, "World Report 2012: Sri Lanka"; Darusman, Ratner, and Sooka, "Report of the Secretary-General's Panel of Experts on Accountability in Sri Lanka," 117–18.
34. Amnesty International, "Sri Lanka: Reconciliation at a Crossroads: Continuing Impunity, Arbitrary Detentions, Torture and Enforced Disappearances," 4.
35. Ibid.

36. S. Thillainathan, "Rehabilitation of Ex-Ltte Cadres, Not Highlighted in Geneva," *Sunday Observer*, March 17, 2013.
37. DeVotta, "Sri Lanka: From Turmoil to Dynasty," 133.
38. Human Rights Watch, "World Report 2012: Sri Lanka."
39. See Amnesty International, "Sri Lanka: Reconciliation at a Crossroads: Continuing Impunity, Arbitrary Detentions, Torture and Enforced Disappearances"; Darusman, Ratner, and Sooka, "Report of the Secretary-General's Panel of Experts on Accountability in Sri Lanka." for a further discussion on these conditions. The assassination of Lasantha Wickramathunga (Editor-Sunday Leader), the disappearance of Pradeep Ekneligoda (Political writer and cartoonist), the attack and fleeing of Upali Tennakoon (Editor-Rivira) and the persecution of Frederica Jansz (Editor-Sunday Leader) are a few specific examples of curtailing dissent.
40. Amnesty International, "Sri Lanka: Reconciliation at a Crossroads: Continuing Impunity, Arbitrary Detentions, Torture and Enforced Disappearances," 4.
41. Colombo as the commercial capital was heterogeneous and displayed the full hybrid nature of the country.
42. See de Mel, Samuel, and Soysa, "Ethnopolitical Conflict in Sri Lanka: Trajectories and Transformations." for a discussion on how language policies resulted in strengthening ethnic concentration and a large number of semi-educated youth feeling restricted to the North and East.
43. LTTE forcibly evicted all non-Tamils from the North and East. In the 48 hours allocated for eviction in the North, a 72,000 Muslims were made into IDPs in 1990.
44. The extent to which the opening of the A9 and the subsequent inter-ethnic interactions contribute to peace become questionable on two points: the military involvement in regulating civil spaces and interactions in the North, and the nature and consequences of local post-war tourism. The Army with their roadside shops, security posts, boat services and general presence primarily caters to the large numbers of Sinhalese tourists visiting Jaffna. The large numbers of tourists from the South assert Sinhalese culture and engage in hostile tourism. Anoma Pieris, "Southern invasions: Post-war tourism in Sri Lanka" *Postcolonial Studies 17*, no. 3 (2014) offers a further discussion. Thus, whether the opening of the A9 has brought about real multiethnic interaction and business opportunities to Jaffna is questionable.
45. Rachel Seoighe argues that the post-conflict reconstruction in the North and East of the country is a continuation of the post-colonial process of Sinhala Buddhist revival. See Rachel Seoighe, "Inscribing the victor's land: nationalistic authorship in Sri Lanka's post-war Northeast," *Conflict, Security & Development* 16, no. 5 (2016).

46. de Mel, Samuel, and Soysa, "Ethnopolitical Conflict in Sri Lanka: Trajectories and Transformations," 98.
47. Tamil is incorporated into the primary and secondary education system at the moment but this is not a compulsory subject that carries weight in the exams. Thus, the attitude towards learning the language is casual.
48. Groups such as *Bodu Bala Sena* and *Sihala Ravaya* emerging at the wake of the armed conflict fuel Sinhala Buddhist extremism in the country. These groups lobbied for banning halal and with seeming state compliance, openly provide leadership to anti-Muslim and to a smaller extent, anti Christian campaigns.
49. Holt, *Aid, Peacebuilding and the Resurgence of War: Buying Time in Sri Lanka*, 74–75. In June 2014, anti Muslim riots in Aluthgama resulted in four deaths and the displacement of nearly 10,000 people.
50. de Mel, Samuel, and Soysa, "Ethnopolitical Conflict in Sri Lanka: Trajectories and Transformations," 101.
51. See Robert D. Kaplan, *Balkan Ghosts: A Journey through History* (London: Picador, 2005).
52. See Kanchuka Dharmasiri, "From Narratives of National Origin to Bloodied Streets: Contemporary Sinhala and Tamil Theatre in Sri Lanka," in *Mapping South Asia through Contemporary Theatre: Essays on the Theatres of India, Pakistan, Bangladesh, Nepal and Sri Lanka*, ed. Ashis Sengupta (Basingstoke: Palgrave Macmillan, 2014) for a detailed discussion of Sri Lankan theatre.
53. In 2012–2013 Jana Karaliya undertook a programme on behalf of the Ministry of National Languages and Social Integration to conduct a series of workshops to promote interethnic understanding and social integration.
54. Though the group experiments with forum theatre, it is not a primary method of engagement. Therefore the focus here will specifically be on their foundational applied theatre performances.
55. Inoka Lankapura, Interveiw with the author, Puttalam, August 28, 2012.
56. These stereotypes are used as a point of analysis here. We need to recognise that the range of attitudes and behaviours of Sri Lankans cannot be reduced to these extreme positions, irrespective of the context.
57. See Cynthia Cohen, "Engaging with the Arts to Promote Coexistence," in *Imagine Coexistence: Restoring Humanity After Violent Ethnic Conflict*, ed. Martha Minow and Antonia Chaves (Hoboken, NJ: Jossey-Bass, 2003), 267–79.
58. Saman Kariyakarawana, "Attitude and Responsibilities of the Southern Academics," in *Dealing with Diversity: Sri Lankan Discourses on Peace and Conflict*, ed. George Frerks and Bart Klem (The Hague: The Netherlands Institute of International Relations, 2004), 102–3.

59. Vidyamali Samarasinghe, "A Theme Revisited'? The Impact of the Ethnic Conflict on Women and Politics in Sri Lanka," *Journal of Women, Politics & Policy* 33, no. 4 (2012): 354.
60. See Augusto Boal, *The Aesthetics of the Oppressed* (London: Routledge, 2006); Sue Jennings and Ase Minde, *Art Therapy and Dramatherapy: Masks of the Soul* (London: Jessica Kingsley Publishers 1993).
61. Leela Selvarajan, interview with the author and Harshadeva Amarathunga, Thambuttegama, February 22, 2008.
62. Sumith Ganangoda, interview with the author and Harshadeva Amarathunga, Thambuttegama, February 22, 2008.
63. Manjula Ranasinghe, interview with the author and Harshadeva Amarathunga, Thambuttegama, February 22, 2008.
64. Parakrama Niriella, interview with the author, Thambuttegama, February 22, 2008.
65. Manjula Ranasinghe, interview with the author and Harshadeva Amarathunga, Thambuttegama, February 22, 2008.
66. Focus group interview with the actors, interview with the author and Amarathunga, Thambuttegama, February 22, 2008.
67. William J. Long and Peter Brecke, *War and Reconciliation: Reason and Emotion in Conflict Resolution* (Cambridge, MA: MIT Press, 2003). Also, see James L. McGaugh, *Memory and Emotion: The Making of Lasting Memories* (New York: Columbia University Press, 2003); Elizabeth A. Phelps and Tali Sharot, "How (and Why) Emotion Enhances the Subjective Sense of Recollection," *Current Directions in Psychological Science* 17, no. 2 (2008).
68. Long and Brecke, *War and Reconciliation: Reason and Emotion in Conflict Resolution*.
69. Marc Howard Ross, "Psychocultural Interpretations and Dramas: Identity Dynamics in Ethnic Conflict," *Political Psychology* 22, no. 1 (2001): 162.
70. Wulf Kansteiner, "Finding Meaning in Memory: A Methodological Critique of Collective Memory Studies," *History and Theory* 2, no. 41 (2002); Marc Howard Ross, "Psychocultural Interpretation Theory and Peacemaking in Ethnic Conflict," *Political Psychology* 16, no. 3 (1995): 526–31.
71. Focus group interview with the actors, interview with author and Harshadeva Amarathunga, Thambuttegama, February 22, 2008.
72. Manjula Ranasinghe, interview with the author and Harshadeva Amarathunga, Thambuttegama, February 22, 2008.
73. Long and Brecke, *War and Reconciliation: Reason and Emotion in Conflict Resolution*, 28.
74. Focus group interview with the actors, interview with author and Harshadeva Amarathunga, Thambuttegama, February 22, 2008.

75. Parakrama Niriella, interview with the author, February 22, 2008 and Parakrama Niriella, interview with the author, August 28, 2012.
76. Ibid.
77. Logananthan's translation of *Metikaraththaya—Mruchchakateeham* in Tamil—drew critical acclaim at its screenings both locally and internationally.
78. Focus group interview with the actors, interview with the author and Amarathunga, Thambuttegama, February 22, 2008.
79. Ibid.
80. Ajanthan Shanthakumar, interview with the author, Puttalam, August 29, 2012.
81. Manjula Ranasinghe, interview with the author and Harshadeva Amarathunga, Thambuttegama, February 22, 2008.
82. Nishanthan Krishna, interview with the author, Colombo, November 2, 2010.
83. Arosha Ranaweera, interview with the author, Puttalam, August 20, 2012; Palitha Abelal, interview with Harshadeva Amarathunga, Puttalam, August 29, 2012.
84. Parakrama Niriella, "Janakaraliya' Mobile Theatre–Sri Lanka," interview by Ajay Joshi, Lanka-e-News, May 22, 2013. http://www.lankaenews.com/English/news.php?id=13689.
85. Roland Bleiker, "Forget IR Theory," *Alternatives* 22, no. 1 (1997).
86. Parakrama Niriella, interview with author, August 28, 2012.
87. Since 2010 Jana Karaliya has gradually started engaging with themes such as the language divide between the Tamil and Sinhala communities, through the content of their plays.
88. Shirin M. Rai, "Analysing Ceremony and Ritual in Parliament," *The Journal of Legislative Studies* 16, no. 3 (2010): 294.

References

Amnesty International. "Amnesty International Report 2012: The State of the World's Human Rights." Amnesty International, 2012.
———. "Sri Lanka: Reconciliation at a Crossroads: Continuing Impunity, Arbitrary Detentions, Torture and Enforced Disappearances." Amnesty International, 2012.
Bleiker, Roland. "Forget IR Theory." *Alternatives* 22, no. 1 (1997): 57–85.
Boal, Augusto. *The Aesthetics of the Oppressed*. London: Routledge, 2006.
Bose, Sumantra. *Contested Lands: Israel-Palestine, Kashmir, Bosnia, Cyprus, and Sri Lanka*. Cambridge: Harvard University Press, 2007.
Bullion, Alan. "The Peace Process in Sri Lanka." In *Conflict and Peace in South Asia*, edited by Manas Chatterji and B. M. Jain, 149–69. Bingley, UK: Emerald, 2008.

Cohen, Cynthia. "Engaging with the Arts to Promote Coexistence." In *Imagine Coexistence: Restoring Humanity After Violent Ethnic Conflict*, edited by Martha Minow and Antonia Chaves. Hoboken, NJ: Jossey-Bass, 2003.
Darusman, Marzuki, Steven Ratner, and Yasmin Sooka. "Report of the Secretary-General's Panel of Experts on Accountability in Sri Lanka." The United Nations, March 31, 2011.
de Mel, Neloufer, Kumudini Samuel, and Champika K. Soysa. "Ethnopolitical Conflict in Sri Lanka: Trajectories and Transformations." In *Handbook of Ethnic Conflict: International Perspectives*, edited by Dan Landis and Rosita D. Albert, 93–118. New York: Springer, 2012.
Department of Census and Statistics - Sri Lanka. "Sri Lanka Census of Population and Housing, 2011." Department of Census and Statistics - Sri Lanka, 2012.
DeVotta, Neil. "Ethnolinguistic Nationalism and Ethnic Conflict in Sri Lanka." In *Fighting Words: Language Policy and Ethnic Relations in Asia*, edited by Michael E. Brown and Sumit Ganguly, 105–39. Cambridge, MA: MIT Press, 2003.
———. "Sri Lanka: From Turmoil to Dynasty." *Journal of Democracy* 22, no. 2 (2011): 130–44.
Dharmasiri, Kanchuka. "From Narratives of National Origin to Bloodied Streets: Contemporary Sinhala and Tamil Theatre in Sri Lanka." In *Mapping South Asia through Contemporary Theatre: Essays on the Theatres of India, Pakistan, Bangladesh, Nepal and Sri Lanka*, edited by Ashis Sengupta, 208–37. Basingstoke: Palgrave Macmillan, 2014.
Fixdal, Mona. *Just Peace: How Wars Should End*. New York: Palgrave Macmillan, 2012.
Goodhand, Jonathan, Jonathan Spencer, and Benedikt Korf, ed. *Conflict and Peacebuilding in Sri Lanka: Caught in the peace trap?* London: Routledge, 2011.
Gunawardana, R. A. L. H. "Roots of the Conflict and the Peace Process." In *Buddhism, Conflict and Violence in Modern Sri Lanka*, edited by Mahinda Deegalle, 177–201. New York: Routledge, 2006.
Harrison, Frances. "Witnesses Support Claim That Sri Lanka Army Shot Prisoners." *The Independent*, February 24, 2013.
Holt, Sarah. *Aid, Peacebuilding and the Resurgence of War: Buying Time in Sri Lanka*. Basingstoke: Palgrave Macmillan, 2011.
Human Rights Watch. "Recurring Nightmare: State Responsibility for 'Disappearances' and Abductions in Sri Lanka." Human Rights Watch, March 6, 2008.
———. "World Report 2012: Sri Lanka." Human Rights Watch, 2012.
Jackson, Richard. "Post-Liberal Peacebuilding and the Pacifist State." *Peacebuilding* 6, no. 1 (2018): 1–16.

Jennings, Sue, and Ase Minde. *Art Therapy and Dramatherapy: Masks of the Soul.* London: Jessica Kingsley Publishers, 1993.
Kansteiner, Wulf. "Finding Meaning in Memory: A Methodological Critique of Collective Memory Studies." *History and Theory* 2, no. 41 (2002): 179–97.
Kaplan, Robert D. *Balkan Ghosts: A Journey through History.* London: Picador, 2005.
Kariyakarawana, Saman. "Attitude and Responsibilities of the Southern Academics." In *Dealing with Diversity: Sri Lankan Discourses on Peace and Conflict*, edited by George Frerks and Bart Klem. The Hague: The Netherlands Institute of International Relations, 2004.
Long, William J., and Peter Brecke. *War and Reconciliation: Reason and Emotion in Conflict Resolution.* Cambridge, MA: MIT Press, 2003.
McGaugh, James L. *Memory and Emotion: The Making of Lasting Memories.* New York: Columbia University Press, 2003.
Phelps, Elizabeth A., and Tali Sharot. "How (and Why) Emotion Enhances the Subjective Sense of Recollection." *Current Directions in Psychological Science* 17, no. 2 (2008): 147–52.
Pieris, Anoma. "Southern Invasions: Post-War Tourism in Sri Lanka." *Postcolonial Studies* 17, no. 3 (2014): 266–285.
Seoighe, Rachel. "Inscribing the Victor's Land: Nationalistic Authorship in Sri Lanka's Post-War Northeast." *Conflict, Security & Development* 16, no. 5 (2016): 443–471.
Rai, Shirin M. "Analysing Ceremony and Ritual in Parliament." *The Journal of Legislative Studies* 16, no. 3 (2010): 284–97.
Richmond, Oliver P., and Ioannis Tellidis. "The Complex Relationship between Peacebuilding and Terrorism Approaches: Towards Post-Terrorism and a Post-Liberal Peace?" *Terrorism and Political Violence* 24, no. 1 (2011): 120–43.
Ross, Marc Howard. "Psychocultural Interpretation Theory and Peacemaking in Ethnic Conflict." *Political Psychology* 16, no. 3 (1995): 523–44.
———. "Psychocultural Interpretations and Dramas: Identity Dynamics in Ethnic Conflict." *Political Psychology* 22, no. 1 (2001): 157–78.
Samarasinghe, Vidyamali. "'A Theme Revisited'? The Impact of the Ethnic Conflict on Women and Politics in Sri Lanka." *Journal of Women, Politics & Policy* 33, no. 4 (2012): 345–64.
Thillainathan, S. "Rehabilitation of Ex-LTTE Cadres, Not Highlighted in Geneva." *Sunday Observer*, March 17, 2013.
Walzer, Michael. *Arguining about War.* New Haven, CT: Yale University Press, 2004.
Working Group on Enforced or Involuntary Disappearances. "Civil and Political Rights, Including the Questions of: Disappearances and Summary Executions: Question of Enforced or Involuntary Disappearances." United Nations, January 18, 2002.

CHAPTER 5

Jana Sanskriti: Transforming Through Empowerment

Jana Sanskriti is a grassroots theatre-activist group from India that addresses structural violence in West Bengal. Jana Sanskriti uses the multivocal and dialogic form of theatre to bring out important but less heard narratives of structural violence into the communal discourse. The theatre group carries out political activism through a number of avenues aiming for the transformation of structural violence primarily in West Bengal. However, this chapter does not aim to present a conclusive picture of the group's activities: instead, it aims to engage with selected elements of Jana Sanskriti that are relevant from a perspective of peacebuilding.

An initial overview of the background within which Jana Sanskriti works outlines the narratives of structural violence in West Bengal, and explores peacebuilding as a means of addressing structural violence. A discussion of Jana Sanskriti's work as a theatre group in this context follows with special attention given to the ways in which Jana Sanskriti embraces multiple voices and a dialogic process within the group structure.

Looking closely at Jana Sanskriti's theatre practice, the chapter highlights two steps in its process of peacebuilding through theatre: performing resistance and initiating transformation. Performing resistance to embedded narratives of structural violence is an integral part of Jana Sanskriti's theatre practice and this resistance, in turn creates a tension, wherein

© The Author(s) 2018
N. Premaratna, *Theatre for Peacebuilding*,
Rethinking Peace and Conflict Studies,
https://doi.org/10.1007/978-3-319-75720-9_5

transformation takes root. Multivocality emerges as a central theme in this process of performing resistance.

Jana Sanskriti's use of theatre visibly transforms narratives of structural violence within two key spheres: political and socio-cultural. Drawing from the broad array of Jana Sanskriti work, the chapter highlights the potentials and limitations of the particular theatre form of Jana Sanskriti.

The chapter concludes with a discussion of two key challenges the group faces: one, navigating a balance between aesthetics and politics in performance; and two, navigating a balance between nurturing a group identity and an individual artiste/activist identity.

Conflict Background

Jana Sanskriti engages with issues of structural violence in West Bengal. Structural violence is an important element in peacebuilding that is rarely discussed from a perspective of art and peacebuilding. Jana Sanskriti's peacebuilding at the community level emerges in tackling some of the rampant issues of structural violence in West Bengal, such as women's rights and political and religious violence.

Structural Violence and West Bengal

Jana Sanskriti's most active and longest standing groups are all concentrated in West Bengal. Its work emerged within the state itself as a response to the structural disparities in the community. Among all Indian states, West Bengal is the thirteenth in size and the seventh in population density, and more than two thirds of its total population fall under the rural category.[1] The overall male-female percentage is roughly divided along equal lines.

Among the many issues of structural violence Jana Sanskriti touches upon, two distinct directions emerge for their relevance to peacebuilding in West Bengal: violence in the political and socio-cultural spheres.[2]

Structural violence embedded in politics invariably shapes lives in rural West Bengal. A key issue here is the elitist and inefficient structures of representation in the political sphere. Election violence is widespread. Residents identify villages where the community perceives being political hatchet men—or goondaism—as their inherited profession.[3] The high frequency of reported incidents of election violence in polls and the state statistics on West Bengal[4] indicate the level of violence ingrained in the state's political structures.

Structural violence in socio-cultural narratives is the other key aspect. Religion and gender-based violence are examples. These often manifest at a family and community level and are further embedded into the everyday life. West Bengal has a relatively low record of religious violence in comparison to other Indian states such as Gujarat. In 2009 and 2010, there were two riots between Hindus and Muslims that resulted in the deployment of the army as a controlling measure.[5] The communal riots in Dhulagarh in 2016 is another example.[6] In contrast, West Bengal's gender-based violence rates high. It consecutively led all twenty-eight states in India in crime against women statistics in 2011 and 2012.[7] Broken down into population statistics, West Bengal constituting 7.5% of the Indian population account for nearly 12.7% of the total reported crimes against women in the country. In the overall 2015 and 2016 Crime Against Women statistics the state comes second to Uttar Pradesh.[8] The situation in West Bengal is dire than the statistics imply in comparison, as the number of reported cases in West Bengal are from less than half the projected female population in Uttar Pradesh. There is a pervasive cultural acceptance for gender-based violence and discrimination at a daily level. Domestic abuse is common, and the state records the highest number of reported crimes in the category of "Cruelty by husband or his relatives" across India. Practices like the dowry system are still prevalent, though its impact has somewhat lessened over the years. Rape statistics in West Bengal are also high, in comparison with the other states. As a number of studies indicate, literacy rates are also a key indicator of structural violence. There is a significant disparity between the rural and urban literacy rates, with the former at 66.08% compared to 81.70% for the latter.[9]

These statistics indicate that structures of violence in West Bengal are at a high level. The narratives of structural violence support and feed each other, thereby creating a tight web that supports the embedded violence in political and socio-cultural structures. This is a cyclic process that reproduces further violence unless it is addressed. Jana Sanskriti's peacebuilding challenges this cycle.

Peacebuilding as Addressing Structural Violence

Addressing structural violence is part of peacebuilding. Scholars continue to call for a broader conceptualisation of violence and conflict that allows for the inclusion of protracted narratives of silent yet visible violence that takes place at an everyday level.[10] As Johan Galtung convincingly argued, marking a milestone in peace and conflict studies, violent social structures of a society unfairly affect a given category or categories of people living in that community.[11] The resulting inequality and discrimination breed violence and create a tension that often manifests as interpersonal, intergroup or intercommunal conflict. To address this, it is important to transform the existing hierarchical structures into a system with a fairer distribution of power.

Peacebuilding incorporates a range of activities within its umbrella that take an immediate focus on ending direct violence, to a long-term focus on addressing root causes of violence, including structural injustices. The locus of peacebuilding from a perspective of structural violence is often the everyday: the everyday manifestations of injustice, discrimination, abuse, and exclusion.[12]

Peacebuilding through addressing structural violence takes on the task of building peace within intangible, embedded narratives of structural violence. Structural violence refers to the limitations, differences and "even deaths" that result when "systems, institutions, or policies" meet some people's needs and rights at the expense of others; and it becomes a matter of peacebuilding when these structures foster inequality between groups—be it ethnic or racial, religious, caste, class, gender, language, or age, thereby propagating direct and indirect violence.[13]

There is a clear correlation between structural violence and direct conflict. Structural violence reproduces itself, ultimately culminating in direct conflict unless there is an intervention. Lisa Schirch highlights this cycle in observing that violent public structures infect the entire culture.[14] Consider economic disparity for an example: Studies verify that there is a strong correlation between economic disparity in a community and the prevalence of everyday violence.[15] Economic disparity is both an indication of structural injustices and a main contributory factor for other root causes of structural violence. It often serves as a fundamental factor for latent conflict, and if allowed to continue unaddressed, manifests as structural violence that inevitably leads to violent conflict. There is also a statistical correlation between structural violence and "higher levels of secondary violence" such as "civil wars, terrorism, crime, domestic violence, substance abuse and suicide."[16] Even at a surface level examination, many armed conflicts reveal that they have roots that extend to structural issues such as inequal resource distribution and inadequate political representation.

Addressing and transforming narratives of structural violence are a prerequisite to a culture of peace. Peacebuilding in this broader form seeks to "prevent, reduce, transform, and help people recover from" violence of all forms, including structural violence that is yet to lead to large-scale "civil unrest."[17] This holistic approach is what Lederach perceives as peacebuilding when he terms it as a process of moving a given population from a condition of extreme vulnerability and dependency to one of self-sufficiency and wellbeing.[18] Bringing the prevalent but less heard narratives of structural violence into the communal discourse, therefore, is an essential component of establishing sustainable peace.

Theatre in India

Theatre as an art form goes beyond the realm of entertainment in India. Many cite Bharata Muni's *Nāṭyaśāstra* dated back to 500BCE–500CE as a key text in this regard. It highlights the importance of performing arts in encouraging self-reflection and engaging the audience in questions of ethics and spirituality. Performances such as *Ramleela* based on *Ramayana* went on for days at an end with the participation of entire villages. Apart from the mainstream narratives of theatre, we can find other local theatre traditions that go back into history among the many and varied cultural communities in India. Take *Band Pather* from Kashmir and *Kattaikuttu* from rural northern Tamil Nadu, as well as many other tribal and folk theatre forms found in Karnataka, Orissa, and Nagaland. All these were means of preserving and communicating stories, and debating questions of ethics at a communal level, while being popular forms of entertainment, expression, and veneration. Consequently, the shared spaces created through theatre were rich platforms for rallying people around political issues and expressing dissent, particularly when it came to the rural areas where access to education was limited.

Capturing the full breadth of theatre projects working on peace in India is a task that goes beyond the scope of this chapter. Nevertheless, commenting on a few noteworthy theatre projects that tackle and encourage reflection on issues of conflict and structural violence is helpful in contextualising the work of Jana Sanskriti.

Issues of structural violence have been the focus of theatre during the colonial period. *Siraj-ud-daula* by the Bengali playwright Girish Chandra Ghosh is an example. The British banned the play for its evident political relevance and the harsh critique of the colonial oppression. We can find activists and plays that tackle similar issues among almost all the major linguistic and ethnic communities at that period in India. The popularity of theatre as a vehicle, and the subsequent formal censorship imposed upon it during the colonial period, indicate the effectiveness of the medium at the community level.

One of the oldest theatre groups highlighting issues of structural violence is the theatre group Jana Natya Manch. Commonly known as Janam, the group focuses on political theatre with particular attention given to workers' and women's rights. Janam's street theatre as well as the proscenium plays voice people's anger and frustration that result from oppressive structures, and the group often works with and trains people from disadvantaged groups on using theatre.[19] Safdar Hashmi, a founding member of the group, was killed as a result of the group's activism. Janam resonates with the work of Indian People's Theatre Association, the well-established and networked cultural wing of the leading community parties of the country.

Activists and groups use theatre to provide a voice for the people. Dalit theatre movement in the 1970s supported the work of groups such as Dalit Panthers that worked to challenge caste discrimination.[20] Kalakshestra Manipur in Manipur is another example where theatre provides a voice to those who are unheard; located at the periphery of the central Indian state, the region is marginalised in terms of mainstream politics and cultural integration. Kalakshestra Manipur uses their work to highlight voices of the indigenous groups and particularly that of women in the region. In doing so, the group actively engages with and addresses issues of structural violence.

Practitioners use theatre to bridge the divides caused by the Indo-Pakistan conflict as well. Theatre groups such as Manch Rangmanch from Punjab and Rangkarmi from Kolkata are examples. The groups as well as their respective directors—Kewal Dhaliwal and Usha Ganguli—collaborated with Pakistani artistes and theatre groups over several theatre projects, organising and performing at theatre festivals in both India and Pakistan.

Other groups and artistes use theatre for its healing capacity. Natrang theatre group in Jammu & Kashmiri is an example. Established in mid 1980s as a vehicle to showcase and express the distinct cultural history of the region, the group has gradually come to use theatre as a tool, through which they can initiate healing and transformation in the war-ravaged community. Nandita Dinesh's work with the Ensemble Kashmir Theatre Akademi also touches upon the healing aspects of theatre.

Though many of these theatre groups and activists engage with issues of conflict, including those of structural violence, this does not indicate continued, sustained work with a given community. The plays often are individual performances or are led by professional artistes, or an external expert who works with the community for a given period produces them. While initiating conversations and healing through such performances are also important, it requires sustained long-term work, integrated with a given community to effect changes in the narratives of structural violence.

Jana Sanskriti

Unlike the Sri Lankan case study where there are clearly defined parties to the conflict, Jana Sanskriti works in a context of everyday violence triggered by structural injustice and discrimination. This shapes the particular nature and approach of Jana Sanskriti: the group is very much a communal movement rooted in the everyday, adopting an everyday lens to approach politics at a larger level.

Background

Jana Sanskriti started in 1985 in West Bengal as an independent organisation using political theatre. Though they work internationally and locally with a number of satellite groups spread throughout India, Jana Sanskriti's primary work base remains the rural West Bengal. Group membership largely consists of male and female agricultural workers. The organisational structure of Jana Sanskriti reflects its bi-fold intentions, with two interrelated teams established in each village—one for performances and another for related political action. Interested individuals can become members of one or both. A core team consisting of eleven members takes key decisions pertaining to the organisation. Each core team member represents a sub group at regional level, which in turn represents the ground level village members.

The main focus of Jana Sanskriti is empowering the oppressed through "scripting power on and off stage."[21] The issues they address are often issues of social and political justice. The group starts its political work within theatre and carries it on through the political mobilisers. The political mobilisers actively rally the community on issues that impact at a general level. Jana Sanskriti's work closely engages with rewriting the established power hierarchies at an everyday level. The work focuses on the so-called "oppressed" communities based in rural districts, largely coming from the working classes. The group's work for peacebuilding is connected with its focus on empowering the powerless.

The emphasis on justice and fairness strongly relates to Jana Sanskriti's take on peacebuilding. Peacebuilding is "as much" about exposing those that hold power in a given situation and working to bring about a more equal relationship among all parties,[22] as it is about addressing direct conflict. Preserving surface level harmony and political order fail to make sense as peacebuilding, if these are done at the cost of justice and fairness. Actions that merely attempt to prevent direct violence in instances of oppression do just that.

Jana Sanskriti uses theatre as a medium due to its aptness in promoting a culture of dialogue. Oppression in its community, as the group argues, is made possible by the pervasive "culture of monologue." A culture of monologue promotes the interests of an elite few, and curtails dialogue and discussion in general. Dialogue between and among different factions of society is an essential faculty of and a crucial first step towards equality and justice in a democracy. Jana Sanskriti works to establish this culture of dialogue where the marginalized factions of the society speak for themselves and stand up for their rights.

Theatre Approach

Jana Sanskriti identifies itself as a political theatre group. Michael Kirby defines political theatre as theatre that is "*concerned* with the state or *takes sides* in politics."[23] Despite practicing political propaganda theatre at its initial stages, along with its development Jana Sanskriti refrained from affiliating with a specific political party. At present the group strongly positions itself on a political standpoint of social justice and engages with local governance through its theatre practice.

Jana Sanskriti uses Theatre of the Oppressed (TO) in general and specifically forum theatre as its medium. This choice is due to the possibilities of dialogue embedded in this particular theatre form. TO is an umbrella term including a number of different theatre forms, developed by Augusto Boal.[24] Each of these has social action at its core and initiates social change by creating a space that encourages the marginalised or the oppressed to speak.

Forum theatre is the primary form of theatre Jana Sanskriti uses in its work, which is also the defining theatre form within the TO school. In forum theatre, the drama actively engages the audience as a part of the play, referring to them as spect-actors. The audience explores the reality of their lives—and the stories they tell themselves about it—through the performance and strive to create new narratives that are emancipatory; stories that transcend the old discriminative versions. Forum theatre encourages the dialogic of theatre, furthering theatre's existing potentials.

Jana Sanskriti adapts Boal's theatre, developed initially in South America and later in Europe, to its particular working context. Local conditions and aesthetics drive these adaptations. These adaptations in turn enhance the theatre's potential for incorporating multiple voices and initiating dialogue. Jana Sanskriti's adaptations in group processes and performances make this evident. A forum theatre performance and discussion is usually a one-off event. Jana Sanskriti makes a fundamental change in this practice by holding repeat performances at a given location, until the discussion comes to a point where its political mobilisers can take it forward. This is a structural adaptation in Jana Sanskriti's use of forum theatre. Another adaptation is incorporating elements from traditional theatre forms. Unlike the classic format of forum theatre, Jana Sanskriti's plays start with a song and also have song and dance incorporated into its body. These are elements where the group borrows heavily from the traditional drama forms in West Bengal such and *Gadjan*. The ensuing multivocality brings Jana Sanskriti's performances close to the local community. The enhanced aesthetic appeal of the resulting adaptation generates local interest, while facilitating openness for the unfamiliar elements of forum theatre within West Bengal. Jana Sanskriti, therefore, embodies multivocality and dialogic in its theatre process.

A further adaptation that enhances the dialogic and multivocality of theatre is Jana Sanskriti's process of scripting a play. Jana Sanskriti's plays focus on communal issues. These could either apply to all of its members or only to a specific group. In scripting a play on a shared issue such as gender discrimination, domestic violence, or election violence, the core team gets together. The voices of village teams directly come into the scripting process, since the core team members represent the village teams. The core team, including the team members and the director, jointly decide upon the script and the particular action sequence that brings out narratives of structural violence through a process of dialogue. The dialogue process constrains positional hierarchy within the organisation. The embedded multivocality and dialogic of the process facilitates voicing specific narratives of structural violence that might not come out in a more power-over setting.

Multivocality and the dialogic embedded in the scripting process continues until it reaches the village level audiences. Once a script is finalised, the core group members take it to the village level and coach the village teams on the performance. Even here, the script is flexible to a certain extent: the context might require adaptations of words, characters or plot twists that differ from the agreed-upon original script. The village teams are free to make these necessary changes, as long as the central message of the drama is left intact. Thus, Jana Sanskriti's performances are flexible. They evolve with the context to be appropriate to and reflective of the places where they are being performed. Also, the play has the freedom to evolve with each single performance turn to better adapt to the changing situations in the locale.

This permitted flexibility within the group processes transcends the centralised power structures seen in the wider community to a considerable extent. Jana Sanskriti's group processes recognise the need for context-based approaches, and work to transform the power hierarchies that come into play in the scripting process of the play. Together, the core group members wield a considerable amount of power in the group. This is remarkable as the members come from diverse educational and social backgrounds that spread across a broad range. Jana Sanskriti, as a theatre organisation working over a long period based in rural Bengal, offers insights on using theatre in peacebuilding through its group practices and theatre approach.

Jana Sanskriti's unique theatre approach raises certain concerns as well: key here is an issue related to performative labour. Rai convincingly argues that the aesthetic refinement of a performance—be it in theatre or in a different political space—calls for an increased effort from some members than the others, depending on their skills and abilities.[25] Unlike it is with a professional theatre group, performance is not a livelihood for most of the Jana Sanskriti actors. Engaging in political theatre, for them, is an activity that has to be squeezed into everyday responsibilities and tasks. This "squeeze" is especially visible with the women's theatre group members. The rehearsals, meetings and group discussions all result in lengthening their workday. The group is well aware of this fact and strives to facilitate the process as much as possible. Nevertheless, with its complex scripting and adaptation process, Jana Sanskriti's theatre approach can ask for a quite high commitment and performative labour input from some members.

Performing Resistance

Jana Sanskriti's peacebuilding takes place through a two-step process: peacebuilding as resistance and peacebuilding as transformation. Jana Sanskriti uses theatre to bring out narratives of structural violence into the communal discourse through these two overarching steps. These steps are often complementary. When manifesting as resistance, Jana Sanskriti's peacebuilding through theatre emerges as resistance to the embedded narratives of structural violence. Through embodying multivocality Jana Sanskriti's theatre creates a space for expressing less heard narratives of violence and bring them into the communal discourse. The performed resistance, in turn, creates the tension from which peacebuilding as transformation proceeds. Thus, Jana Sanskriti's theatre brings out and creates tension in existing violent and exclusive structures, aiming for their transformation at a community level.

This section examines Jana Sanskriti's process of using theatre to perform resistance towards embedded narratives of structural violence in West Bengal, which in turn results in the creation of a tension from where transformation can happen. Performing resistance at Jana Sanskriti, again, is a twofold process. On the one hand, it is carried out onstage as an expression of the multivocal form of theatre. On the other hand, it is carried out offstage, through the group practices and community level political activism.

Narratives of gender discrimination—a prevalent but insidious element of structural violence in West Bengal—provide a fertile ground. How Jana Sanskriti elicits the narratives, and the ways in which the group engages with existing patriarchal practices to resist and create a tension within patriarchal structures deserve particular attention.

Performing and Encouraging Onstage Resistance

Jana Sanskriti's onstage resistance is a combination of provoking resistance through the performances and encouraging resistance from the audience. Key tools in this are the scripting and performance of the play and the onsite forum discussion. Both target and actively encourage multivocality.

The script makes the narratives of structural violence explicit, while grounding it in the real experiences of people from the community.

In order to achieve this, Jana Sanskriti adopts a joint scripting process together with the core group members who are part of and share the everyday realities of the communities with/for whom they perform. The script is grounded in the regular expression of the community members. The narrative of gendered violence usually comes from where it is felt powerfully: at the intersections of different narratives of structural violence. In performing this script back to the community, in the format of a rapidly tightening web of structural violence onstage, the performance challenges the veneer of social acceptance a little further, each time.

Take the play *The Brick Factory* for example:

The Brick Factory is from the regular repertoire of Jana Sanskriti that touches upon many facets of interconnected structural violence. It is written in 1997 and has been widely performed since then. The protagonist of the story is Phulmoni, a woman worker at a brick factory. The women are paid lower wages than men and the contractor exploits both the men's and women's labour by refusing to pay overtime. The workers unite in a feeble attempt to ask for fair wages. The contractor strategically uses the patriarchal rhetoric of "keeping women under male control" to undermine workers' unity, thereby effectively curtailing any joint action among men and women. Phulmoni in the next scene is pressured into granting sexual favours to secure her job and to protect her husband from being taken to the police. Though her husband is aware of the situation he is helpless to intervene. In the final scene Phulmoni is judged by an all-men village *Panchayat*[26] that finds her guilty of "polluting the culture" by going in search of work to the city and having a sexual relationship with the contractor. Her husband is also punished for his compliance.

In this play, the layered oppression Phulmoni has to undergo disturbs the audience and evokes responses. Also the type of the issue—women working in the city and having to undergo sexual exploitation—provokes spectator responses. Urban migration is a common occurrence and as such, is a pertinent issue to the community in general.

The forum discussion is another site where provocation takes place: the Joker's role takes that on, inviting and encouraging the audience to express resistance. The actor playing the role of the oppressor too provokes the spectators to go deeper with their responses. This engagement potentially results in a dialogue that presents an authentic challenge, a possible turning point for the drama to unfold in a different path. The script enhances the relevance to the audience and together with the forum discussion it engages and provokes spectactors to perform resistance.

In performing resistance to the established structural narratives on gender discrimination, the forum discussion embodies multivocality and dialogic. Consider a forum discussion of *The Brick Factory* that took place in Shyamnagar. Here, the multivocality and the dialogic bring out complexities, voices and questions through the forum discussion. The Joker actively encouraged expression from and facilitated dialogue among the audience, utilising the flexibility and space of theatre to accommodate different voices. The spect-actor interventions touched upon different dimensions and complexities of asking for and providing labour equality for women. While one spectator voiced that "girls are also a part of life, so they are equal", another claimed they "provide equal labour." In response to a comment that women cannot work as much as men, a woman asked "why not provide appropriate work for women? You give everyone the same work." The multivocal and the dialogic form of forum theatre here, backed up by Jana Sanskriti's encouragement of expressing resistance, created a space safe for these different voices in the community to emerge and engage in a dialogue. A 10-year-old boy demonstrates the potential of this space in a warmly received intervention: "both work equally, why are they [women] low? Everyone's hunger is the same." These probing questions during the forum discussion arise from the tension created in performing resistance to the everyday narratives of structural violence.

Jana Sanskriti's work in performing resistance and the forum discussion enhances the audience's analytical skills in engaging with narratives of structural violence. The community in Shyamnagar went beyond the immediate situation to discover the underlying narratives of structural violence. Pradeep, the core group member who played the Joker's role in this performance, points out that Jana Sanskriti goes from the "particular to the general", that it connects from the "incident to the system."[27] They encourage the audience or the spect-actors to make the connection between isolated incidents of oppression as performed in *The Brick Factory,* and the larger web of structural violence—such as gender discrimination and economic exploitation—that fosters such actions. The Joker plays a central role here in leading the discussion from the particular to the general.

Jana Sanskriti's continued engagement indicates progress in the communities. The interventions I observed indicate that the spectators chose a strategic approach towards the interventions. In an article published in 2004, Dia Mohan discusses the tendency of the spect-actors to provide conventional or magical solutions to Phulmoni's plight: such as for Phulmoni to leave the factory or refuse the contractor's advances, jeopardsing their family income and her husband's safety.[28] As she points out, these solutions do not take into account the complexity or the systemic nature of the issues at stake. The spect-actor interventions I witnessed for *The Brick Factory* in 2012 progress beyond this initial point. Instead of focusing on the last scene where the oppression is at its most evident, the 2012 interventions focused on challenging the system of patriarchy at its early stages. Spect-actors accurately identified and intervened from the beginning, when the contractor started using patriarchal rhetoric to undermine workers' unity. Thus, the audience responds to the structures, instead of getting caught up in the particular incident. The spectators are capable of identifying the violence of patriarchal structures emerging in the drama at its earlier phases. This skill indicates the enhanced capability of the community developed over the years in locating the root of the issue and performing resistance to the underlying violent structures.

There are further examples to the fact that Jana Sanskriti has cultivated keen analytical skills among its audience. The spect-actors are adept in intervening before the narratives of structural violence become stronger, and respectively, harder to tackle. In building peace within structural violence, locating and starting from the weak links of the narratives makes the intervention relatively easier. The difference between interventions made for *The Brick Factory* that Mohan commented on in 2004 and the interventions I observed in 2012 indicate the shift in the spect-actors from the personal to a systemic approach. In 2012, the audience is adept at identifying and picking out the patriarchal thread of structural violence at its initial phases of introduction, where it is yet to be reinforced by the traditional and political authorities of *Panchayat*. The authority figure that attempts to divide the workers by drawing on patriarchal rhetoric is relatively easier to engage with. He is an individual, not an institution. His apparent exploitation of the workers relates to the personal grievances of both the men and the women, thus making him a weak link in the interconnected web of structural violence. In the 2012 interventions, it is here that the community first intervenes. The multiple voices coming from the audience, replacing one spectator after another, drawing from counter narratives to patriarchy, keeps the play from moving towards its climax.

Jana Sanskriti's onstage performance of spect-actor resistance, thus, revolves on themes of fairness and equality. The dialogue of *The Brick Factory* focused on the expressions of equal and fair workplace treatment for women. In the dialogic engagement of forum discussion, the spect-actors clearly connect Phulmoni's predicament with the underlying violent patriarchal structures. Asserting the depth to which this connection is made would require further research. Yet it is clear that here, Jana Sanskriti's performances and forum discussions onstage achieve the connection from "particular to the general" in relation to prevalent patriarchal structures.

Encouraging Offstage Resistance

Jana Sanskriti brings out structural narratives by encouraging performing resistance offstage. Active cultivation of the faculty is visible in group practices that connect with community level political activism. The resistance to and dialogue on the oppressive patriarchal structures extend to offstage activism within group members' lifeworlds. The group's standpoint on the practice of dowry—traditionally offered by the bride's family to the groom—demonstrates this. Male members of Jana Sanskriti refuse a dowry when they get married. This act takes place at the boundary of private and public spaces, stronger for its symbolic significance in an increasingly market driven society. To refuse the dowry, the groom often has to stand up against his family network that holds a considerable amount of power within his lifeworld. Almost every household in Jana Sanskriti's working areas has extended families, many with more than three married siblings sharing the parent's house and lands. Refusing the dowry automatically becomes a public declaration of non-compliance with multiple established structures of power. At times, the pressure can be overwhelming. Mohan refers to a Jana Sanskriti member who chose to elope with his bride when his family insisted on a dowry.[29] Another offstage resistance to the patriarchal norms at the group level is the formation of women's theatre groups. Seeing women active in the public space provides role models for other women in the community, and broadens gendered boundaries. These actions "breach the normative order of domination"[30] and as such, are acts of performing offstage resistance to violent patriarchal structures at different levels, through the group practices and norms. Jana Sanskriti's offstage activism draws public attention to the prevalent but less heard structural violence that operates at a daily level.

Performing resistance offstage through Jana Sanskriti's political team brings narratives of structural violence into the communal discourse. Jana Sanskriti's political mobilisers encourage and rally the community to take a stand on key issues. Take the issue of alcoholism, assumed to be at the root of extensive domestic violence in the area: in late 2011 and 2012, Jana Sanskriti mobilised the community to protest against illegal alcohol production in the area and to take concrete action to challenge the issue.

Jana Sanskriti welcomes performing resistance offstage, even when it is directed at its own work. An interesting example elaborates this: *The Brick Factory* came into being as a result of an act of resistance from the audience to another drama, *Sarama*. In *Sarama*, the unmarried female protagonist is raped. Defying convention and social norms, she chooses to press charges against the rapists, and to raise the baby. An NGO supports her and the story ends with a positive note. While the play received appreciation from the average crowd, a woman in Birbhum supported by other females in her community challenged the ending for its credibility. Rape from authority figures was a daily reality for female workers in *The Brick Factory*, where the woman's family worked for as long as she knew. Protest was hardly a choice since the entire family's livelihood depended on the exploiter himself. There were no NGOs to support them. This woman's vocal resistance to what she saw as an unrealistic story, brought out the prevalent but less heard narratives of structural violence many undergo on a daily basis, into the communal discourse. The act of resistance expressed by the community resulted in the production of *The Brick Factory*. Jana Sanskriti performs and encourages resistance to the embedded structural narratives onstage as well as offstage.

These seemingly small acts in fact construe the infrapolitics of peacebuilding as it is seen in Jana Sanskriti. The performed resistance makes up the "daily confrontations, evasive actions and stifled thoughts."[31] Through performing resistance on and offstage utilising the dialogic and multivocality of theatre, Jana Sanskriti is continually pushing and testing the boundary of what is deemed permissible.[32] It is a constant process of performing resistance in the public and private spheres, trying to bring out the insidious politics of social and political structures into the public space of theatre and communal discourse. As Scott points out, resistance expressed in public is irrevocable: once the act of public defiance is done, it will "fundamentally alter" the social relationships unless it is beaten back; even when it is beaten back and forced to hide, an irrevocable change has already occurred.[33] He observes that the act of being staged moves the questionable ethics associated with relations of subordination from a shadowy existence to the public limelight, thereby stripping away the veneer of acceptance and pseudo legitimacy that covers its questionable ethics. Believing the injustices do not happen and that we are helpless at the face of it, becomes a luxury that we can no longer afford, with the consistence performing of resistance that reveals the existing violent structures in public. The act of doing so unsettles and creates tension among the unjust narratives. This process of resistance aimed at freedom from structural violence or structures of conflict as critical agency gives rise to local, embedded processes of peacebuilding. It is a process that enables the "subjects to produce peace" instead of "producing subjects."[34] The resistance Jana Sanskriti performs on and offstage addressing narratives of structural violence is indeed the foundation of the peace they build at the community level. The tension created herein prepares the ground where transformation takes place.

Triggering Transformation

Peacebuilding as Transforming Narratives of Structural Violence
The second level of Jana Sanskriti's peacebuilding process is initiating positive transformation in narratives of structural violence. The tension created from performing resistance to the embedded narratives of structural violence, brings up the respective narratives into communal discourse. To complete its peacebuilding process, Jana Sanskriti seeks to take the performed resistance and the resulting tension forward, to positively transform these very narratives of structural violence in rural Bengal.
Specifically, the discussion will look at the ways in which Jana Sanskriti's use of theatre transforms narratives of structural violence in the political and socio-cultural spheres at a community level. These spheres overlap. The pertinent issues often arise as a result of a network of structural narratives that span multiple spheres. The process of transformation Jana Sanskriti aims for, too, is multi-pronged. Political and socio-cultural spheres come to the fore for their relevance within the community. The analysis primarily borrows from and is located within Jana Sanskriti's scripts, dramaturgy, and interviews. Looking at this

process reveals how Jana Sanskriti's onstage interventions lead to offstage transformations.

Transforming Narratives in the Political Sphere

In the political sphere, Jana Sanskriti brings out the elitist and inefficient structures of political representation of people into the communal discourse in order to initiate their transformation. Through its work, the group questions the authenticity and sincerity of political structures in representing citizens at two levels: at the village and state level political representation and at trade union's worker representation.

The play *Gayer Panchali—The Song of the Village*—brings out the injustice of political structures at village level representation into the communal discourse. The very structures established to ensure democracy and fair representation at the village level obstruct these principles due to embedded elitism and corruption. Jana Sanskriti questions the functioning of the Integrated Rural Development Program (IRDP) through *Gayer Panchali*.[35] Though the programme was introduced for the benefit of the lowest rung of agricultural workers, it fails at the implementation level. Mohan observes that the loan distribution through IRDP articulates "feudal relations between villagers and money-lenders, subject to the paternalistic expectations of politicians and the demands of political party loyalty."[36] The play depicts how, at the *Panchayat* level, IRDP funds are being used for the benefit of *Panchayat* leaders themselves, who are middle and large level farmers. The dialogue among the *Panchayat* leaders makes this evident: "Those of us in the organisation are primarily middle and big peasants. The government has said that the IRDP loans should go to poor agricultural workers. So in that case, we are ignored as if we are the scum that floats off the tidal wave."[37] This corruption is not a one-off act: it is part of a wider practice of corruption that has encompassed the entire political system. The *Panchayat* Head justifies taking the loans in saying: "[i]f we distribute all the loan money to the poor farmers based on the beneficiary list, then our organisation will die"[38] and he counters the rare voice within the *Panchayat* for the fair distribution of the loan with "[i]n the end, I had to raise fifty thousand rupees to get this position as *Panchayat* head. Are you suggesting that I will not recuperate that sum? How idiotic?"[39] The play continues to discuss further incidents of corruption at the *Panchayat* level that prevents the population from receiving fair political representation at community level. Despite being a democracy, what exists at the village level is more akin to a feudal practice, with the feudal lords being the political elite. Politicians forget the spouted principles and proffered promises during the election time with impunity. Jana Sanskriti brings this issue back into the communal discourse through the script: "all these principles and commitments don't make politics. We give promises knowing we will not abide by them."[40] The audience as voters are aware of this. But they are helpless in standing up against the political leaders due to the structural power invested in these corrupt politicians through the state. Finally, when the voters with sticks, corner the local politician and question him, he threatens the community in turn: "Do you know that we are leaders? We have the police and administration in our hands … I will not give any more. I will make it impossible for you."[41] The actor infuses the dialogue with symbolic action by grabbing the sticks from people's hands and pointing these back at the people. Thus, Jana Sanskriti makes it apparent to the audience that democracy and the structures that are supposed to protect them are being used for the benefit of political elites. The politician breaks into a song, drawing a parallel between the power of the stick and democracy:

> "In my hand, I have democracy's stick …
> … bathed in blood
> While it sings a religious tune
> With great faith."[42]

Democracy, symbolised through the stick, is the rhetoric the state draws on to keep people under control. Religion and nationalism are also pliable narratives the politicians draw on to collude with democracy.

The dramaturgy of each scene too constructs a vivid imagery of oppression. This is especially evident in the third scene where the *Panchayat* leaders sit down in discussion about the IRDP loan distribution. The seats here are the commoners, using their bodies to form seats for the politicians. The image of oppression presented in the scene is vivid: it connotes that the *Panchayat* leaders have come to and stand in power by oppressing the very people they are supposed to represent. Thus, the feudal imagery of leaders sitting upon the backs of human beings emphasise the absence of democratic principles.

Jana Sanskriti emphasises that despite the popular rhetoric, there is very little change in people's everyday lives. The so-called democratically elected politicians are representative only in name: in reality, the elitist structures of political bodies articulate a feudal relationship. The character of a grandpa, traditionally a voice of wisdom and authority, expresses this sentiment in the same scene: "They are feudal lords, feudal lords, feudal lords! In our grandfather's generation, these feudal lords would run the neighbourhood and now the vote-seekers have taken their place."[43] *The Song of the Village* as one of the first dramas of Jana Sanskriti, captures the violence in the structures of political representation at the community level. Not only is the local political body corrupt in the use of funds allocated for the general public, but it also controls the administration body and the police. With the incorporation of these bodies into the corrupted elitist boat, the people are left with hardly any accessible venues of structural support at the village level. Jana Sanskriti, through its work, brings these silenced narratives of Jana Sanskriti into the communal discourse. (Fig. 5.1)

The play *Where We Stand* brings out the inherent violence of the political structures at the higher echelons. The scenes in the play, like most other Jana Sanskriti plays, are disconnected: the only connection binding them together is the different aspects of oppression the

Fig. 5.1 Last scene of the Jana Sanskriti play *Where We Stand*

characters face. The elitist political structures depicted here focus on protecting the interests of the politicians at the cost of social harmony. The third scene presents how politics manipulate, and at times ignite, the Hindu and Muslim religious tensions and caste affiliations for securing votes.[44] Here, a telephone conversation takes place between leaders of different political factions such as Hindu and Muslim fundamentalist parties and Dalit voters. The conversation revolves around the destruction of a Mosque. The concern of the politicians here is not the impact of religious fundamentalism or violence upon the community, but the impact of this incident on securing minority votes in the upcoming election: as the play says, "[h]ow to get the minority vote into our bank, how to mollify the minority to vote for us."[45] The focus on securing minority votes feeds the narratives of enmity between religions, further sabotaging remaining hopes for tolerance and coexistence. Leaders representing Hindu and Muslim parties collaborate at the top level for securing power, while communities at ground level are encouraged to fight with each other. The telephone conversation ends with: "Then let's work together ... I will scratch your back, and you will scratch mine."[46] Jana Sanskriti plays reveal the existing political sphere to be structured in a way that maintains communal division and hatred—be it ethnic, religious, caste or party affiliations—to ensure the preservation of the political elite.

By bringing these ignored and silenced narratives of structural violence into the communal discourse, Jana Sanskriti encourages people to face the situation: to unite and initiate transformation of the politically oriented divisions and the narratives of structural violence that goes with the separation.

A key element in this transformation is empathy. Shanthi, a supporter of Jana Sanskriti from its early days, relates a story on how some party hooligans who sought to intimidate and kill the founder Sanjoy Ganguly later turned into supporters of the organisation. The work of Jana Sanskriti in Medinipur district in 1980s questioned the reasons behind political violence between parties at ground level when the party heads collaborate at state level. Party hooligans from the area were sent to intimidate Jana Sanskriti to stop its work. The group responded by continually inviting the hooligans to attend the performances. The hooligans, according to Shanthi, ended up becoming friends with Sanjoy Ganguly and in a display of a turn of heart, offered to kill those who sent them in the first place. This offer reflects simply an act of giving up one system of violence and adopting another. Satya, another founding member, recalls the long process of discussions they had with such a person: "we were telling him repeatedly that you have no rice in your family, and the person you are going to beat also doesn't have any rice in their family. And he eventually listened."[47] This is where empathy takes place and anger ceases to become the defining factor of a relationship. Accessing empathy opens up alternative paths beyond the conception of the regular conditioned discourse. However small, it leads to a positive transformation of the narratives of violence within the political structures. The former party hooligan is no longer a willing follower or a captive of those violent structures. His refusal to take part in the structural violence that is perpetuated through his body is a direct result of Jana Sanskriti activism. The transformation is triggered from the empathy that is developed with the person on the "other side", the person who is also a victim of the same violent structures.

The elitist and corrupt political structures co-opt political representation of the civilians in other arenas like trade unions and police. Jana Sanskriti brings this out into communal discourse, facilitating its transformation. *Where We Stand* also portrays trade union leaders' corruption and how they protect their own interests at the cost of abiding by ethical and moral obligations. The first scene in *Where We Stand* discusses the death or the assassination of Bikas, a jute mill worker. Someone shoots Bikas from the factory owner's car and later on, leaves his body on the railway tracks, in a futile attempt to fake an accident. The factory workers mourn Bikas, seeing him as someone who sacrificed his life for workers' rights. Tarit, the trade union leader who is also a member of the parliament, appears at the scene. His protests against the murder last only until the factory owner offers him a bribe. The play captures the nuances of offering and accepting bribes, and the facile justifications for the corruption—that this is "the party of the poor" and "this is how [they] are able to run the party."[48] Tarit manipulates the communist rhetoric to pacify the outraged workers and to convince them to return to work. Presenting this sequence on the stage is powerful since it directly challenges the corrupted system in West Bengal, a stronghold of the Communist Party of India (Marxist). It opens up the disjuncture between the public and private faces of trade union representatives to the communal discourse. The administration and police again are co-opted into these violent structures of the political system, thereby further expanding the cohort of elites benefiting through the structural violence in the political system.

The play calls for the transformation of structural violence in the political sphere: it asks the spect-actors for "a little bit of conscience" for "our nation's politicians" who suffer from a "dearth of conscience" and have "become animals."[49] *Where We Stand* urges for transformation from the side of the politicians as well as from the side of the people: the latter makes the dialogic of the drama more powerful, as it strongly encourages individuals to rethink their own roles in this system. For the elitism in political structures including the politicians, police, ministers and business, the actors claim, "for this you are responsible. I am responsible. We are all responsible."[50] Jana Sanskriti holds everyone, including themselves, responsible for giving birth to the corrupted, violent structures, for nurturing them and for permitting the exploitation to continue. Jana Sanskriti goes beyond performing a story to planting the seeds of transformation within people, encouraging them to discuss their responses to this call in the forum space for dialogue.

The communal discourse around the narratives of structural violence in the existing politics, results in the mobilisation of neutral communal forces to represent community interests at village level. The offstage activist team of Jana Sanskriti carries out this work by having representatives in *Panchayat* meetings and organising lobbying for a fairer distribution of funds among the community under government programmes. Through creating a system of representation devoid of political party affiliations, the exclusions and violence of the existing political structures are mitigated to a certain extent. While this is outside the state political structure, it marks the starting point of an organised movement that expresses its frustration and mistrust of the existing political structures.

Transforming Narratives in the Socio-Cultural Sphere

Another sphere in which Jana Sanskriti's peacebuilding becomes apparent is the socio-cultural sphere. On and offstage activism together work to transform socio-cultural narratives. Firstly, onstage spect-actor interventions initiate transformation within individuals and create ripples in the communal discourse that extends the impact of intervention. Secondly, onstage performance extends to offstage activism that in turn leads into transformation in the socio-cultural sphere.

Gender in general, and domestic violence in specific, is an apt lens to explore Jana Sanskriti's performance related transformation of socio-cultural narratives. Even though Jana Sanskriti engages with a number of socio cultural narratives, focusing on a single issue facilitates looking at the different ways in which Jana Sanskriti initiates transformation in this particular narrative. According to 2011 crime statistics of India, 43.4% of all reported crimes against women are a result of cruelty by husband and relatives.[51] Domestic violence is therefore a key narrative of structural violence in the socio cultural sphere, in need of transformation.

Transformation Through Onstage Spect-actor Interventions

Onstage spectator responses to the inherent violence in gender narratives brought up through Jana Sanskriti's performances indicate the transformation that has taken place within the socio-cultural sphere. The patterns of responding to patriarchal systems are changing. This transformation is evident in how certain performances were received by the audiences in 2012. Spect-actor responses have transformed over the years, probably as a result of the continued engagement and encouragement of Jana Sanskriti. The disparity between the spect-actor interventions to *The Brick Factory* as Dia Mohan noted it in 2004, and the interventions I observed in 2012, arise due to this transformation. As discussed earlier, the interventions I observed were hardly conservative or magical. The spectators demonstrated a perceptive take on the extended network of patriarchy and intervened at the initial stages of its manifestation in the play. They touched upon key points of contention to initiate a dialogue instead of simply providing a solution for the character in the story. Thus, a progressive transformation in the spect-actor responses over the years in engaging with violent socio-cultural narratives is evident.

The spect-actor interventions for *A Story of One Girl*—a play about a young wife who's married off as a child without a full dowry, later falling sick and subjected to abuse by her alcoholic husband—indicate a transformation in the narratives of passive acceptance of domestic violence. The spect-actor responses come from different points of view, such as the wife's parents, the husband's parents, a neighbour, the wife, and the extended families. Thus, the spectators identify a range of intervention points throughout the course of the play. The play is at its early stages of performance, being a recent production. Nevertheless, the interventions point towards standing up to the violence and injustice, instead of the culturally conditioned and sanctioned responses of submission and tolerance. Thus, spect-actor interventions indicate a transformation in the narratives of passive submission to the violent structures within the socio-cultural sphere. Chittaranjan marks a clear link between this on-site performance of resistance and the reduction of domestic violence in the community. He notes that it is difficult for women to speak out since they are trained to remain silent, but that things are changing: "now they protest. In the intervention part of the drama they come out and protest. And when they go home in their family they protest. This is why the domestic violence is reduced."[52] Thus, the community perceives the spect-actor interventions transforming patriarchal narratives onstage to have an impact on their private lives.

Onstage Interaction Leading to Offstage Transformation

The process of triggering transformation within violent structures in the socio-cultural sphere extends beyond spect-actor intervention: as indicated earlier, community and group members acknowledge that onstage transformations of violent patriarchal narratives are consciously carried offstage and has resulted in contributing to larger general changes in pertinent communal narratives. Personal narratives that come from both Jana Sanskriti and community members testify: several women mention instances of marriages without dowry for themselves, their sisters or cousins and trace the link back to the impact of the performances and forum discussions. Malathi's[53] personal story of negotiation is a case in point: "we managed to get my own sister married without a dowry. I have taken part in Jana Sanskriti work and forums and when the groom asked for a dowry, I told them about this play we have seen in the village, *Shonar Meye*. And I shared some of the things we discussed at the forum about [the practice of] dowry. Afterwards the groom agreed to marry my sister without a dowry." Forum discussions work as a point that initiates transformation and as a resource for people to draw from, in negotiating dowry requests in real life. These can effectively dissuade the groom from demanding a dowry. This is one example of a concrete change made in the lifeworld of the community that is traced back to the forum discussions and participation. Many others exist at the community level. In similar ways, onstage performance can effectively extend into the offstage transformation of discriminatory patriarchal structures.

Offstage negotiating and transformation of domestic violence is a delicate process. It often takes the personal intervention of a group member. The issues would generally arise during the performance, but not necessarily in it. In his interview, Chittaranjan, a core team member recalls an incident where the performers pointed out a person in the audience who regularly beats his wife.[54] Kavita, another core team member from the same area, tells me of an incident when a woman spoke to her during a forum and said that her husband beats her after consuming alcohol.[55] An audience member notes an attempt by a chronic alcoholic to justify the husband's violent behaviour in an intervention. The approach of the team is the same in these instances: they visit the family at an appropriate time and speak with the abuser, and elders if required. Though this is not sufficient to completely stop the abuse, the visits considerably reduce the violence. Almost all the team members I spoke with recall many similar incidents. Thus, personal intervention stemming from the moral responsibility of activism is common among the field members of Jana Sanskriti, and form a crucial part of bringing out less heard narratives of gender violence into the communal discourse.

The impact of this responsibility and the commitment to embodying the transformation is evident among many a group member. Once again, take a prominent core team member who married a woman from the same village, a woman who was abused and deserted by her husband. Dia Mohan also refers to a similar case.[56] These are radical moves in the rural Bengali context, where there is little possibility of a second marriage for a woman and widows and deserted women are especially shunned and marginalised for their lifetime. In response to my observation that this could not have been easy, Chittaranjan asks "what is the meaning of it if we do not live according to the values we talk about?" Thus, the personal action is not solely personal: it is seen as an embodiment of the values they stand up for, through Jana Sanskriti's work. There is a clear connection and awareness between the group work and personal action. Jana Sanskriti embodies the values of democracy and equality through its group practices, and these are in turn reflected in the actions of the individual members. Especially in a close-knit community, such concrete actions pioneer social transformation. The transformation triggered through these practices is highly effective, as it leads from example. It creates model stories of transformation that bring in the underlying narratives of structural violence into focus and constantly challenge them within the communal discourse.

Conclusion

Jana Sanskriti uses theatre to bring out important but less heard narratives of structural violence into communal discourse. Multivocal and dialogic form of theatre emerges as a key element in this process. The act of performing resistance encourages, empowers, and actively brings out the marginalised and less heard voices on issues of structural violence. A dialogue facilitated among and between these voices on and offstage, initiates transformation in the communal discourse.

Performing resistance and initiating transformation are only two overarching steps in the process of bringing out less heard narratives of structural violence into the communal discourse through Jana Sanskriti's theatre. The process of peacebuilding it leads to is rather complex and multi layered.

The theatre space itself symbolises a transgression into the public space, drawing a parallel with the process of bringing out narratives of structural violence into the communal discourse. Sticks—*lathi's*—frame Jana Sanskriti's performance space on the ground and these sticks are also used as a symbol of power, often oppression, in the forum play. Inviting the spectator onstage is an invitation to shake oneself free from the barrier of oppression and enter into the sphere of power. Crossing the line of sticks to enter the theatre space becomes an act of transformation for the audience members. She or he claims the public space to express oneself, turning the action into a symbolic act of being momentarily free from the structures that silence and prevent the voices of rural Bengali's from entering the public space.

Jana Sanskriti emphasises the narratives of structural violence by bringing together everyday performativity alongside staged performances, effectively disrupting the ideological boundary between reality and fiction. The action of entering the theatre space becomes a vehicle for questioning the moral and political divisions that keeps afloat societal norms and structures such as gender, caste, religion, and state.[57] Transformation of reality and fiction takes place with the on and offstage mobilisation of Jana Sanskriti. It blurs the ideological division between reality and fiction. Thus, the moment of stepping onstage and rehearsing an alternative power relation and norms, initiate transformation of the reality of spect-actor's lives. The tension created in disrupting the ideological boundary between fiction and reality is what creates the space for contemplation and action that transforms the violent structures. Jana Sanskriti provides a rare case where staged performativity is placed alongside with everyday performativity, resulting in an interactive and often progressive "making and unmaking of power relations"[58] which the theories of performativity that deals separately with these concepts is yet to do. Bringing together the everyday performativity and staged performativity is an element of theatre that comes out in both Jana Sanskriti and Jana Karaliya, the groups for whom theatre is a way of life.

The composition of Jana Sanskriti plays lends to the philosophy that drives it. The striking scenes of oppression the group often creates the beginning and invariably at the end of plays, scenes interposed with evocative folk-songs, and dividing sequences with local dance patterns all contribute: this particular way of "framing and sectioning" invites a fresh, critical perspective.[59] The space provided here through music and dance is quintessential: it is what holds the emotion in place and keeps it grounded in the narrative. These aesthetic elements allow time for individuals to process what they see onstage and engage with it from a perspective that balances emotions with a critical, analytical mind. Yarrow too notes that the interspersed drama and song at critical points of the drama allow different perspectives to emerge.[60] It creates the space for and facilitates the resistance provoked by Jana Sanskriti dramas to emerge as transformation.

Jana Sanskriti's link with emotion is what facilitates transformation of narratives of structural violence through its theatre practice: however, in order for positive transformation, the driving emotion has to be a result of a dialogic process. An immediate, reactive response to oppression or resistance is insufficient. The immediate tension in the embedded narratives of structural violence helps Jana Sanskriti take the expression of resistance towards a point of disquiet. The transformation resulting from expressing resistance can be either positive or negative, but emotion needs to come into play to facilitate this step either way. The campaign against illegal alcohol production Jana Sanskriti carried out in 2011 and 2012 illustrates this factor. The group moved into mobilisation too early: they held a series of performances on alcohol addiction and domestic violence, building resistance for the connected narratives within the community. However, Jana Sanskriti's political team moved into mobilisation before the emotional transformation could take place, as it was evident from spect-actor responses at the time. The community rallied by anger instead of empathy, destroyed illegal alcohol production points in the area as a result of a public protest. Here, performing resistance led to action, without actually going through a dialogic process that transformed the released emotions. The pent up collective pain, when tapped into, broke free in the form of anger; a familiar way of responding that perpetuate structural violence. Rage and similar emotions thus fuelled the actions. Instead of being non-violent, this transformation resulted in violent action propelled by a larger community consciousness. While the expression was sufficient in gaining community attention for the particular type of structural violence perpetuated through alcoholism, the dialogue was insufficient in actually bringing the community towards a point of disquiet, to a point of deeper contemplation. Engaging in a dialogue on the violence at the community level is important for positive transformation. Otherwise, the process of performing resistance simply leads to reaction instead of transformation, which replicates the familiar narratives of structural violence.

This chapter demonstrated that Jana Sanskriti works for peacebuilding at the community level, through bringing prevalent but less heard narratives of structural violence into the communal discourse. There are two steps in its process: performing resistance and initiating transformation. In performing resistance, the group embodies multivocality, and actively brings in less heard narratives of structural violence into the communal discourse through its dramas. At the second step, Jana Sanskriti primarily relies on dialogue as a tool for initiating transformation. The dialogic faculty embodied in forum theatre comes to the fore here. The organisation uses the forum discussions to initiate verbal, performed, and symbolic transformation onstage. The local community offers ample everyday examples of this transformation being carried offstage. However, the action offstage is not always positive: it can be reactive instead of transformative and as such, can be violent.

The turning point in positive transformation through Jana Sanskriti's theatre practice is in continuing with the dialogue till it generates empathy. Empathy comes to the fore as what sets apart the successful examples of transformation with Jana Sanskriti, both onstage and offstage. This process is not easy; it commands a considerable amount of time, resources and skills, as well as insight into the communal psyche. Merely being convinced of the worthiness of the idea or the need to transform narratives of structural violence is insufficient. It requires a deeper understanding of the relations between the oppressive structures and oppressed, that generates empathy within the community consciousness. It is this empathy that pushes the problem beyond a certain person or a group to the abstract social structures at the root of the problem. The individuals who perpetrate violence are a part of that system. In order to transform conflict dynamics, the focus needs to be at the systemic level and not the isolated incident. Jana Sanskriti, through the multivocal and dialogic form of theatre, focuses on bringing out less heard narratives of structural violence into the communal discourse.

Notes

1. Office of the Registrar General & Census Commissioner - India, "Provisional Population Totals Paper 2 of 2011 (India & States/Uts)" (Ministry of Home Affairs, Government of India, 2012), http://www.censusindia.gov.in/2011-prov-results/paper2/census2011_paper2.html.
2. Economic sphere is another key area Jana Sanskriti addresses. This is often seen as an outcome of the already established hierarchies in the socio-cultural or political spheres, and as such, the group approaches unequal economic or resource distribution from the perspective of these two spheres.
3. Satya Ranjan Pal, interview with author, Badu, October 12, 2012; Sanjoy Ganguly, interview with the author, Badu, October 18, 2012.
4. See Staff Reporter, "Violence Mars Municipal Elections in West Bengal," *The Hindu*, May 14, 2017, http://www.thehindu.com/news/national/violence-mars-west-bengal-municipal-elections/article18451094.ece.
5. See "Hold West Bengal Rural Polls in Three Phases," *The Hindu*, January 13, 2013.
6. Swati Sengupta, "The Truth Behind the Riots in Bengal that the Media Doesn't Report," *Huffingtonpost* India, December 27, 2016, https://www.huffingtonpost.in/2016/12/26/the-truth-behind-the-riots-in-bengalthat-the-media-doesnt-repo_a_21642420/.
7. National Crime Records Bureau - Ministry of Home Affairs, "Crime in India - 2011 Statistics," (New Delhi: National Crime Records Bureau, 2012).
8. National Crime Records Bureau - Ministry of Home Affairs, "Crime in India - 2015," (New Delhi: National Crime Records Bureau, 2016) and National Crime Records Bureau - Ministry of Home Affairs, "Crime in India - 2016 Statistics," (New Delhi: National Crime Records Bureau, 2017).
9. See Robin Luckham, "Whose Violence, Whose Security? Can Violence Reduction and Security Work for Poor, Excluded and Vulnerable People?," *Peacebuilding* 5, no. 2 (2017) and Helen Berents, "An Embodied Everyday Peace in the Midst of Violence," *Peacebuilding* 3, no. 2 (2015).
10. Government of India, "Provisional Population Totals Paper 2 of 2011 (India & States/Uts)," 48.
11. See Johan Galtung, "Violence, Peace, and Peace Research," *Journal of Peace Research* 6, no. 3 (1969) and *Peace and Social Structure* (Copenhagen: Ejlers, 1978) for a further discussion.
12. See "Violence, Peace, and Peace Research."
13. Lisa Schirch, "Strategic Peacebuilding—State of the Field," *Peace Prints: South Asian Journal of Peacebuilding* 1, no. 1 (2008): 7.

14. Ibid.
15. See Hanne and Gudrun Østby Fjelde, "Economic Inequality and Inter-Group Conflicts in Sub-Saharan Africa, 1990–2008," *Unpublished Paper Presented at the Inequality, Grievances and Civil War* (Zurich, November 2011); Christopher Cramer, "Does Inequality Cause Conflict?" *Journal of International Development* 15, no. 4 (2003); Dia Da Costa, "Introduction," in *Where We Stand*, Sanjoy Ganguly (Kolkata: CAMP, 2009); and Carles Boix, "Economic Roots of Civil Wars and Revolutions in the Contemporary World," *World Politics* 60, no. 3 (2008).
16. James Gilligan, *Preventing Violence* (London: Thames & Hudson, 2001), 39.
17. Lisa. Schirch, *The Little Book of Strategic Peacebuilding: A Vision and Framework for Peace and Justice* (New York: Good Books, 2004).
18. John P. Lederach, *Building Peace: Sustainable Reconciliatin in Divided Societies* (Washington, DC: U.S. Institute of Peace, 1997).
19. Shayoni Mitra, "Dispatches from the Margins: Theatre in India Since the 1990s," in *Mapping South Asia Through Contemporary Theatre: Essays on the Theatres of India, Pakistan, Bangladesh, Nepal and Sri Lanka*, ed. Ashis Sengupta (Basingstoke: Palgrave Macmillan, 2014).
20. Barbara R. Joshi, ed., *Untouchable!: Voices of the Dalit Liberation Movement* (London: Zed Books, 1986).
21. 'Scripting power on and off stage' is a commonly used term for the work of Jana Sanskriti, among its members and publications by and on the organisation.
22. Kevin Clements, "Peace Building and Conflict Transformation," *Peace and Conflict Studies* 4, no. 1, article 2. (1997), http://nsuworks.nova.edu/pcs/vol4/iss1/2.
23. Michael Kirby, "On Political Theatre," *The Drama Review: TDR* 19, no. 2 (1975): 129.
24. Theatre of the oppressed has sometimes been categorised as applied theatre due to the core of social consciousness shared by both the genres. I will consider them as separate genres due to the wide scope of theatrical forms deriving from each and the specific focus of Theatre of the Oppressed.
25. See Shirin M. Rai, "Political Performance: A Framework for Analysing Democratic Politics," *Political Studies* 63, no. 5 (2015) for a further discussion on performative labour.
26. *Panchayat* is the official administrative division in the village, somewhat similar to a village council.
27. Pradeep Haldar, interview with the author, Digambarapur, October 5, 2012.

28. Dia Mohan, "Reimagining Community: Scripting Power and Changing the Subject Through Jana Sanskriti's Political Theatre in Rural North India," *Journal of Contemporary Ethnography* 2, no. 33 (2004).
29. "Reimagining Community: Scripting Power and Changing the Subject Through Jana Sanskriti's Political Theatre in Rural North India," *Journal of Contemporary Ethnography* 2, no. 33 (2004): 200.
30. James C. Scott, *Domination and the Arts of Resistance: Hidden Transcripts* (New Haven: Yale University Press, 1990), 203.
31. Raymond D'Angelo, *The American Civil Rights Movement: Readings & Interpretations* (Guilford, CT: McGraw-Hill/Dushkin, 2001), 586.
32. Scott, *Domination and the Arts of Resistance: Hidden Transcripts*, 200.
33. *Domination and the Arts of Resistance: Hidden Transcripts*, 215–16.
34. Oliver P. Richmond, "A Pedagogy of Peacebuilding: Infrapolitics, Resistance, and Liberation1," *International Political Sociology* 6, no. 2 (2012): 115.
35. This is a nationwide programme initiated in 1980 for poverty alleviation.
36. Da Costa, "Introduction," 12–13.
37. Sanjoy Ganguly, *Where We Stand* (Kolkata: CAMP, 2009), 31.
38. Ibid.
39. Ibid.
40. Ibid.
41. *Where We Stand*, 36.
42. Ibid.
43. *Where We Stand*, 33.
44. *Where We Stand*, 138–40.
45. *Where We Stand*, 139.
46. *Where We Stand*, 140.
47. Satya Ranjan Pal, interview with the author, Badu, October 12, 2012.
48. Ganguly, *Where We Stand*, 131.
49. *Where We Stand*, 133–34.
50. *Where We Stand*, 134.
51. National Crime Records Bureau - Ministry of Home Affairs, "Crime in India - 2011 Statistics," 399.
52. Chittaranjan Pramanik, interview with the author, Digambarapur, October 6, 2012.
53. Malathi Basu, interview with the author, Sundarban, October 7, 2012 (pseudonym used).
54. Chittaranjan Pramanik, interview with the author, Digambarapur, October 6, 2012.
55. Kavita Bera, interview with the author, Digambarapur, October 7, 2012.
56. Mohan, "Reimagining Community: Scripting Power and Changing the Subject Through Jana Sanskriti's Political Theatre in Rural North India," 200.

57. Da Costa, "Introduction," 11.
58. Da Costa, "Introduction," 12.
59. Ralph Yarrow, "[People Playing People in India: Sanjoy Ganguy] in Sanjoy Ganguly," in *Where We Stand: Five Plays from the Repertoire of Jana Sanskriti* (Kolkata: CAMP, 2009), 7.
60. Ibid.

References

Berents, Helen. "An Embodied Everyday Peace in the Midst of Violence." *Peacebuilding* 3, no. 2 (2015): 1–14.
Boix, Carles. "Economic Roots of Civil Wars and Revolutions in the Contemporary World." *World Politics* 60, no. 3 (2008): 390–437.
Clements, Kevin. "Peace Building and Conflict Transformation." *Peace and Conflict Studies* 4, no. 1, article 2. (1997). http://nsuworks.nova.edu/pcs/vol4/iss1/2.
Cramer, Christopher. "Does Inequality Cause Conflict?" *Journal of International Development* 15, no. 4 (2003): 397–412.
D'Angelo, Raymond. *The American Civil Rights Movement: Readings & Interpretations*. Guilford, CT: McGraw-Hill/Dushkin, 2001.
Da Costa, Dia. "Introduction." In *Where We Stand*, edited by Sanjoy Ganguly, 9–20. Kolkata: CAMP, 2009.
Fjelde, Hanne, and Gudrun Østby. "Economic Inequality and Inter-Group Conflicts in Sub-Saharan Africa, 1990–2008." *Unpublished Paper Presented at the Inequality, Grievances and Civil War*. Zurich, November 2011.
Galtung, Johan. *Peace and Social Structure*. Copenhagen: Ejlers, 1978.
———. "Violence, Peace, and Peace Research." *Journal of Peace Research* 6, no. 3 (1969): 167–91.
Ganguly, Sanjoy. *Where We Stand*. Kolkata: CAMP, 2009.
Gilligan, James. *Preventing Violence*. London: Thames & Hudson, 2001.
Office of the Registrar General & Census Commissioner - India. "Provisional Population Totals Paper 2 of 2011 (India & States/Uts)." Ministry of Home Affairs, Government of India, 2012. http://www.censusindia.gov.in/2011-prov-results/paper2/census2011_paper2.html.
Joshi, Barbara R., ed. *Untouchable!: Voices of the Dalit Liberation Movement*. London: Zed Books, 1986.
Kirby, Michael. "On Political Theatre." *The Drama Review: TDR* 19, no. 2 (1975): 129–35.
Luckham, Robin. "Whose Violence, Whose Security? Can Violence Reduction and Security Work for Poor, Excluded and Vulnerable People?". *Peacebuilding* 5, no. 2 (2017): 99–117.

Lederach, John. P. *Building Peace: Sustainable Reconciliatin in Divided Societies.* Washington, DC: U.S. Institute of Peace, 1997.

Mitra, Shayoni. "Dispatches from the Margins: Theatre in India Since the 1990s." In *Mapping South Asia Through Contemporary Theatre: Essays on the Theatres of India, Pakistan, Bangladesh, Nepal and Sri Lanka*, edited by Ashis Sengupta, 64–102. Basingstoke: Palgrave Macmillan, 2014.

Mohan, Dia. "Reimagining Community: Scripting Power and Changing the Subject Through Jana Sanskriti's Political Theatre in Rural North India." *Journal of Contemporary Ethnography* 2, no. 33 (2004): 178–217.

National Crime Records Bureau - Ministry of Home Affairs. "Crime in India - 2011 Statistics." New Delhi: National Crime Records Bureau, 2012.

———. "Crime in India - 2012 Statistics." New Delhi: National Crime Records Bureau, 2013.

———. "Crime in India - 2015." New Delhi: National Crime Records Bureau, 2016.

Rai, Shirin M. "Political Performance: A Framework for Analysing Democratic Politics." *Political Studies* 63, no. 5 (2015): 1179-97.

Staff Reporter. "Hold West Bengal Rural Polls in Three Phases." *The Hindu*, January 13, 2013.

———. "Violence Mars Municipal Elections in West Bengal." *The Hindu*, May 14, 2017. http://www.thehindu.com/news/national/violence-mars-west-bengal-municipal-elections/article18451094.ece.

Richmond, Oliver P. "A Pedagogy of Peacebuilding: Infrapolitics, Resistance, and Liberation1." *International Political Sociology* 6, no. 2 (2012): 115–31.

Schirch, Lisa. *The Little Book of Strategic Peacebuilding: A Vision and Framework for Peace and Justice.* New York: Good Books, 2004.

Schirch, Lisa. "Strategic Peacebuilding—State of the Field." *Peace Prints: South Asian Journal of Peacebuilding* 1, no. 1 (2008): 1–18.

Scott, James C. *Domination and the Arts of Resistance: Hidden Transcripts.* New Haven: Yale University Press, 1990.

Sengupta, Swati. "The Truth Behind the Riots in Bengal that the Media Doesn't Report," Huffingtonpost India, December 27, 2016. https://www.huffingtonpost.in/2016/12/26/the-truth-behind-the-riots-in-bengalthat-the-media-doesnt-repo_a_21642420/.

Yarrow, Ralph. "People Playing People in India: Sanjoy Ganguly." In *Where We Stand*, 5–8. Kolkata: CAMP, 2009.

CHAPTER 6

Sarwanam: Speaking for the People

Sarwanam, a theatre group based in Kathmandu, Nepal, is the focus of this final case study chapter. The two previous case study chapters of the book respectively explored how theatre brings parties and narratives in conflict together in Sri Lanka, and how theatre is used to address structural violence in West Bengal. This chapter shares some similarities with these two case studies, but adds a complementary and a different aspect of using theatre for peacebuilding.

Sarwanam uses the dialogic and multivocal form of theatre to make excluded citizens' perspectives a part of the public discourse on conflict. The chapter sets out to examine how: background information on the Nepalese conflict and the theatre group helps situate Sarwanam within its working context. Exploring the theatre practice of Sarwanam highlights how theatre opens up possibilities of conversation between parties and narratives in conflict. This discussion outlines the ways in which Sarwanam uses theatre to make excluded citizens' perspectives a part of the public discourse on conflict. A close examination of two key dramas of the organisation—*Sakuni Pasa Haru* (*Sakuni's Tricks*) and *Itihasko Banki Pristha* (*Remaining Page of History*)—and analysing the different ways in which these dramas use theatre to make excluded citizens' perspectives a part of the public discourse on Nepalese conflict, enables getting a deeper understanding of the theatre practice of the group. Finally the chapter highlights the challenges faced by the organisation in relation to its particular theatre style and practices. The challenges in navigating aesthetics and politics and the personal as well as artistic identities within the group arise as two key themes in the concluding discussion.

Conflict Background

Nepal presents a somewhat unique context for South Asia. Unlike the other two case studies, Sarwanam's work takes place within the environment of an internationally negotiated peace agreement following the Maoist insurgency and people's uprisings against the state power. The resulting conflict discourse, therefore, revolves around the key parties of the negotiation process. This setting of a relatively stable negotiated peace necessarily shapes the approach of Sarwanam in using theatre for peacebuilding in Nepal.

The introduction into the Nepalese conflict offered here is brief. This description is only intended to be a general picture of the situation that will assist in contextualising the activities of the theatre group. By no means does it purport to be a comprehensive description of the Nepalese conflict.

Nepal

Nepal has a current population of 26.49 million and falls into the category of least developed countries in the world. The gap between male and female literacy rates respectively standing at 75.1 and 57.4%[1] exemplify the strong patriarchal culture in the country. Nepal has one of the highest rates of child labour as well as gender-based violence and domestic violence against women.[2] The stratification in the country is also reflected in other factors such as caste and economic disparity. The average income in Kathmandu is estimated to be "five times higher than" the average "income in the mid-western districts", referred to as the Maoist heartland."[3] Apart from the apparent political reasons, these social and structural issues also significantly contributed to the Nepalese conflict, leading scholars to comment that the conflict was the "cumulative effect of more than 345 years of exploitation."[4]

Conflict Outline

A series of political events resulted in the Nepalese conflict. A monarchy that secured its freedom through an agreement with the British Raj, Nepal is free from the colonial history most other countries in South

Asia share. A multi-party democracy was introduced in the country for the first time by the ruling monarch in 1959 but was shortly curtailed in 1960. A repressive non-party system of councils called *Panchayat*, allowed the king to exercise sole power during this period. After widespread civil disobedience campaigns also known as People's Movement I in 1990, the King restored democracy.[5] However, this democratic system—launched within narrow party politics and elite power struggles—failed to deliver the benefits of democracy to the people. Many outside the urban high caste elite circles remained feeling excluded despite the newly established democratic system.[6] Upreti perceives the Maoist insurgency led by the Communist Party of Nepal (Maoist) (CPN(M))[7] that broke out in February 1996 as a violent expression of people's frustration stemming from the disappointed hopes on fair democratic governance.[8] The Maoist insurgency intensified in its scale and scope during the next ten years and the King dissolved the parliament and postponed elections indefinitely. Frequent changes in the government and a short-lived ceasefire in 2003 all contributed to a growing sense of political instability. Declaring emergency law and deploying the Royal Nepal Army to suppress the rebels drew further international attention to the Nepalese conflict. In 2005, the governing political parties came together in a Seven Party Alliance and reached an agreement with CPN(M) on a programme to restore democracy in the country. This united leadership succeeded in rallying the public momentum once again for a protest for democracy in which "people in massive strength came out on the street and challenged the royal regime."[9] This mass protest, known as People's Movement II, resulted in reinstating democracy once again. The ten-year insurgency formally ended in November 2006 with the signing of the Comprehensive Peace Accord (CPA) between the government and the CPN(M). Subsequently, as per the demand of the CPN(M), the monarchy was abolished in 2007. The constitution of Nepal was successfully passed in September 2015 after several complications.

The Peace Process

There are two significant elements of the Peace Process that shaped the post-conflict context of Nepal: United Nations presence in the country as a monitoring body and the Constituent Assembly (CA) that was elected to draft a new constitution for the country.

Among the various UN missions in Nepal the Office of the High Commissioner for Human Rights (OHCHR) and the United Nations Mission in Nepal (UNMIN) played an important role in the conflict. During the peace process, OHCHR monitored the human rights situation together with UNMIN. UNMIN is a special political mission with a limited mandate, established in January 2007 through a Security Council Resolution at the request of the Seven Party Alliance and the CPN(M). According to its mandate, UNMIN aimed to create a "free and fair atmosphere" for electing the Constituent Assembly and for the implementation of the peace process. UNMIN left on the 15 January 2011 failing to see its mission to an end.[10]

The CA was responsible for drafting and delivering a new constitution for Nepal, following the aspirations of the people's movements. The interim constitution provisioned for the CA in 2007 and it was elected to office in 2008. It consisted of 601 members appointed to office through different democratic processes. In its first meeting, the CA declared Nepal a republic, thereby effectively putting an end to the monarchy. From then on, progress towards drafting a constitution for the country through a consensus process became an uphill journey. Different political factions had conflicting interests and the CA self-extended its term four times.[11] The Supreme Court dissolved the CA after the 27 May 2012 and ruled that elections for appointing a new CA would be held later in the year. Following elections in 2013, a second CA took oath on 21 January 2014, and produced a new constitution that was endorsed by 538 out of 598 members and came into effect on 20 May 2015. Despite its seeming success at the parliamentary level, protests against the constitution are rife at the periphery of the state. Calls for greater inclusion of minority and marginalised groups, including non-gender discriminatory citizenship provisions, are key demands. Indigenous groups and districts in the Terai region along the southern border of the country are at the forefront of the protests. India also demanded amendments to the constitution and took a political stance by supporting an unofficial blockade at the India–Nepal border. The consequent humanitarian and political crisis, amidst the rebuilding efforts of the 2015 earthquake, brought further strife to the fledgling state. Despite the promise of the peace agreement and the effective reintegration or absorption of Maoist fighters respectively into the community or the state armed forces, persisting political instability among other reasons prevent laying a solid foundation for sustainable peace in Nepal.

Perspectives from Margins

The primary discourse on conflict is often centralised around both the conflict timeline and the major conflicting parties. Sustainable peacebuilding necessarily takes a more proactive approach towards engaging with the communities that are affected by conflict, irrespective of their political affinities. People feel the conflict and the ensuing political process differently than their leaders, who are at the centre of the conflict and the peace process. This section explores the impact of Nepalese conflict from a citizens' perspective.

Unpredictability and the tension that comes with it are significant factors that characterise life in a conflict zone. The daily routines of farming, cooking, sleeping and child-rearing continued in rural Nepal, where the most violent confrontations between the Maoists and the army took place. These apparently calm, familiar routines dominated the lives of most and could have been affected any time by "unexpected terror and violence."[12] Nepal holds the highest number of newly reported enforced disappearances in the years between 2002 and 2005[13] and as such, the unpredictability and the tension in everyday lives during the conflict has been very real and tangible for those at the ground level.

People were caught between two regimes, placed in a position where they often had no alternative but to be subjected to violence by both the army and the Maoists. They were being forced to provide food and shelter as well as donations to the Maoists on the one hand, and were left vulnerable to state retaliation and abuse of power on the other. By 2000, the Maoists relied increasingly on staying within close proximity to the village to meet their needs.[14] A woman relates how she was forced to cooperate despite the risks: "I told them ... 'if you stay here and the army arrives then all my family will be killed'... I begged them not to stay and they left after they had eaten."[15] A relatively well-off Kathmandu resident observes that being asked for "donations" is an experience he had to go through several times during the conflict and that he had to pay whatever amount the Maoist representatives demand without raising any questions.[16] Those who paid, ran the risk of facing the wrath of the state security forces and legal actions against them.

Those who resisted the pressure, were often directly or indirectly punished in some manner.[17] An ever-present tension pervaded people's everyday lives, as one interviewee pointed out: "We didn't know what time we are going to be trapped ... That time we were afraid of the government and Maoists equally."[18] Apart from these isolated incidents, the Maoists forcefully confiscated the property deeds of major landowners intending to "redistribute them among villagers."[19] These actions placed the civilians vulnerable to the state power. Amnesty International reports that the local administration provided the security forces with lists of people who were accused of giving food or shelter to the Maoists or attending Maoist meetings: and this led to frequent "house-to-house searches" at "night and in large numbers" where arrests were made without sufficient evidence.[20] Civilians were, therefore, forcibly drawn into the tug of war between the parties.

Violence and abuse by both the sides were widespread, with frequent incidents of civilian death. The number of "extrajudicial killings and disappearances by Security Forces" rose dramatically since 2001, after declaring emergency law and mobilising the Royal Army to suppress the insurgency.[21] The reported conflict-related killings come from "all but two of Nepal's 75 districts"[22] and both the army and the Maoists are listed as perpetrators.[23] Apart from these reported incidents, there are many that went unreported: the theatre group members have a number of stories where they either experienced or heard about deaths of civilians that went unreported and often accepted with a helpless resignation.[24]

Forced recruitments and infrastructure destruction by the Maoists also intensified the pressure on people. Women and children were especially vulnerable to forced recruitment.[25] There is documented evidence of parents being ordered to send their children to Maoist cultural groups, or outright abductions of women and children for political indoctrination and militia membership.[26] Infrastructure, such as schools and government offices, located in the regional districts of Nepal were closed or banned by the Maoists,[27] and there were almost no state interventions to reopen these.

Rape was also a frequently used weapon in the conflict, reportedly, primarily by the Security Forces. The Institute of Human Rights Communication in Nepal noted that hardly any action was taken whenever the authorities were informed of rapes or acts of sexual violence committed by the Security Forces.[28] The strong gender stereotypes and the hierarchy in the Nepalese society resulted in "normalising" and "legitimizing" violence against women[29] and in reducing the reported number of rapes. Being raped multiple times was seen as yet another reality of life in certain villages in remote areas: a woman notes that there were hardly any women in her village who have not been raped at least once.[30]

Thus, Nepali citizens in the remote areas of the country where the conflict was felt the most, were caught up in the tug of war between the Maoists and the Security Forces. As Hutt aptly puts, "[i]t really was a case of two regimes, in which villagers had to choose between support, acquiescence, opposition or flight."[31] Irrespective of what they chose, the strain of the conflict upon the people is still felt within the community.

Challenges for Sustainable Peacebuilding at a Community Level

Though the armed conflict abated with the signing of the CPA, there are still several issues that hinder peacebuilding in the community.

The impact of the conflict is still felt among the community in many ways, such as the unresolved issues of disappearances, displacement and restorative justice for crimes committed. These are major challenges, crucial for sustainable peacebuilding, that need to be addressed. International Committee of the Red Cross (ICRC) records indicate that by the end of 2011, there were 1406 active cases for disappeared people[32] and the numbers indicate only a minor improvement since then. Individuals as well as families resorted to fleeing as their last resort and some were forcibly evicted by CPN(M), who seized their lands.[33] These issues are yet to be satisfactorily resolved,[34] despite provisions to that effect in the CPA.

Procedure on restorative justice for the crimes committed during the conflict is another area at issue. The domestic justice system is strongly accused by the local as well as the international human rights defenders of being partial. Some organisations went so far as to jointly state that there is "virtually no prospect of success" for those who are seeking justice through the domestic justice system for crimes committed by State agents.[35] Bertelsmann Stiftung claims that not even a single person or a political organisation has been held accountable for human rights violations up until 2016.[36] While a few cases did go through the judiciary system since 2014, these have been rare; even when successful, the sentences were disproportionately light. In fact, many of those accused of human rights violations directly or indirectly continue to receive protection from those who are in power.[37] The political parties in the government have repeatedly attempted to either withdraw cases or bring about propositions to allow immunity for human rights abusers linked with the conflict.[38] The two commissions established in 2015 tasked with investigating human rights violations during the conflict indicate a half-hearted attempt at justice with in-built loopholes for amnesty and light sentences. There is little evidence that a genuine political will to implement an impartial restorative justice process exists even a decade after the civil war. Restorative justice is a key element in the war-to-peace transition process of a conflict. Nepal needs resolution that comes through transitional justice in order to provide justice to the people and to satisfy the expectations of its citizens.

Political instability poses another obstacle to sustainable peacebuilding at the ground level. The inability of the CA to deliver a constitution until September 2015 indicates a fragile balance of power. Violent protests characterised the period after September 2015, a testimony to the ethnic fragmentation of the communities and the tensions that exist among the people. Despite the democratic system, the voices of the people remain almost unheard. The political parties including CPN(M) that were in the CA are accused of serving their own interests at the cost of the public interest, and of abusing "social harmony and tolerance" to "strengthen their power base."[39] At the district level the fragility is further intensified due to the absence of elections for a decade and the recent signs of ethnic identity politics.[40] Ethnic organisations as well as armed groups are reportedly abusing communities in the Terai and Eastern hill regions without fear of prosecution.[41] After two decades, local elections take place for the first time in this sensitive environment in 2017.

The rulers coming into power after signing the CPA also failed to address the structural root causes of the Maoist insurgency. Therefore, the reasons such as poverty and discrimination that drove people to take up arms remain the same, or at times, have worsened. Human Rights Watch finds that the government has made "little progress" in achieving social, cultural and economic rights during the post-conflict period.[42] Given that the Nepalese conflict is also seen as a political conflict with social and political transformation at its heart,[43] addressing these aspects become even more important. The grievances of people remain the same until the root causes are addressed. Upreti perceives this failure to be the result of intentional activities serving the self-interest of powerful elites.[44]

During the conflict and the peace process, the Nepalese citizens' voice was generally heard in certain circumstances like mass demonstrations. The space for citizens' participation was limited in terms of political decision-making during the conflict, and continues to be so after the signing of the CPA. The peace process is critiqued as "non-transparent, elite-centric and ... exclusionary in nature."[45] The implementation of the Local Peace Committees is also seen to be highly politicized.[46] The citizens' voice is largely excluded from the public discourse on conflict. Adopting inclusive practices that satisfactorily address community grievances without falling back into the dynamics that characterised the previous eras is very much a contemporary challenge for Nepal. For this, we need non-violent strategies to bring out the citizens' voice; strategies that can make the so far excluded citizens' voice a central element of the public discourse. It is here that Sarwanam's theatre has significance as a peacebuilding approach.

Theatre in Nepal

Theatre in Nepal is diverse, given the diversity in ethnic, cultural, and indigenous groups. Theatre artists engaged with contemporary issues through different forms of theatre. Starting from 1950s, theatre activists such as Bal Krishna Sama made what was previously seen as an elite art form into a platform where stories of ordinary people's everyday lives were acted out. This act of expanding the breadth of theatre itself was political at the time. Subsequently, activists such as Ashesh Malla and Sunil Pokharel introduced and used street theatre to support people's movements for democracy. Theatre gained popularity among the people as a result, and developed a reputation as a tool in people's politics. Censorship and state repression prevailed during the periods of turmoil, and banning plays with political content, arresting artists who campaigned for democracy, and using physical violence against them, were common during the pre-democracy period of the country.

The theatre group Aarohan along with Sarwanam played a key role in Nepali politics. While Sarwanam led by Ashesh Malla continued developing its own theatre format, Sunil Pokharel left Sarwanam in the early 1980s to form Aarohan. Aarohan initiated national theatre festivals in Nepal and used these spaces to rally artists together to stand against the politics of the period. The plays of the group are diverse. The repertoire includes street theatre and proscenium plays, as well as western adaptations and scripts by local playwrights. Abhi Subedi's *Agniko Katha* (*Story of the Fire*) relates to the disruption the conflict had on traditional social foundations, while *Thamelko Yaatra* draws an allegory with the disintegrating urban social structures as a result of the conflict. The collectively developed play *Bhitta* is noteworthy for its take on the polarised Nepalese conflict, and the symbolic emphasis placed on the fact that people only have themselves to rely on, in order to survive the violent times.

Introduction of forum theatre and playback theatre are also important milestones in using theatre for peacebuilding in Nepal. Both the theatre forms create space for voicing people's opinions. Forum theatre is known as "Kachahari theatre" in Nepali. Kachahari is a meeting process used to resolve issues at the village level during the *Panchayat* rule. Coined by Sunil Pokharel, the localised name draws attention to the potential for discussion and dialogue embedded in forum theatre. Ghimire Yubaraj, Founder and Artistic Director of Shilpee Theatre and a practitioner who worked closely with Pokharel to develop forum theatre in Nepal, perceives the term to be a constant reminder about the depths theatre has to reach in order to truly offer a voice to those who are at the margins.[47] He notes that Kachahari courts, while providing a space for conflict resolution where villagers could speak out, was never truly representational. The voices of the local elites and culturally privileged were heard louder and more often. Through plays such as *Naari* that engage with gender discrimination, Yubaraj strives to use Kachahari theatre to do what the Kachahari courts failed to do; to cut through the many layers of oppression and offer a space for the voices that are the least heard in Nepali society. Playback theatre is also adapted to make meaning within the local narratives, and is commonly known as "Chautari Natak" in Nepali. This too creates a meeting point and a dialog space for people and to share their experiences of conflict and listen to that of others. Civil society groups use both these theatre forms as informal mediation tools in Nepal.

Theatre groups also engage with other facets of complex Nepali politics. Take Mithila Natyakala Parishad in Janakpur that works to preserve the Mithila theatre tradition. The group engages in the debate for a separate state for the region, through their plays and cultural activism. Shilpee Theatre and Madalenas Nepal, along with many other theatre groups, draw attention to women's issues through their performances. Sadbhawa theatre brings together younger artistes with the talent and passion for social change in a platform where they themselves take leadership.

Many groups including Aarohan, Shilpee, and Mandala theatre practice theatre for development and engage with urban as well as rural issues. Different forms of theatre such as mime are also used to engage with contemporary politics. *Naya Nepal* (New Nepal), a satirical play by Achel Natya Samuha supported by Manthan Theatre of India is an example.

The variations in the theatre groups and the development of different theatre forms in Nepal indicate the significance of bringing theatre closer to people and using it as a platform where people's narratives can be represented. The latter is especially important in the polarised conflict narratives within which the Nepali peace process takes place. Despite being effective in reaching into certain communities or groups of people, not many theatre groups or plays succeed in actively seeking out and engaging with communities at the periphery at a broader level or engaging with conflict issues in a way that focuses on the voices of and brings together the fractured community. Language, infrastructure, as well as access pose obvious barriers here. Given that these communities suffered the most from the conflict, looking into theatre efforts that make excluded citizens' perspectives a part of the public discourse on conflict is important in discussing how theatre can be used for building peace in Nepal.

Sarwanam

Background Information

Sarwanam started in 1982 as a theatre group. The founder, Ashesh Malla, sees it as the initiation of a social movement since the group from its inception performed to bring out the voice of the people and to protest against the exclusion and oppression Nepal's citizens. Sarwanam is based in Kathmandu though Ashesh Malla as well as many of the longest-standing members of the group comes from districts outside the capital. Membership is usually established through an informal process and calls for continued participation in the activities of the group over several years. Sarwanam has its own performance centre in the capital that contains a theatre, a café, a gallery, a library, an office and a workshop space. The group owns the building, and the financial resources for its construction are generally seen as the savings of the team in the paid theatre projects they undertake for NGOs and INGOs. The organisational structure of the group reflects two main bodies: the artistes' team and the management team. The management team is smaller and consists of the older members of the group, while the artistes' team is made up of the regular group members. The teams overlap in some cases and the daily functioning of the centre is seen as a responsibility of the entire group.

Theatre Approach

The dialogic and the multivocality of the theatre group primarily comes out in the theatre form and performances of Sarwanam. The group has developed its own alternative theatre style in order to make theatre more accessible for the people. Specifically, Sarwanam performances use minimal props in an effort to make theatre more affordable to produce and convenient to perform. Leading theatre personalities in the country commend Ashesh Malla on the simplicity of Sarwanam's costumes and props, seeing these as a way to overcome a central challenge the theatre practitioners face in South Asia.[48] Sarwanam plays are seen as low budget productions that are not low budget in the performance.

The particular theatre form of Sarwanam has a strong resemblance to street theatre. Ashesh Malla is key in introducing street theatre to Nepal, and the influence of street theatre is evident even in the proscenium plays of the group. Strong emphasis on symbolic gestures and mime can break through language barriers and as such, Sarwanam perceives their alternative theatre to embody democracy and freedom.[49] The symbolism opens up the plays for multiple interpretations, thereby enhancing its dialogic potential and multivocality. The group tours regional districts of Nepal at least once every year with a short performance—the members identify these national tours as an effort to bring themselves closer to the audience and to carry on their activism among larger audiences.

The thematic engagement of Sarwanam plays is a key area where multivocality and the dialogic of its theatre are highlighted. Ashesh Malla, who is also the theatre director of the group, writes all the plays of the group.[50] As established earlier, the political parties and the government are both accused of excluding people from the public decision-making and the elite-centric peace process. Including excluded citizens' perspectives in the public discourse becomes a necessity for sustainable peacebuilding. Passive acceptance or avoidance of the atrocities committed is widely seen as a coping mechanism of the local population.[51] Thus, engaging with these issues from a citizen's perspective and making the citizens' voice part of the public discourse on conflict become imperative for the reconciliation of the conflict and to achieve sustainable peacebuilding. Sarwanam dramas directly engage with political issues such as the absence of democracy and the aftermath of conflict in Nepal from a citizen's perspective. Abhi Subedi, a noted theatre personality and a critic, observes that the way in which Sarwanam highlighted the corruption in the society and the suppression and violence people experience at a daily basis, opened a new chapter in Nepali theatre.[52] Articulating these issues as openly as Sarwanam did during the *Panchayat* rule, he argues, was a feat beyond the capabilities of a politician of the period. A long-term member observes that they have always tried to produce dramas around the feelings and problems of the people from remote areas of Nepal.[53] Accordingly, in using the multivocality and the dialogic of theatre to make excluded citizens' perspectives a part of the public discourse, Sarwanam addresses a distinct gap in Nepalese peacebuilding.

Group Practices

Sarwanam uses theatre to make excluded citizens' perspectives part of the public discourse on Nepalese conflict. Sarwanam's contributions in this can be discussed under two main sections: through group practices and performances.

Group practices include the way in which the group is shaped. Sarwanam incorporates certain elements in its group practices that enhance its accessibility to people from different groups, and encourages dialogue among them.

Open to All

The group membership is open to all: this encourages the participation of individuals irrespective of their caste, ethnicity, class, religion or age. At present, the group has members from the higher castes such as Brahmin as well as those from lower castes. The members come from different districts in Nepal and belong to different sub-ethnic communities and are from the two primary religions in Nepal: Hinduism and Buddhism. Members' ages vary from 73 to 17. The economic levels as well as employment indicators of the group are diverse. However, for a large majority of the members in the artistes' group, there is a strong pattern of families with economic hardships where income is largely derived from cultivating their own lands. This pattern is not reflected among the management team: the management team is from Kathmandu and are well established and economically stable. A pertinent factor here could be that management team members are relatively older than the artistes' group members, and are all except one,[54] employed outside the theatre group. Nevertheless, the fact that the artistes' group is open to those who are from the regions with little financial capability indicates that there is little discrimination on the socio-economic factors within the group. Gender is another strong discriminatory element in Nepalese society. Group practices inevitably reflect this to a certain extent, but there are often instances when these boundaries are unsettled. For example, the preparation of lunch and cleaning, work typically regarded as women's, is carried out according to a roster and therefore is done by both the males and females in the artistes' group. However, tasks such as controlling the lighting or the sound system of the theatre, still very much remain in the male domain.

This is not to say that preferential treatment is absent: tasks such as controlling the lighting or the sound system of the theatre still very much remain in the male domain. Also, the team overlooks the service rosters and duties outside the theatre space when it applies to certain members. This variation is present in other domains as well.[55] The outsiders also note this privileging and some even go so far as to see Sarwanam as being centred on the director, and the group members to "push up Mr. Malla."[56] Thus, the openness of group membership does not necessarily indicate equal treatment within: there are subtle hierarchies in the group dynamics that determine the place of each individual within the group and the space within which they are allowed to vary from the standard expectations in performing their roles.

Group Commitment

The commitment of the team is another factor that supports Sarwanam's role in making excluded citizens' perspectives a part of the public discourse. As a whole the artistes are ethically motivated and perceive the commitment to the group as their primary responsibility, even to a point of enduring practical risks and economic hardships as a result.

Ashesh Malla and the team outline numerous situations where they had to face the wrath of both the Maoists and the Police during performances. The Maoist groups directly and indirectly threatened and attacked the group when they carried plays on human rights and democracy to the villages prior to and immediately after signing the CPA, but

Sarwanam members managed to escape without serious harm. The state security forces questioned and harassed the team during performances in Kathmandu and sometimes in the regions. Still, surprisingly, some members related instances when both the Police and Maoists provided protection for their travel during intense conflict periods.[57]

In several interviews with the artistes, it became apparent that performing at Sarwanam is dissociated with its financial element, even when the performances are undertaken as part of a funded project. An actor, married with a child in kindergarten, says that he had to work somewhere as "they" [the organisation] do not have enough money to pay a salary. There seems to be a tension between being expected to attend regular rehearsals or perform duties at the organisation and having to earn their livelihood elsewhere while. Ramesh acknowledges that he is "working very hard in the morning shift in the office and come here [Sarwanam] in the evening [when there are rehearsals]"[58] in order to juggle both the responsibilities. Another factor that contributes to this situation is the perception of theatre as an industry. Theatre is not seen as an economically productive activity as another artiste observes: "here in Nepal there is an economic crisis and we have to look for any job."[59] It is interesting to note that while theatre in this case is not seen to be capable of generating sufficient income for an artiste to maintain his/her family, in working together, it succeeded in fundraising for setting-up group infrastructure.[60] However, with the construction of the Sarwanam building, a path with the potential of leading to economic sustainability opens up for the full-time artistes' team members. Many in the artiste team now have hopes for a bright future in which there will be a steady income.[61] Achieving sustainability will be a significant milestone for the group as well as for theatre practices in South Asia.

Sarwanam's perception of being a part of the team is more akin to performing a "higher duty" than earning a livelihood, thereby further dissociating it with its financial element while intensifying the group commitment. During the forum discussion and in the personal interviews, team members often compared the group to a "place of spiritual worship" (*mandir*) and the director Ashesh Malla to a father, citing his care and unwavering support offered within the organisation as well as with any other issues arising in their personal lives.[62] The organisation and the work they undertake there are frequently regarded as personal commitments or ethical responsibilities. Shiva's view on being ethically responsible as an actor captures this: "I cannot drink as I work against it [alcoholism] through drama, I have to answer to the audience so I cannot do any wrong." This ethical responsibility is generated through organisational conditioning to a certain extent. In referring to former members who left the organisation as a result of a disagreement about financial issues, the artistes as well as the management team evokes the rhetoric of "good" and "bad" people. Those who remain at Sarwanam are seen as "good people" as it is a place where only the "good" can remain.[63] The hamartia of the "bad people" who left the organisation is their desire for "money and power", and "ambition."[64] The resignations are seen as a desertion, a "betrayal of the family." Thus, the ethical commitment of the artistes emerges not only from a sense of altruism but also from a polarised and a charged group culture.

While there is acceptance for the group to voice dissent on the different elements of performance, there is little space to raise questions about the financial decisions of management. This underplaying of the financial element simultaneously brings out the other benefits the group has within Sarwanam: the sense of family is a primary motivation. Apart from this, several actors cite self-satisfaction of being in theatre and specifically theatre that engages with issues of people from rural Nepal, and the resulting recognition as benefits.[65] Building up a reputation is particularly seen to compensate for the financial hardships they undergo: "We have poor economic conditions but we can expect a future. We believe that though we do not have money, we have fame."[66] The sense of ethical responsibility that pervades Sarwanam works to keep the team together, to continue their efforts at making excluded citizens' perspectives a part of the public discourse even amidst practical difficulties.

These dynamics are similar to what some scholars see between the Chinese state and society. Ling highlights the similarities that exist between filial devotion and state obedience, and argues that this is yet another way of naturalising the moral authority of the society's superiors.[67] Sarwanam indicates a similar pattern. The team members regard the director with a combination of filial and spiritual devotion. The moral authority he has within the group is naturalised and derives from the broader discourse of duty and obligation that exists within the Nepalese society. Ling observes that private property, if it is possible to accrue, could offer an escape from structures of parental governance.[68] This is a challenge for Sarwanam since the members are expected to prioritise the organisation's work unless there is an even higher moral obligation in place. A number of Sarwanam members find the theatre group their sole source of income. The combination of naturalised moral authority, exclusive economic reliance and the absence of transparency on financial issues within Sarwanam can create space for exploitation or abuse of the members trust.

Enhanced Accessibility of Theatre

Another factor pertinent to group practices that makes the theatre space multivocal, is Sarwanam's enhanced accessibility to the audience and artistes. The construction of its own theatre hall addresses a crucial point that affects proscenium theatre: the financial capabilities that are needed to hire a performance space. This financial requirement restricts proscenium theatre and can pose a major threat to the production of a play. However, through building its own theatre hall, Sarwanam has ensured having a space to perform in the capital only at its maintenance costs. Thus, the group has considerably enhanced its accessibly to a proscenium theatre space with the construction of the Sarwanam building. The theatre hall, the gallery and the workshop hall are also rented out to other organisations at a daily fee, or based on an alternative arrangement that is agreeable to both the parties.[69] Doing so enhances the accessibility of theatre for other directors and groups as well. The income generated through the complex is expected to create sufficient salaries for the Sarwanam artistes and thereby solve the issue of insufficient financial compensation that has by necessity prevented some artistes from engaging full-time at Sarwanam.

Process of Coming Up with a Drama

The multivocality and the capacity for dialogue within the group are evident in the process of deciding a theme for the next drama and during the rehearsals. The drama to perform is decided as a result of a group discussion, taking into consideration the current political situation of the country and the best approach to make citizens' voices heard in this context. Despite the "guru" culture prevalent within the group, the group members voice their hesitancies on the director's choices and at times, get them overturned through a subtle process of dialogue. The group, unhappy with the drama *Ek Rath* for which they were rehearsing in June 2012, instead suggested choosing something that did not engage with the revolution so explicitly. After an extended discussion where several members voiced their concerns, the director/play writer agreed to dismiss *Ek Rath* and perform *Remaining Page of History* as their second drama at the Sarwanam theatre. This is a case in point where the multivocality and the dialogic embedded in the group practices became evident.

Practices of Performance

Practices of performance are the other main way in which Sarwanam's contribution in making excluded citizens' perspectives a part of the public discourse on conflict can be conceptualised. Three aspects of Sarwanam's theatre productions are relevant for this discussion: the chosen theatre form, taking theatre beyond the capital and the key themes of Sarwanam dramas. These aspects are important in discussing the ways in which multivocality and the dialogic emerge through Sarwanam dramas.

Theatre Forms: Street and Proscenium

Sarwanam practices street and proscenium theatre and in both these theatre types, use what they call "an alternative theatre form." This theatre form is designed to make theatre more accessible in terms of communication and required resources. Sarwanam's alternative theatre style uses a minimal number of props and requires very little stage management and costumes. These reduce the costs of producing a drama, and enhance the aptness to perform in remote locations with minimal facilities. Consequently the plays increase their accessibility for the average person. Putting up a play with little resources enhances the multivocality of theatre. Further, Sarwanam plays often emphasise mime and have exaggerated symbolic body movements. These elements reduce the cost of production and enhance the effectiveness of the medium. Strong emphasis on symbolic gestures and mime can break through language barriers and as such, Sarwanam perceives alternative theatre to embody democracy and freedom. Breaking down traditional theatre practices to move forward with a less ornate, less flowery theatre at the beginning of 1980s was seen as a significant development. The minimalist approach is often appreciated as a factor appropriate for the Nepali context. Further, the enhanced symbolic movements and the limited use of verbal dialogue support taking the expression of theatre and the dialogue that takes place between the drama and audience to a different level than those of the verbal and the mere performative. Audience members as well as veteran theatre artistes identify this as a positive factor that characterises Sarwanam productions.[70] These features open up paths for a stronger emotional narrative and powerful communication. However, while the theatre form is appropriate for street theatre and is largely successful, questions arise on the extent to which it is appropriate for the proscenium theatre.[71]

National Tours

The national drama tours are the primary way in which Sarwanam engages with and makes its theatre accessible to those who live outside the capital. Here the group uses street theatre, where a makeshift stage is marked with chalk dust on a small clearing near a bazaar (Fig. 6.1).

Undertaking national tours deepen the group's capacity for dialogue and enable them to listen to the people living in the regional districts

Fig. 6.1 Sarwanam performing in a school during a national tour

and vice versa. The group has a deeper understanding of the conflict dynamics and the suffering of the people because of the national tours. Nhucche observes that he understood the real meaning of a Maoist as a result of a national tour in which they encountered villagers who are familiar with Maoist fighters.[72] Almost all the group members have at least one story where they had a deeper glimpse into the daily fear that permeated the lives of the rural Nepali communities. The dramas facilitate dialogue by inference, and by the actual engagement of the artistes. Many recall instances where certain scenes in the performances reflected actual incidents that were taking place at that moment, such as being surrounded by police or the Maoists when a similar scene was unfolding in the drama during a village performance. Difficult circumstances the communities have to tolerate in silence become part of the public discourse along with their portrayal in the drama in front of the actual perpetrators of violence.

Further to this, the actors initiate dialogue among the audience before or/and after the drama during the national tours. Shiva relates an incident where they engaged in a dialogue with the Maoists before the performance in order to explain the purpose of the drama.[73] Such communication is important since it presents a third voice, a voice devoid of political affiliations or motivation that raises people's concerns. After the street theatre performances, artistes take time to talk with the audience about what they saw and to take the audience's point of view and get feedback; this again facilitates bringing in different voices and enhances the dialogic capacity of the theatre. It leads to deeper conversations on the dramatic themes.

Further, on the national tour as well as on the proscenium dramas, the group makes slight adaptations in the dress and language in order to provide a fair representation of different ethnic groups, and to easily fit within a given community. For example, while an actor might wear a shalwar kameez that is the typical men's wear in the hill country, he might change into a sarong when the team performs in Terai, the region adjoining India. Doing so enhances the group's accessibility for the local communities and facilitates Sarwanam's acceptance.

Themes Call for Democracy

The final and the most important point in Sarwanam's theatre that contributes to making excluded citizens' perspectives a part of the public discourse on conflict is the themes of its plays. In general, Sarwanam plays revolve around issues pertaining to human rights and democracy. The performance takes a neutral point of view that is affiliated neither with the Maoists nor with the government. Often, the plays initiate dialogue on the people's suffering that results from the conflict. The most common strategy of coping with the conflict is noted to be "avoidance or passive acceptance of the prevalence of either party."[74] Through its performances portraying the people's situation on stage, Sarwanam aims to break this silence. The portrayal thus speaks to the audience, on one hand presenting what goes on and initiating a dialogue from that point onwards, and on the other hand, relating to those who have experienced the situation by enabling identification with the characters. While the allegations in the dramas are quite powerful, Sarwanam often refrains from making direct accusations: "We did not directly criticise them [the Maoists] but we changed the costumes, names, things like that ... We do not directly say 'this is you we criticise'." The final identification is left to the audience even though the characters are laden with ample symbolic insinuations: "People can realise this is for me if they see, but we do not point to them." The group can thus present a neutral front while making its statement. The seeming indirectness provides protection from the parties of the conflict, as acknowledging the portrayal as their own would have been an acknowledgement of the violence they perpetuate. Ramesh recalls that this very indirectness saved them during a national tour: "We thought that they would arrest us at that time because we were talking about the conflict and referred indirectly to the Maoists too ... Even though the Maoists got angry, they couldn't do anything about it because they couldn't admit it is about them." Sarwanam dramas, therefore, strive to make the excluded citizens' perspectives a part of the public discourse by utilising multiple avenues to bring out different voices thorough theatre, in ways that encourage and initiate dialogue among and between the theatre product and its audience.

Thematic Engagement with Conflict

Thematic engagement is a central way in which Sarwanam engages in peacebuilding. The group often uses stories or legends from the Nepali culture or stories with symbolic significance to bring up excluded citizens' perspectives to the fore in public discourse. Addressing disruptive and divisive turns in Nepali politics is seen as a group duty to the society or the country.[75] Here, the dialogic and the multivocality of theatre is embedded in the thematic composition of the plays. In order to further explore the different ways in which Sarwanam strives to make excluded citizens' perspectives a part of the public discourse, the discussion will focus on two dramas that capture different aspects of Sarwanam's approach for peacebuilding in the following section. With the first drama, *Sakuni's Tricks*, Sarwanam uses theatre to address the rationale by reinterpreting a Sanskrit epic according to the present context; it is primarily for the proscenium theatre, has a printed script, and is relatively longer than the usual Sarwanam drama. With the second drama, *Remaining Page of History*, Sarwanam uses theatre to speak to emotion. *Remaining Page of History* is produced for both proscenium and street theatre. It has only a few dialogues and does not have a formal script. Most of the drama is performed through mime and therefore presents an appropriate example of the symbolic theatre form of Sarwanam.

Sakuni's Tricks: Using Theatre to Address the Rationale

The discussion of Sarwanam's utilisation of *Sakuni's Tricks* or *Sakuni Pasa Haru* to make excluded citizens' perspectives a part of the public discourse through thematic engagement with the conflict has three main sections: the first section provides a brief introduction to the play followed by a general outline of its plot and its relevance to the context in order to ground the ensuing discussion. The second section discusses *Sakuni's Tricks*'s dialogic seen in the ways in which it draws from the history to relate to the present. The third section discusses the play's multivocality seen in its potential for different interpretations, and the ways in which these interpretations present insights on the people's voice. The last section touches upon the challenges the group faces in relation to *Sakuni's Tricks* (Fig. 6.2).

Sakuni's Tricks is a proscenium play of Sarwanam. Reinterpreting *Mahabharata*, the longer of the two Sanskrit epic poems,[76] it utilises theatre's to create a space that enables shifting between the epic and modern. *Mahabharata* narrates the story of Kurukshetra War, a war between the Kaurava and Pandava princes. Given its close association with Hinduism, *Mahabharata* holds a fundamental place in shaping the Nepali culture, perceptions, and beliefs.[77] Woven around a scene from the original canon, *Sakuni's Tricks* is presented in highly poetic language and addresses the rationale of the audience. The play explores the post

Fig. 6.2 A scene from *Sakuni's Tricks* performed at the Sarwanam theatre

and pre conflict power struggle in Nepal in order to frame the exclusion of people's voice in the higher tiers of Nepali politics. It invites the audience to scrutinise local politics from a third point of view. When *Sakuni's Tricks* was performed in Sarwanam Theatre in April 2012, the play attracted theatregoers and practitioners alike with its script and the potential of application to the present Nepali context. The background music of the play is provided with only a few instruments that succeeded in emphasising the significance of the scenes. It is seen as music that "goes with the mood; powerful and [capable of] generate[ing] emotions."[78] The language of the play is highly literary and has more verbal communication than other Sarwanam plays. Nevertheless, it embodies the characteristic Sarwanam theatre style of exaggerated mime and a minimalistic production.

General Outline of the Plot
Sakuni's Tricks depicts a scene between the Kauravas and Pandavas. The play starts from a scene in the original story where the three princes—Yudhistira, Arjun, and Duryodana together with their uncle Sakuni

engage in a game of dice. Duryodana and Sakuni are the Kauravas while Yudhishtira and Arjun are Pandava brothers. Halfway through the game, the play deviates from the original story and Yudhistira, traditionally representing the good and the ethical "white" side proposes having an election to determine the ruling party instead of going to a war as warring is obsolete. Duryodana announces an election after being cajoled into it by his uncle Sakuni. Sakuni is a keen strategist who is interested in maximising his power. The Pandavas, knowing this, lure Sakuni to their side with offers of Ministerial positions and financial remunerations. People's protests and cries are heard on killings, poverty, drought and similar issues in the background while the Pandavas, together with Sakuni, count the commissions they gain from the international projects and donations launched in the country. In due course the Pandavas win the election and the people's cries repeat. These are pointedly ignored in favour of the celebrations and personal gains. Two things hold the narrative together: one is the narrator who comes onstage to introduce or analyse certain scenes and the other is Dritarashtra, the blind Kaurava king. The scenes unveil in answer to Dritarashtra's questions. After the victory of the election, Dritarashtra enters the stage appearing outraged at the actions and demands that the play be stopped; he takes off his costume and refuses to take part in the drama any longer where tactics of Yudhistir or Dhuryodana or Sakuni come into play. He claims to be a teacher, a common person and refuses to be Dritarashtra any longer and stands facing the surprised actors on the stage with his back to the audience.

Correlating Political History
The political parties in Nepal are widely held to be responsible for the initiation and escalation of conflict due to their failure in reforming the governing system and reducing poverty. They are accused of contributing to the escalation of conflict with their struggle for power within and between parties.[79] Floor crossing, corruption and bribery to form a government, are seen as the norm, leading to the escalation of people's frustration and the conflict. A factor that seriously impaired the progress during the ceasefire is the lack of honesty in implementing agreements signed within and between parties.[80] The result, according to Upreti, was a peace process that is "non-transparent, elite centric and consequently, exclusionary in nature."[81] The political parties were more interested in reaping the benefits of development funding the country

garnered than a genuine effort for post-conflict recovery and peace-building. An audience member's opinion resonates this frustration: "it [*Sakuni's Tricks*] was a reflection of our society. Our present leaders are for people, of people, speak for people, are democrats or Marxists; and their ultimate goal is to hold the power and just lead. This is what was shown in the play; it was the real portrayal of our present scenario."[82] Using allegory, *Sakuni's Tricks* explores the current political situation in Nepal and at the end, raises the frustrated citizens' voice.

Dialogic of Sakuni's Tricks: Drawing from the History to Relate to the Present
Sakuni's Tricks draws from the history to relate to the present, thereby exemplifying the ways in which reinterpreting an epic to reflect upon present issues can enhance its impact. It forms a bridge between the past and present, engaging with the past in order to initiate dialogue on the present.

The familiarity with the epic and the depth to which it is ingrained within us function to enhance a reinterpretation of the story in several ways. It is an act of engaging with something that is already known to the audience and as such, it speaks to a part that already exists within the individual. With *Sakuni's Tricks*, it speaks to *Mahabharata*, which some compare to the Bible in its significance in the Indian subcontinent.[83] Relating to this known part of ourselves is easier than introducing something that is unfamiliar. One way this contributes is through making the play more memorable. Familiarity with *Mahabharata* ensures that *Sakuni's Tricks* stays with the audience beyond the theatre space. The familiar narrative of the epic plays with existing thought patterns, and there is more curiosity and interest in the audience when it comes to engaging with the new twists in the play's narrative. The familiarity also means that there could be an extra degree of willingness when it comes to reflecting upon the story, a certain openness that might not be there for a play that is solely on the current political situation. By presenting a reinterpretation of *Mahabharata*, Sarwanam takes the play and its message closer to the people.

Another central way in which using *Mahabharata* serves to enhance the dialogic impact of *Sakuni's Tricks* is through the contrast in characterisation. The reinterpretation invites the audience to witness characters from the epic re-cast in political dynamics that bear a close symbolic resemblance to the Nepal political context after the conflict. While

Sakuni's Tricks is based on the general framework of *Mahabharata*, it takes the story beyond the framework of the epic. Instead of the dichotomous characterisation seen in the epic with a stark separation between good and evil with clear white and black characters, the reinterpretation introduces grey characters. The characters of the epic no longer remain pure; they are conflicted by desire for power and material gain. With the presentation of unexpected character developments, *Sakuni's Tricks* invites the audience to engage in a dialogue between the already known characters of the epic and the newly introduced modern interpretations of these characters.

The reinterpretation flows along different lines than the original, in a continual process of being in a dialogue between the two readings. The juxtaposition effectively changes the existing story in our minds. *Mahabharata*, as a fundamental epic of the Indian subcontinent, is intertwined with the construction of identities. The ripples evoked from it in the reinterpretation, form new links and relate to the present day in hitherto unexpected ways that can have far reaching consequences. When these changes are the result of seeing the story in a different way, of seeing the present situation in another way, it carries more weight than an original script does. The association with the epic already takes us into a deeper level of relating to the story. Instead of constructing something anew, *Sakuni's Tricks* with its reinterpretation of *Mahabharata*, invites the audience to rewrite the existing foundation of the epic along with their understanding of contemporary politics. The resulting understanding and realisation are thereby made more powerful and deeper, as well as inclusionary.

Multivocality of Sakuni's Tricks: Different Interpretations

Drawing from the analogy of *Mahabharata* is particularly apt for the Nepali context. As discussed above, one reason is the religious and mythological background and the impact that connection has on the audience. Another is the multiplicity of interpretations it holds for the audience. The ensuing multivocality opens the play up for diverse, overlapping, and at times contradictory, perspectives.

An interpretation by Bijaya Bishport places Sakuni, the floor-crosser in the election, as a third power outside the country that expects to benefit from an internal conflict in Nepal. For him, Sakuni represents the interventions of India and America.

Priya offers a more plausible and a pertinent interpretation by seeing the Pandava's as the Maoists. Just like the Pandava princes in the

Mahabharata had to leave the palace and spend twelve years in the jungle devoid of all the familiar comforts, Priya points out that the Maoists leaders also had to leave their homes and live in the jungle for several years. She perceives the Pandava princes of Yudhistira and Arjuna as an analogy for the Maoists. Similar to the Pandava princes representing all that is good and ethical for the people in the country, the Maoists at one time held out hope of an ethical state for the Nepalese: "The people had hope and aspirations that when those Maoist leaders do come to power, they will do something new for the country, people would get jobs, good education. There will be no corruptions and so on."[84] However, unlike the Pandavas in the epic and very much like the Pandavas in *Sakuni's Tricks*, when the Maoists came to power they continued the practice of exploitation and suppression evident in existing politics. Priya asserts that while "the Pandavas who went to the forest and came back to their country did good for their country in the past, ... these people [Maoists] who left their homes and so on [and] went to [the] forest [and] again came back, they didn't [do] anything. They were like [the] others. They were like Kauravas."[85] Manoj—another audience member—supports this view, saying that the Maoistsforgot their ideological beliefs once they entered mainstream politics in the post-war period.[86] His interpretation goes beyond the mere allegation to the post-conflict power struggle that leaves the citizens' perspectives unheard. It actively makes a correlation between the key parties of the conflict and the heroes of the drama, firmly establishing the contradictions with the original epical characters. Possibility for multiple interpretations enhances the appropriateness of the drama and its resulting impact upon the audience.

Another factor that highlights the multivocality brought through *Sakuni's Tricks* is located in the way the characters are interpreted. Priya notes "there is no difference between Kauravas and Pandavas. The gods have been mixed. There is no white and black difference. Now the Pandava's too have become like the Kaurava's."[87] Here, Priya highlights the importance of adapting to a new value system, to a new thinking pattern, as the old yardsticks are no longer meaningful within the modern period. The drama urges democratic Nepal to acknowledge the changes that have been brought about, and to act accordingly. It reminds us of the fallibility of rulers, with the old one-dimensional characters being obsolete: instead there are complex characters that defy categorisation. Characters that are flexible and fallible. It is here that checks and balances in a governing system become important, and a democratic constitution and a regulated election procedure become imperative. Building people's trust on a new constitution and a fair political system is a pre-requisite to a stable peace in Nepal.[88] These exist in order to ensure that the rulers serve citizens' interests. With the absence of such security as it is in a Nepal that is in frequent political turmoil, it is easy to exclude the citizens' grievances.

The call for change is supported by a general interpretation of *Sakuni's Tricks*'s plot. Through introducing *Mahabharata*, Sarwanam brings in the voice of the traditional, the religious. At the same time, by reinterpreting the story, Sarwanam contradicts the conventional reading and calls for a reinterpretation of the traditional that is appropriate for the modern circumstances. War is no longer an appropriate strategy for the modern context, though it was the decisive factor for the Kauravas and Pandavas. Election—and democracy—has their place. The monarchy is obsolete, and accordingly, power rests with the people. Exposing the weak points of party politics on-stage invites the people to question the rulers. The traditional subordination to the rulers is no longer appropriate as the current leaders do not serve the public interest, even if they indeed start off with honest intentions. The play subtly nudges the public to take a more active role in the country's post-conflict proceedings in order to ensure that the public interest is served. With its references to the Sanskrit epics that draw an ironic parallel with the present day politics, *Sakuni's Tricks* presents a rational insight into the post-conflict situation. It emphasises the necessity to move on and take charge of the people's power by the people, instead of entrusting it to the politicians and parties that are mostly corrupt and severs only their own interests.

The conclusion of the play also has several potential interpretations relevant to the discussion. By prefacing Om Mani Sharma's refusal to take part in the drama as Dritarashtra with "I am happy being a common person. I don't want to be Dritarashtra", the play brings the viewer back to the fatalistic, numbed position of refusing to take any action because of the pent up frustration. Instead of actively motivating the public to take any action, it merely reflects the frustration of the people, the disappointment they have suffered as a result of being constantly betrayed by the political parties: the parties that one after another proclaimed to represent the interest of the people to no avail. The climax of the drama is built up to voice the people's pent up frustration that is by and large ignored and goes unheard by the political elite of the post-conflict era. This dramatic presentation of the frustrated public voice has a significance that extends beyond the mere expression: it calls for a renewed disquiet that lies heavily upon the present. In certain instances, it indicates that the right leaders are not yet in power,[89] or that the country is looking for a good leader.[90] Yet again, it is interpreted as citizens being aware of the corruption within politics and refusing to play along anymore.[91] Standing up against the politicians as a common citizen is seen as an assertion of the people's rights including the right to speech and people's power. The two People's Movements for democracy, while being spearheaded by the political parties, drew in massive public support turning it into a real people's demonstration. The resulting disquiet of Om Mani Sharma's declaration hints at this dormant potential of the Nepali public. The ending takes the play beyond the despair Davis identifies as characteristic of the post-conflict Nepali theatre.[92]

Sakuni's Tricks's potential for multiple interpretations also works to protect the theatre group from any resultant threats that might arise due to its political significance. The group has ample experience of being at the receiving end of threats and harassment meted out by political hooligans before and during conflict. Protecting itself from risks is an important factor. Shyam notes that with *Sakuni's Tricks*, "[n]o one can blame us [the group]" even though "they feel that they are scolded. Even when someone raises a question, we say [that] we are talking about *Mahabharata*."[93] Here, the criticism of Nepali politics is presented in the guise of a reinterpretation. The message it conveys is symbolic and ultimately rests with the viewer's interpretation. Characters, costumes and the language of the play all retain their reference to *Mahabharata*. The political significance comes only from the content of the story. Despite the strong criticism it raises against the politicians, *Sakuni's Tricks* has sufficient subterfuge to protect the group members from political threats.

Challenges in Relation to the Play
Sakuni's Tricks has received strong critiques on certain aspects of the play too. An overarching generalisation levelled by several audience members is that due to the very frustration people experience as a result of the political power struggle in the country, the people have become disinterested in anything to do with politics.[94] Based on this, one person questions the assumption that *Sakuni's Tricks* makes people think about the present situation. The play is critiqued for certain parts of its acting. While Ram playing Dhuryodana has received critical acclaim, several

other actors can be questioned on their ability to deliver a convincing act, including Vinmaya who plays the narrator. The narrator's delivery of lines can improve in its evocation. While being powerful and descriptive most of the time, her presentation style has little variation according to the scene to be presented. The movements and gestures of the actors also appear repetitive at times. The "composition of movement blocking" is the same throughout all the disagreements that take place in the drama.[95] The language of the script, while being praised for its highly literary narrative, makes itself vulnerable to critique by being beyond the reach of everyday usage. Team members noted the difficulties they had with rehearsing; the audience members noted the difficulties they had with understanding certain conversations in the play; the scriptwriter, Ashesh Malla, noted that the beauty of the script made it difficult for the average person to grasp the full meaning. The use of highly literary language here is justifiable on the grounds that such language is apt for a reinterpretation of *Mahabharata*. However, it is important to ensure that the language does not become a barrier to communication. These challenges—while presenting factors that need to be revisited in terms of a reproduction of the play—do not unduly undermine the political significance of *Sakuni's Tricks*. It is regarded as a play "beyond time"; something that will continue to have significance irrespective of the temporal conditions or political contexts in Nepal.[96]

Remaining Page of History[97]: Using Theatre to Speak to Emotion

Sarwanam's thematic engagement with the conflict is evident in the play *Remaining Page of History* or *Itihasko Banki Pristha*. The way in which Sarwanam utilizes the play to make excluded citizens' perspectives a part of the public discourse on conflict can be discussed under three main sections: the first section provides a brief introduction to the play outlining the plot. The second section discusses the ways in which the dialogic of theatre has been utilized in the play through the body and emotions. The third section explores the multivocality and how the citizens' voice has been brought forward through the drama. Finally, there is a discussion on the challenges observed in relation to this drama.

Introducing Remaining Page of History

Remaining Page of History outlines the citizens' suffering during the Maoist insurgency in Nepal, with a particular focus on women. A team member sees it as a drama that reveals the "black scars of the society" resulting from the conflict.[98] The data presented earlier in the chapter on the citizens' everyday lives during the conflict from reports of international human rights monitoring missions resonate rather closely with the harsh narrative, adding to its plausibility. It can be performed either as a proscenium or a street play and was performed for the first time at Sarwanam theatre in July 2012. Here, Sarwanam uses theatre to create a symbolic space capable of addressing the emotions of the audience. The story uses minimal dialogue and the narrative consists largely of symbolic mime. The little language that is used in the play is everyday conversational diction. This, together with the emphasis given to the symbolic and mime, enhances the accessibility of the drama to people from different educational and language backgrounds.

The plot of *Remaining Page of History* revolves around a family living in the rural Nepal during the Maoist insurgency. The characters remain nameless. The family has a father, a young daughter, a son and his wife. An old couple in the village serves the task of establishing the story's context in the beginning, as the story does not have a narrator. Two Maoists coming from the forest see the son chopping firewood near the house and intimidate him. The wife also comes out and together they plead to be left alone, when the army appears. The son and the wife run inside the house while the Maoists exit the stage. The army, after a futile chase of the Maoists, stumbles upon the house again. They take the son away for questioning, beating and pushing away the father and the wife who protest. The following day the old woman and the man from the village point towards the dead body of the son, and the body is taken for burial in a procession. The women in the village force the wife to go through rituals of widowhood and wear widowhood symbols, such as breaking her bangles and wrapping her in a white saree instead of the bright red clothing she wore so far. After the end of the funeral, the father decides to leave the village with the daughter and the daughter-in-law. On the way, the daughter falls sick and passes away. Further along, the father also dies after being caught up in a cross fire between the army and the Maoists. The daughter-in-law, now isolated, buries him as best as she can. She continues her journey alone and is set upon by three men who rape her. Afterwards, she commits suicide by hanging herself. The play ends with her body under a dim red light while a dancer dressed in black and wearing long hair loose, comes on stage and performs a dance.[99]

Dialogic: Through the Body and Emotion
Through *Remaining Page of History*, Sarwanam thematically engages with the conflict and uses the dialogic of theatre to make excluded citizens' perspective a part of the public discourse on conflict. The body and emotion form the vessel that brings forth the dialogic.

The highly stylized symbolic representation of *Remaining Page of History* primarily uses the body movements and facial expressions for communication, instead of dialogue. The choice limit verbal communication locates the dialogic of theatre firmly within the symbolic. The dialogue in the play is limited to establishing the narrative's foundation. Therefore, after the first few scenes, the drama almost entirely relies upon symbolic mime as its mode of communication. As a result, the scenes are imbued with intensified tension and become powerfully evocative and moving. Ashesh Malla argues that even if the voice is left out, drama still has the use of body movement and facial expression: if the actor or actress is capable of delivering a balanced presentation of body and emotion onstage, that will ensure establishing a relationship with the viewer.[100] The absence of extensive props, costumes and lighting further contribute to bring the body to the fore as the primary conveyor. The body becomes the vehicle for the dialogic, automatically relating to the audience at a level that rarely achieved when communicating through language.

In *Remaining Page of History*, supported with its symbolic presentation revolving around the body, emotion serves a dialogic function with the audience by establishing a connection that resonates with what is being performed onstage. The narrative itself is apt for this: it invites the audience to resonate with the vivid emotional display of the symbolic mime, harnessing empathy with the victims of conflict. The reviews call that *Remaining Page of History* "recreate the angst and confusion that prevailed in the country during that period" and goes on to "give audiences a sense of the grief and sorrows that have become part of the lives of all those affected by the 10-year conflict."[101] Furthermore, the play captures the emotional intensity of the period. It expresses the feelings of pain and loss throughout the drama, inciting anger at the injustices committed. These are the encompassing feelings of the period. Performed onstage, the play evokes corresponding emotions from the audience. An audience member notes that the play has the potential to draw the audience into it, blurring the "line between real and unreal": for her, this resonance with the play has a cathartic effect, that is irrevocably connected with the emotions it generates.[102] The social and political significance of emotions takes place here in this dialogic resonance (Fig. 6.3).

The social and political significance of emotions in constituting an imagined community is evident in the final scene of *Remaining Page of History*. The final dance takes place in a dim light, with the hanging body of the protagonist under a spotlight as the background. A single actress with long loose hair, dressed entirely in black, performs a Kali Tandav dance, representing the building outrage and anger of women who suffer the most as a result of conflict. According to Hindu Mythology, Kali Tandav is a dance form from the repertoire of Lord Shiva's Tandav dance, which is at the "source of the cycle of creation, preservation and dissolution."[103] The Kali Tandav is danced to evoke the power of Durga, the goddess of revenge, primarily associated with female anger and destruction. Thus, the dance becomes a deification of the righteous anger that arises, from the women who suffered from the conflict in particular, and from the citizens whose suffering during the conflict has been overlooked at best and betrayed at worst, by the political

Fig. 6.3 A scene from *Remaining Page of History*

elite, in general. Also, it can be interpreted as an expression that encompasses the audience's responses to the drama: an onstage enactment of the feelings of anger and violence. The dance engages in relating to and representing the communal feelings evoked during the performance. The last scene, therefore, is a continual process of dialogue between the stage and the audience, between the individual and the society. While the dance is powerful and does express the violence of the pent up anger and frustration, the scene is quite short. Arguably this aspect of revenge is seen to be conducive for peacebuilding, as it provides consolation and empowerment for the women who have suffered from the conflict in different ways.[104]

Multivocality in Remaining Page of History
Here I look at how multiple voices are facilitated through *Remaining Page of History*, effectively making the excluded citizens' voices heard within the public discourse.

The scene composition of *Remaining Page of History* conveys its multivocality. Multivocality is performed on-stage with the simultaneous happenings going on under three spotlights towards the end of the first scene. Most of the characters in the story appear onstage at this point when the connections are yet to be established. A rather small stage is shared by three very different groups, each highlighted by a separate spotlight. The setting leaves no doubt that these three scenes take place in separate places at the same time. The groups burst into activity when it is their turn, and remain either frozen or dimly illuminated when it is the turn for another group to act. The activities of the groups are rather a contrast to each other: one a conversation between an old man and a woman in the village; another a domestic scenario in a village with a father, a young daughter and a daughter-in-law; and the final a group of singing and dancing young men. The interconnections between the groups become apparent only later on. The old man and the woman turn out to be residents of the same village where the domestic scene takes place. Young men from the other group reappear in the course of the play as Maoists, army, and hooligans. These diverse characters bring out the different facets of the society that exist within the same conditions, yet respond to and feel the ramifications of the conflict differently. It presents the different viewpoints and voices on conflict.

Another factor facilitating the inclusion of different voices is the anonymity of the characters. The namelessness enhances the story's generic format: stripping the characterization to the bare necessities becomes a strategy that facilitates relating at the level of emotion. It takes the interpretation beyond a particular person or a family or a caste, to encompass in general the villagers who suffered from being caught in-between the fighting parties. This generic nature leaves sufficient flexibility for the audience to relate to the characters, whether they are from the rural or the urban. It is seen as "drama close to the heart."[105] The symbolic presentation style also leaves the narrative open to different interpretations, thus ensuring ample room for multivocality. Hence the story is left open for the representation of multiple voices.

This expression of the different dimensions of people's voice in turn encourages the audience to explore whether the civilians' sacrifices have been sufficiently acknowledged. Even though the politicians at either side of the conflict work together at the decision making level today, some of the major problems of the country still remain unanswered. For example, due to the absence of a proper reconciliation process, the violence perpetuated during the conflict period by both the army and the Maoists remains unaddressed. *Remaining Page of History* questions whether the people's suffering has been of any avail in this case. With the dissolution of the Constituent Assembly at the time, this question lurked quite close to the surface of public conscience. Sarwanam points out the costs of conflict upon the communities and brings up the people's voice. These actions signify the political elite's responsibility to acknowledge and respect the citizens' perspectives. The group draws attention to the core issues for which people fought, the issues for which people suffered. Sarwanam taps into this repository of common experiences during the conflict and represents it as the people's voice, expecting to impact the current politicisation and corresponding corruption to a certain level through that.

Challenges

Remaining Page of History receives critiques on some elements. While the symbolic presentation together with minimal dialogue contributes to the emotional address of the play, the audience members and external artistes question the excessive and at times inaccurate, use of mime.[106] Arguably, mime is used excessively in certain instances such as in depicting conversations between family members. However, there are many instances where the mime is put to excellent use to convey external factors that verbal dialogue would sound artificial in doing. An example is when the army chases the Maoists. The scene effectively conveys stretching over time and distance with only a few minutes of activity. Another example would be the scene where the protagonist is raped: here, three men in black pants come on stage, surrounds the isolated woman, and one drags her *dhupatta* (a long scarf similar to a shawl) and mimes licking it from one end to the other in exaggerated action while the woman writhes on the floor at the opposite end of the stage. The other two men imitate the same action with their hands. The scene ends with the three men dragging themselves away from the stage in a process, bent in double, arms hanging down and being obviously devoid of all energy. The evocativeness of this would be extremely difficult to capture except with the mime. Another critic argues that the absence of dialogue in some ways slow down the pace of the drama, depriving "the audience from connecting with its sentiments."[107] Once again this is arguable, as the narrative appears to flow smoothly and through the entirety of the drama. The only place where the pace seemed to slow down is during the first part of the family's journey, after they left the village. However, this is due to a weakness in the script and the direction rather than an absence of dialogue. Finally, *Remaining Page of History* also faces the generic critique raised on almost all the Sarwanam performances: that of the actors failing to do justice to the characters.[108] It is apparent the group needs to improve their skills—especially with regard to the proscenium stage—in order to meet the audience expectations and the general theatre standards of the present.

Overall Challenges for the Theatre Group

Sarwanam has a history of over 25 years of working for democracy in Nepal and is an established organisation in the country. The group already has certain strategies in place to mitigate external challenges that limit its work. What I discuss here are only a few recurring points that negatively affect the groups' productions and ideology.

While Sarwanam's theatre invariably presents plays that address a political situation, there are occasions when it requires aesthetic fineness. Lack of refinement becomes a challenge only because the group presents itself as a professional theatre group. Sarwanam plays are widely appreciated and even recommended for its script and plot. However, as it was noted in the discussion of the two plays, there are frequent critiques raised when it comes to the performance level. These critiques are raised about weak points in acting and direction. The acting is termed as "monotonous" and "repetitive"[109] and an audience member calls some of the miming as "mistaken action." Given that Sarwanam promotes its own theatre style based on emphasised body movements and facial expressions, it is particularly important to make maximum use of the bodily expression as actors. The group needs to explore a wider range of bodily expression instead of being limited to a few, over-used gestures and patterns. Weak points in characterisation are also evident in some dramas: this is tied in with gaps in the play's direction. Another factor that needs to improve is the script: given the prominence of mime and symbolic in Sarwanam plays, the scripts need to be more detailed. At the moment the scripts contain dialogues, and display either a total absence of or a bare minimum of instruction when it comes to mime and symbolic performance. For example, *Remaining Page of History* only has a partial script for the sections with dialogue in it. The rest is developed during rehearsals together with the director and the artistes. While this is liberating in some aspects, it also imposes serious limitations upon the final performance or the capacity to replicate the play. It is not surprising, therefore, that mime and symbolism, while being effectively communicative, fails to reach the expected audience standards of "realistic" in its delivery.[110]

The group is entering a new phase of its growth and as a result, improvements in the aesthetic quality of the plays can be expected. Finishing construction of the Sarwanam building provides them with a regular rehearsal location and the income the building generates offers hope of receiving a sufficient income through group activity. These are external facilitators for delivering a high quality performance. However, external factors alone would not be sufficient. Most of the artistes' team at Sarwanam has been with the group for over six years. It appears that the actors need further skill training that goes beyond what is available within the group. Working in collaboration with other directors[111] and groups could be a way of overcoming this challenge.

The team's didactic approach towards the work they do can also become an issue. It reflects the assumed power hierarchies of being a part of the theatre group: this attitude can be counterproductive to the overall group objectives. The actors often regard their work as "teaching" and "lessons" and "advice": the people from rural Nepal are referred to as "uneducated" "simple people" who are "grateful" to the knowledge they bring. Such an attitude indicates a didactic tendency among the performers. It is important to address this conception as otherwise it runs a risk of undermining the principles the group stands up for, such as democracy and respecting the wisdom of the citizens.

Conclusion

Sarwanam has been politically active as a theatre group during most of the recent political transitions in Nepal. The peacebuilding approach it takes reaches into the social fabric, addressing an irrepressible issue that has been, and is at the heart of different conflict dynamics: the exclusion of people's voice from the public discourse. As the reports from international human rights organisations as well as personal stories from Nepal point out, the Maoist insurgency took place on the topography of everyday civilian lives. However, the peace process largely took place within the upper echelons of the political elite. Sarwanam, through its theatre, strives to make excluded citizens' perspectives a part of the public discourse on conflict. It is here that Sarwanam's significance as an organisation using theatre for peacebuilding takes place.

This chapter demonstrated how Sarwanam contributes to peacebuilding in Nepal through using the multivocality and dialogic of theatre to make excluded citizens' voices part of the public discourse on conflict. It explored the ways in which Sarwanam uses theatre to bring out excluded citizens' perspectives under two broad themes: the group practices and the practices of performance. The group practices were found to be inclusionary and ethically committed: the practices of performances were also inclusionary and dialogic in its structure and implementation. The thematic engagement of the plays with the conflict situation was at a high level. Each of the two plays explored present a unique approach to the conflict situation, while bringing out excluded citizens' perspectives using complex dramatic techniques and forms. *Sakuni's Tricks* addresses the rationale, inviting the audience to intellectually engage with the issues by reinterpreting the Sanskrit epic *Mahabharata*. *Remaining Page of History* addresses emotions of the audience, presenting a narrative of the conflict's impact upon local people. The first focuses on a political analysis to establish the absence of people's voice at the governance level, while the latter focuses on a ground level story to bring out the neglected suffering of people.

Therefore, it becomes apparent that Sarwanam creatively utilises the imagined space of theatre and the dialogic and multivocal form of theatre to serve its purposes. Through the freedom it grants to the artist, Sarwanam emphasises political situations where the citizens' voice is absent or unheard, highlights certain incidents to ensure that the people's voice is heard, and makes correlations that are intended to make the audience contemplate and take action. It uses the aesthetic "ability to step back, reflect and see political conflict and dilemmas in new ways"[112] and proclaims the excluded citizens' perspectives as a part of the public discourse on conflict with renewed vigour. Contrary to what Davis argues about Sarwanam and post-conflict Nepali theatre, plays of the group do not fall into and remain within a feeling of despair. While resonating with the pervading sense of despair and connecting with the suffering of the people, the plays aim to shake people up from this state with their powerful and moving endings. This combined passion and commitment for art and politics sets Sarwanam apart from other theatre groups and characterises its contribution to using theatre for peacebuilding.

NOTES

1. Central Bureau of Statistics - Government of Nepal, "Nepal in Figures 2013" (Central Bureau of Statistics, Government of Nepal, Kathmandu, Nepal, 2013).
2. Friedrich Ebert Stiftung, "Nepal in the Year 2012: A Glance" (Friedrich Ebert Stiftung, 2013), 62.
3. Michael Hutt, ed. *Himalayan People's War: Nepal's Maoist Rebellion* (London: C. Hurst & Co. Ltd, 2004), 17.
4. Bishnu R. Upreti, *Nepal from War to Peace: Legacies of the Past and Hopes for the Future* (New Delhi: Adroit Publishers, 2009), 23.
5. Amnesty International, "*Nepal: A Spiralling Human Rights Crisis*," (Amnesty International, April 04, 2002), 10.
6. "*Nepal: A Spiralling Human Rights Crisis*," (Amnesty International, April 04, 2002), 11.
7. Subsequently known as the Unified Communist Party of Nepal (Maoist) and Communist Party of Nepal (Maoist-Centre).
8. Upreti, *Nepal from War to Peace: Legacies of the Past and Hopes for the Future*, 23.
9. *Nepal from War to Peace: Legacies of the Past and Hopes for the Future*, 50.
10. Friedrich Ebert Stiftung, "Political, Economic and Social Development in Nepal in the Year 2011" (Friedrich Ebert Stiftung, 2011).
11. Friedrich Ebert Stiftung, "Political, Economic and Social Development in Nepal in the Year 2011."

12. Judith Pettigrew, "Living between the Maoists and the Army in Rural Nepal," in *Himalayan People's War: Nepal's Maoist Rebellion*, ed. Michael Hutt (London: C. Hurst & Co. Ltd, 2004), 262.
13. United Nations Office of the High Commissioner for Human Rights, "Nepal Conflict Report 2012," (United Nations Office of the High Commissioner for Human Rights, October, 2012), 46–47.
14. Judith Pettigrew discusses these changing condition in Pettigrew, "Living between the Maoists and the Army in Rural Nepal."
15. "Living between the Maoists and the Army in Rural Nepal," 267.
16. The citizens had no means of verifying whether the claimants were Maoists or not: thus, as a repercussion, they were susceptible to impersonators who were interested in posing as Maoists for financial gains.
17. Amnesty International, "Nepal: A Spiralling Human Rights Crisis," 7.
18. Pratham Baral, interview with the author, Kathmandu, June 10, 2012 (pseudonym used).
19. Amnesty International, "Nepal: A Spiralling Human Rights Crisis," 7.
20. United Nations Office of the High Commissioner for Human Rights, "Nepal Conflict Report 2012," 46, and also Amnesty International, "Nepal: A Spiraling Human Rights Crisis."
21. "Nepal Conflict Report 2012," 46–47.
22. Ibid., 15.
23. This attack was followed by the retaliatory killing of 11 individuals by around 300 Maoists, including a 14-year-old boy on 15 April 2005. At the same incident, 11 houses were burned and at least 1000 people fled to India. See "Nepal Conflict Report 2012," 95 and Pettigrew, "Living between the Maoists and the Army in Rural Nepal" for a detailed discussion.
24. One such story Meena shared is about a young boy they met in a national tour. The group was looking for a place to sleep at night, and a boy from the village took them to the nearby school where they could spend the night. Meena and the others heard gunshots in the middle of the night. In the morning, they discovered that entire family of the young boy had been shot the previous night, because one of the siblings was accused of supporting the Maoists.
25. There is also evidence of children being used by the Royal Nepalese Army as informants or spies. See United Nations, "Nepal's Hidden Tragedy: Children Caught in the Conflict," (United Nations, 2006).
26. Mandira Sharma and Dinesh Prasain, "Gender Dimensions of the People's War: Some Reflections on the Experiences of Rural Women," in *Himalayan People's War: Nepal's Maoist Rebellion*, ed. Michael Hutt (London: C. Hurst & Co. Ltd, 2004), 163. United Nations, "Nepal's Hidden Tragedy: Children Caught in the Conflict."

27. Amnesty International, "Nepal: A Spiralling Human Rights Crisis," 7.
28. Institute of Human Rights Communication, "Sexual Violence in the 'People's War': The Impact of Armed Conflict on Women and Girl in Nepal," (Kathmandu: IHRICON, 2007).
29. Retika Rajabhandari and Women's Rehabilitation Centre, *Violence against Women in Nepal: A Complex and Invisible Reality* (Kathmandu, Nepal: WOREC, 2006), 4; Women's Rehabilitation Centre, *Anwesi: A Year Book on Violence against Women 2008* (Kathmandu, Nepal: WOREC, 2008), 12.
30. United Nations Office of the High Commissioner for Human Rights, "Nepal Conflict Report 2012."
31. Hutt, *Himalayan People's War: Nepal's Maoist Rebellion*, 19.
32. International Committee of the Red Cross, "Nepal Annual Report" (ICRC, 2011), 230–31.
33. United Nations Office of the High Commissioner for Human Rights, "Nepal Conflict Report 2012," 15.
34. Friedrich Ebert Stiftung, "Nepal in the Year 2012: A Glance."
35. TRIAL (Swiss Association against Impunity) et al., "Nepal: Written Information for the Adoption of the List of Issues by the Human Rights Committee with Regard to Nepal's Second Periodic Report (Ccpr/C/Npl/2)," http://www2.ohchr.org/english/bodies/hrc/docs/ngos/TRIAL_Nepal_HRC108.pdf; ibid.
36. Human Rights Watch, "Nepal: Country Summary," (Human Rights Watch, January 2012).
37. Ibid.
38. Amnesty International, "Amnesty International Report 2012: The State of the World's Human Rights," (London, UK: Amnesty International, 2012), 250.
39. Friedrich Ebert Stiftung, "Nepal in the Year 2012: A Glance."
40. Ibid.
41. Human Rights Watch, "Nepal: Country Summary."
42. Ibid.
43. Upreti, *Nepal from War to Peace: Legacies of the Past and Hopes for the Future*, 32.
44. *Nepal from War to Peace: Legacies of the Past and Hopes for the Future*, 23.
45. Ibid., 427.
46. Friedrich Ebert Stiftung, "Nepal in the Year 2012: A Glance."
47. Ghimire Yubaraj, personal communication with the author, June 01, 2017.

48. Bijaya Bishport, interview with the author, Kathmandu, June 12, 2012, and Yubaraj Ghimre, interview with the author, Kathmandu, June 18, 2012.
49. Nepal consists of a large number of ethnic identities and tribes that identify with their own languages and dialects. Thus, limiting language use in the plays enables the audience to identify with the characters with relative ease.
50. There have been exceptions as well. Consider the two following examples: A 2010 street theatre tour sponsored by Amnesty International where the script was by Krishna Pradhan (more information on this can be found at http://www.amnestynepal.org/content/news/48/CARAVAN-ON-RIGHTS-OF-THE-MIGRANT-WORKERS.html). Secondly, Ashesh Malla's daughter, Sampada Malla, co-directed a performance in 2011.
51. Upreti, *Nepal from War to Peace: Legacies of the Past and Hopes for the Future*, 428.
52. Abhi Subedi, *Nepali Theatre as I See It* (Kathmandu: Aarohan, 2006).
53. Om Mani Sharma, interview with the author, Kathmandu, June 08, 2012.
54. The only member of the management team who works exclusively at Sarwanam is Harsha (pseudonym used). Harsha is married to a someone from a well-off family in Kathmandu and as such, has no pressing financial difficulties.
55. In meetings, rehearsals and performances, certain individuals received more space for speaking up, and there was a marked tolerance for tardiness, mistakes, and interruptions when these came from the same individuals. They enjoyed the power to handle organizational equipment and were encouraged to take part in activities that went beyond acting such as direction, production, technical, and technological aspects of producing a play.
56. Bijaya Bishport, interview with the author, Kathmandu, June 12, 2012.
57. Ram Shrestha, interview with the author, Kathmandu, June 14, 2012; Shyam Khadka, interview with the author, Kathmandu, June 14, 2012; Shiva Adhikari, interview with the author, Kathmandu, June 13, 2012.
58. Ramesh Khadka, interview with the author, Kathmandu, June 15, 2012.
59. Ibid.
60. The end of my research period coincided with the beginning of Sarwanam's journey towards sustainability. The artistes for the first time after the construction of the hall, received a substantial payment for a drama tour carried out for an INGO in May 2012. This led one artist to exclaim "oh, we received so much money this time, so much!"

61. Ram Shrestha, interview with the author, Kathmandu, June 14, 2012; Tika Bhakta, interview with the author, Kathmandu, June 17, 2012; Sabithri Malla Kakshapati, interview with the author, Kathmandu, June 17, 2012; Shyam Khadka, interview with the author, Kathmandu, June 14, 2012.
62. Ramesh Khadka, interview with the author, Kathmandu, June 15, 2012; Meena Khadka, interview with the author, Kathmandu, June 15, 2012; Vinmaya Prajapati, interview with the author, Kathmandu, June 13, 2012; Tika Bhakta, interview with the author, Kathmandu, June 17, 2012.
63. Ramesh Khadka, interview with the author, Kathmandu, June 15, 2012; Sabithri Malla Kakshapati, interview with the author, Kathmandu, June 17, 2012; Om Mani Sharma, interview with the author, Kathmandu, June 08, 2012.
64. Ibid.
65. Ramesh Khadka, interview with the author, Kathmandu, June 15, 2012; Tika Bhakta, interview with the author, Kathmandu, June 17, 2012; Nhucche Shrestha, interview with the author, Kathmandu, June 17, 2012.
66. Ramesh Khadka, interview with the author, Kathmandu, June 15, 2012; Shyam Khadka, interview with the author, Kathmandu, June 14, 2012.
67. Lily H. M. Ling, "Rationalizations for State Violence in Chinese Politics: The Hegemony of Parental Governance," *Journal of Peace Research* 31, no. 4 (1994): 397.
68. Ibid.
69. Yubaraj Ghimre performed his drama at Sarwanam theatre without paying the daily fee for renting the theatre, based on the agreement that the first three days of ticket earnings go to Sarwanam as payment.
70. Audience Forum interview, interview with the author, Kathmandu, June 19, 2012; Bijaya Bishport, interview with the author, Kathmandu, June 12, 2012; Yubaraj Ghimre, interview with the author, Kathmandu, June 18, 2012.
71. Anjay Dahal (interview with the author, Kathmandu, June 15, 2012 [pseudonym used for identification]) and Yubaraj Ghimre (interview with the author, Kathmandu, June 18, 2012) as well as several reviews in newspapers, term *Sakuni's Tricks* as 'overacting' and 'being full of similar gestures'.
72. Nhucche Srestha, interview with the author, Kathmandu, June 17, 2012.
73. Shiva Adhikari, interview with the author, Kathmandu, June 13, 2012.
74. Upreti, *Nepal from War to Peace: Legacies of the Past and Hopes for the Future*, 428.

75. Om Mani Sharma, interview with the author, Kathmandu, June 08, 2012.
76. The other is *Ramayana*.
77. Its significance is compared to the Bible or the Quran: William J. Johnson, *The Sauptikaparvan of the Mahābhārata: The Massacre at Night* (Oxford: Oxford University Press, 1998), ix.
78. Pratham Baral, interview with author, Kathmandu, June 10, 2012.
79. Upreti, *Nepal from War to Peace: Legacies of the Past and Hopes for the Future*, 29.
80. *Nepal from War to Peace: Legacies of the Past and Hopes for the Future*, 427.
81. Ibid.
82. Priya Chhetri, Interview with author, Kathmandu, June 06, 2012 (Pseudonym used).
83. William J. Johnson, *The Sauptikaparvan of the Mahābhārata: The Massacre at Night* (Oxford University Press, 1998), ix.
84. Priya Chhetri, interview with the author, Kathmandu, June 06, 2012.
85. Ibid.
86. Manoj Shankar, interview with the author, Kathmandu, June 19, 2012 (pseudonym used).
87. Priya Chhetri, interview with the author, Kathmandu, June 06, 2012.
88. Upreti, *Nepal from War to Peace: Legacies of the Past and Hopes for the Future*, 187.
89. Krishna Pradhan, interview with the author, Kathmandu, June 10, 2012.
90. Tika Bhakta, interview with the author, Kathmandu, June 17, 2012.
91. Ibid.
92. Ashis Sengupta, ed. *Mapping South Asia through Contemporary Theatre: Essays on the Theatres of India, Pakistan, Bangladesh, Nepal and Sri Lanka* (Basingstoke: Palgrave Macmillan, 2014).
93. Shyam Khadka, interview with the author, Kathmandu, June 14, 2012.
94. Anjay Dahal, interview with the author, Kathmandu, June 15, 2012; Bijaya Bishport, interview with the author, Kathmandu, June 12, 2012.
95. Bijaya Bishport, interview with the author, Kathmandu, June 12, 2012.
96. Priya Chhetri, interview with the author, Kathmandu, June 06, 2012.
97. Also referred to as *Banki Pristha* or *Remaining Page*.
98. Tika Bhakta, interview with the author, Kathmandu, June 17, 2012.
99. This is a Kali Tandava dance, a dance for the goddess Kali that expresses women's anger and brings about destruction.
100. Ashesh Malla, interview with the author, Kathmandu, June 23, 2012.
101. Manisha Neupane, "Scars of War," *The Kathmandu Post*, July 10, 2012.
102. Priya Chhetri, interview with the author, Kathmandu, June 06, 2012.

103. Lipika Das, "Shakespeare in Odisha: A Study of Selected Odia Translations," *Odisha Review* (May 2012): 51.
104. Tika Bhakta, interview with the author, Kathmandu, June 17, 2012.
105. Nirmala Harun, interview with the author, Chitvan, May 4, 2012.
106. Anjay Dahal, interview with the author, Kathmandu, June 15, 2012; Bijaya Bishport, interview with the author, Kathmandu, June 12, 2012.
107. Neupane, "Scars of War."
108. Ibid.; Yubaraj Ghimre, interview with the author, Kathmandu, June 18, 2012.
109. From several newspaper reviews, discussions with audience members and also, an observation of Ashesh Malla himself.
110. Anjay Dahal, interview with the author, Kathmandu, June 15, 2012; Yubaraj Ghimre, interview with the author, Kathmandu, June 18, 2012; Priya Chhetri, interview with the author, Kathmandu, June 06, 2012.
111. Sarwanam tends to work exclusively with Ashesh Malla, except for a very rare instance when the group would work for a public production with another playwright/director.
112. Roland Bleiker, *Aesthetics and World Politics* (Basingstoke: Palgrave Macmillan, 2009), 2.

References

Amnesty International. "*Nepal: A Spiralling Human Rights Crisis.*" Amnesty International, April 4, 2002.
———. *Amnesty International Report 2012: The State of the World's Human Rights*. London, UK: Amnesty International, 2012.
Bleiker, Roland. *Aesthetics and World Politics*. Basingstoke: Palgrave Macmillan, 2009.
Central Bureau of Statistics - Government of Nepal. "*Nepal in Figures 2013.*" Central Bureau of Statistics, Government of Nepal, Kathmandu, Nepal, 2013.
Das, Lipika. "Shakespeare in Odisha: A Study of Selected Odia Translations." *Odisha Review* (May 2012): 45–52.
Friedrich Ebert Stiftung. "Political, Economic and Social Development in Nepal in the Year 2011." Friedrich Ebert Stiftung, 2011.
———. "*Nepal in the Year 2012: A Glance.*" Friedrich Ebert Stiftung, 2012.
Human Rights Watch. "*Nepal: Country Summary.*" Human Rights Watch, January 2012.
Hutt, Michael, ed. *Himalayan People's War: Nepal's Maoist Rebellion*. London: C. Hurst & Co. Ltd, 2004.
Institute of Human Rights Communication. *Sexual Violence in the "People's War": The Impact of Armed Conflict on Women and Girl in Nepal*. Kathmandu: IHRICON, 2007.

International Committee of the Red Cross, Nepal Annual Report. "Nepal Annual Report": ICRC, 2011.
Johnson, William J. *The Sauptikaparvan of the Mahābhārata: The Massacre at Night*. Oxford: Oxford University Press, 1998.
Ling, Lily H. M. "Rationalizations for State Violence in Chinese Politics: The Hegemony of Parental Governance." *Journal of Peace Research* 31, no. 4 (1994): 393–405.
Neupane, Manisha. "Scars of War." *The Kathmandu Post*, July 10, 2012.
Pettigrew, Judith. "Living between the Maoists and the Army in Rural Nepal." In *Himalayan People's War: Nepal's Maoist Rebellion*, edited by Michael Hutt, 261–84. London: C. Hurst & Co. Ltd, 2004.
Retika Rajabhandari and Women's Rehabilitation Centre. *Violence against Women in Nepal: A Complex and Invisible Reality*. Kathmandu, Nepal: WOREC, 2006.
Sengupta, Ashis (ed.). *Mapping South Asia through Contemporary Theatre: Essays on the Theatres of India, Pakistan, Bangladesh, Nepal and Sri Lanka*. Basingstoke: Palgrave Macmillan, 2014.
Sharma, Mandira, and Dinesh Prasain. "Gender Dimensions of the People's War: Some Reflections on the Experiences of Rural Women." In *Himalayan People's War: Nepal's Maoist Rebellion*, edited by Michael Hutt, 152–65. London: C. Hurst & Co. Ltd, 2004.
Subedi, Abhi. *Nepali Theatre as I See It*. Kathmandu: Aarohan, 2006.
TRIAL (Swiss Association against Impunity), CVSJ (Conflict Victim's Society for Justice), PPR (Forum for the Protection of People's Rights) Nepal, HimRights (Human Rights Monitors), NEFAD (Network of Families of Disappeared and Missing), THRD Alliance (Terai Human Rights Defenders Alliance), and OTV-Nepal (VIctim's Orphan Society of Nepal). "Nepal: Written Information for the Adoption of the List of Issues by the Human Rights Committee with Regard to Nepal's Second Periodic Report (Ccpr/C/Npl/2)." http://www2.ohchr.org/english/bodies/hrc/docs/ngos/TRIAL_Nepal_HRC108.pdf.
United Nations. "*Nepal's Hidden Tragedy: Children Caught in the Conflict.*" United Nations, 2006.
United Nations Office of the High Commissioner for Human Rights. "*Nepal Conflict Report 2012.*" Geneva: United Nations Office of the High Commissioner for Human Rights, October 2012.
Upreti, Bishnu R. *Nepal from War to Peace: Legacies of the Past and Hopes for the Future*. New Delhi: Adroit Publishers, 2009.
Women's Rehabilitation Centre. *Anwesi: A Year Book on Violence against Women 2008*. Kathmandu, Nepal: WOREC, 2008.

CHAPTER 7

Conclusion

Exploring art for peacebuilding is a search for the transformative power of what reaches us amidst the emotional and political turmoil of conflict. It is an act of studying what exactly it is that moves us to recognise, acknowledge, and connect with our own humanity as well as that of the enemy, at a time when our worlds as we know them are collapsing around us. At a time when calculated rational arguments and well-formed policy frameworks fail to make sense to our humanness, art can create subtle yet powerful ripples in our communal spaces; ripples that can either die out, or if appropriately used, connect and amplify to encompass an entire nation.

This book set out to explore the role theatre as an art form plays in conflict transformation in South Asia. It has done so first with a conceptual overview and a discussion that established the significance of art and theatre in addressing the gaps within contemporary peacebuilding discourse, and second, with an empirical study that focused on three cases from Sri Lanka, India, and Nepal. Through a careful examination of the case studies, it demonstrated that theatre as a form of art working at an everyday level within communities, can make a significant contribution to building peace.

How exactly does theatre work for peacebuilding? The empirical analysis elicited the multivocal and dialogic form of theatre as the underpinning quality that facilitated conflict transformation across the three case studies. Multivocality facilitates the expression of varied, contradictory voices that often go unheard within the prevalent mainstream discourse of a given conflict. Strategies embodied within the group processes, theatrical form, and the imagination of theatre, can bring out these voices at different stages of the theatre production. The dialogic form of theatre enables the expression elicited through multivocality to initiate a conversation between parties and narratives in conflict, within and beyond the theatre space. Peacebuilding and conflict transformation emerge therein. The multivocal and dialogic nature of theatre is particularly suited to express local complexities, and open up possibilities for communication between parties and narratives in conflict. Consequently, theatre and arts as an approach, contributes to peacebuilding by offering a different, resilient approach that can encompass the many complexities in a conflict context.

Theatre for peacebuilding offers an alternative path within prevailing approaches to peacebuilding. The key debates in peacebuilding have arrived at an impasse between the overall statebuilding and society-building approaches to peacebuilding. Emerging literature on a hybrid approach to peacebuilding, draws attention to the need for the discipline to incorporate peacebuilding strategies that can work at an everyday level within local communities. Theatre as an approach to peacebuilding locates itself and takes its significance precisely at this point. Despite its widespread use in conflict situations and its potential in peacebuilding, theatre has received relatively little academic attention.

The empirical contribution of the book facilitates a better understanding of the role of theatre for peacebuilding, through exploring three relevant longstanding theatre groups from South Asia. Jana Karaliya uses theatre to create a space where parties and narratives in conflict can come together. Being a multi-ethnic, bilingual, mobile microcosm that lives and travels together, Jana Karaliya's approach is embedded within and responds to the ethnic and political dynamics of the Sri Lankan conflict and post-conflict situation. Jana Sanskriti contextualizes and uses forum theatre to bring out prevalent but less heard narratives of structural violence in West Bengal. Through group practices and performances, Jana Sanskriti performs resistance to and triggers transformation within the narratives of structural violence at the community level. Sarwanam makes excluded citizen's perspectives a part of the public discourse on conflict in Nepal through theatre. The group developed a symbolic theatre form and used this to draw out the citizens' voice omitted from the public discourse on peacebuilding, and to connect with and speak to both the rational and emotional sensibilities of the audience through its plays.

The analysis across the cases points to the importance of finding a balance between multivocality and dialogic in utilising theatre for peacebuilding. Balance is key for initiating a shift in the polarised narratives that prevail during conflict. Theatre for peacebuilding initiatives can run the risk of focusing on one to the exclusion of the other. Such an exclusionary focus on one element is again detrimental or prevents theatre from reaching its full potential in peacebuilding. When theatre is highly multivocal but less dialogic like Jana Karaliya, theatre is not being utilised for its full potential. When theatre is highly dialogic but fails to be sufficiently multivocal, like it was in Jana Sanskriti's anti-alcohol protest that turned violent, the discussion would not necessarily reach the depths it could and the results could be neutral or detrimental to peacebuilding. The point of balance is highly context specific and differs for each theatre group and for each theatre initiative.

The empirical analysis also points to the possibility of seeing theatre for peacebuilding as resistance in a given situation. Practitioners use theatre to perform resistance to divisive or dominant narratives at the early stages of peacebuilding. The multivocal and dialogic form of theatre can empower the silenced voices in conflict contexts to speak out and perform resistance to violence and injustice: this resistance, in turn, due to the absence of physical violence and the separation from the outer world allowed through the permeable membrane of theatre's imaginary, facilitates a dialogue within and between narratives and parties in conflict. The dialogue, as a starting point for transforming relationships, is an act of performing resistance to the existing conflict-prone narratives.

All three cases demonstrated some elements of challenging the existing hierarchy or prevalent conflict narratives in a context to develop a momentum for peace: Jana Karaliya articulates narratives of ethnic unity and coexistence in the context of Sri Lanka. Instead of being the norm, the multi-ethnic, bilingual group starts off as being the alternative in the midst of established conceptions of ethnic separation. Jana Karaliya works in this context, subtly challenging the prevalent stories of separation and carving out common ground. Jana Sanskriti in India openly challenges the existing narratives of structural violence in search of emancipation and empowerment of the working classes. The community actively participates in challenging these hierarchies on and off stage. The transformation of these oppressive narratives is seen as a precondition for an authentic peace. Sarwanam in Nepal protests the post-peace agreement actions of the political elite and resists keeping the civilians in the margins of sculpting justice distribution. It continues to project the citizens' voice into the public discourse on conflict.

Facilitating Peacebuilding Through Theatre

Incorporating strategies that initiate, embody, and promote multiple voices and dialogue can enhance the potential of peacebuilding through theatre. Multivocality and the dialogic can be integrated into different aspects of theatre to bring conflict parties together. Group composition and mobility, production elements such as the scripting process and flexibility offered through different theatre types, and audience engagement are examples of such aspects.

When appropriately contextualised, the elements that facilitate multivocality and dialogic of theatre as seen in each case study, can be accelerators in developing theatre for peacebuilding initiatives. Thus, these pointers need to be contextualised. These elements can be discussed under two themes: context related and activism oriented.

The first context related element that can facilitate the multivocal and dialogic form of theatre for peacebuilding, is the level to which art and its appreciation prevail in the local context. Interest in the art form is a powerful motive to bring people together. In the case of Jana Karaliya, this is what brings the community to the mobile theatre every afternoon; with Sarwanam, this is what makes people trickle down from the hills at the sound of the group's drum and songs announcing its arrival. With Jana Sanskriti, this is what makes the community engage with the same forum play over and over. Interest in theatre can also be an indicator of the support a group receives for its peacebuilding activities. The more a community is attuned to the arts and see it as part of their everyday activities, the more apt they are to support, spend time on and engage with it, and therefore, benefit from the potential of theatre for peacebuilding.

The second context related factor that positively contributes to the process of peacebuilding through theatre is the sensitivity of the group to local politics. Awareness of the nuances and local complexities of conflict and politics can significantly contribute to peacebuilding, especially through a highly flexible medium like theatre. As Jana Karaliya demonstrates, this awareness helps in avoiding pitfalls and utilising the flexibility of theatre to find alternative ways of carrying out peacebuilding even in challenging circumstances. The group consciously refrained from directly engaging with conflict issues through its dramas during the war period, in order to ensure group safety and viability. This self-imposed censorship is a calculated strategy to survive in a highly volatile and a fragile political situation. Such sensitivity is crucial for determining the success of the overall theatre for peacebuilding initiatives. The theatre initiatives are inevitably shaped by the political situation, and generally aim to respond to the existing conditions while avoiding punitive action. Sensitivity to the local politics is therefore an important factor for peacebuilding through theatre.

The third context related factor that contributes to peacebuilding through theatre is group resilience. Resilience of a theatre group is important to ensure continued peacebuilding. The more a group embraces strategies of resilience, the more likely it is to survive. As the case studies amply demonstrated, these strategies of resilience can vary depending on the context and group nature: Jana Karaliya adapts to the existing conditions by expanding and contracting the group, and group activities. It takes political sensitivities into account in shaping the group approach and activities to ensure its survival: similarly, it takes financial sustainability into account in planning activities such as periods for rehearsals, performance schedules, touring and breaks. Jana Sanskriti in West Bengal has members who live and perform in their own villages, thereby reducing the financial obligations incurred in maintaining a full-time theatre group. What results is a versatile group with a relatively simplified process of production. Sarwanam has come up with a strategy to ensure resilience through constructing a theatre complex for the group. The infrastructure potentially generates sufficient income to financially sustain the group, freeing it from reliance on external funding sources. Having its own performance centre, thus, allows Sarwanam to fully focus on theatre. Incorporating strategies for resilience is an important factor to consider in developing theatre initiatives for peacebuilding.

The first activism oriented factor that contributes to peacebuilding through theatre is the engagement with the community. This is twofold: the length of engagement and regular contact with the community outside the theatre space. While isolated performances can also make a significant impact, when a theatre group engages with a given community over an extended period, the potential for initiating change increases. Jana Sanskriti's practice of recurrent performances of the same forum play in a given location for a period, and Jana Karaliya mobile theatre performances over a three-month period testify to this. In both these cases, taking the time to work with the people ensures that the silences existing at different levels get an opportunity to be heard, and to engage in dialogue through theatre. It further ensures that the moments of healing, empathy, transformation or communication, initiated through the multivocal and dialogic form of theatre are nurtured until they firmly take root. Witnessing the concrete impact of their work further motivates the activists. Regular performances over an extended period enhance the impact of using theatre for peacebuilding. Consistent contact with the community outside the theatre space is also an important factor that comes into play in relation to a group's engagement for peacebuilding. All three groups studied in this book ensure their accessibility to the community after the performances and on an everyday basis.[1] The audience gets to interact with the actors outside the theatre space at a personal level, taking theatre for peacebuilding beyond the limitations of theatre and further integrating the message of peacebuilding to the lives of ordinary people. It also becomes a forum for gaining popularity and thereby, influence. Engagement with the community is an element that needs to be taken into account in approaching peacebuilding through theatre.

The second activism oriented factor that contributes to theatre for peacebuilding is the existence of political action that stems from or carries forward the theatre group's work. Pre-planned political action that goes along with the performance can significantly enhance the impact of theatre for peacebuilding. Numerous commentators such as Niriella admit that the next step would require bold initiatives at a more high-profile political level that will utilise the transformation initiated at ground level.[2] Jana Sanskriti has aligned itself with appropriate national level institution-led movements at times when their mutual agendas for social change overlapped. Such political mobilisation need not necessarily start at the high-profile level: as it does with Jana Sanskriti, theatre can easily become the seed for and contribute to a community level people's movement for justice that results in tangible positive outcomes. Through its interrelated theatre and political work, Jana Sanskriti is able to effect concrete village level change in the communities where it works. What is necessary for such a process is deliberate political action found upon insights gained from the multivocal and dialogic form of theatre for peacebuilding. The level, to which the political movement is embedded in, based on, and authentic to the theatre process and its outcomes, is likely to positively correlate with its impact upon the community.

The third activism oriented factor that contributes to theatre for peacebuilding is the ethical commitment of the group. Ethical commitment emerges as a significant element among the case studies, holding them together amidst financial and other hardships. This commitment is two-fold: ethical commitment to the group objectives for peacebuilding, and preserving this integrity in the group processes. The group aims—in the cases I studied—became a uniting force for the individuals within, and they in turn, expected the group processes to embody and be true to these principles. Theatre groups for peacebuilding succeed in winning the trust of their audience and sustaining themselves over a long period when they demonstrate ethical commitment in these two ways.

This book examined a selective array of avenues and actions available once peacebuilding enters the space of theatre. The theatre groups discussed serve as a testimony to the alternative approaches to peacebuilding that are uniquely moulded by and address the complexities and traces of conflict found in the local context. Given this context-specificity, multiplication or generalisation of the same models could be problematic. The contribution of the study is found in the theoretical reasoning that emerged as a central theme in all three case studies: multivocality and the dialogic. Through its multivocality, theatre can empower the silenced voices in conflict contexts to speak out and preform resistance to intolerable conditions and injustice. This resistance, due to the absence of physical violence and the separation from the outer world allowed through the permeable membrane of theatre's imaginary, facilitates a dialogue within and between representatives from different parties. Such dialogue, in turn, leads to a transformed relationship. It is the initial step in envisioning a collaborative future. Incorporating theatre opens alternative avenues through which we can approach and build peace.

Art based approaches can play a significant role in broadening the boundaries of peacebuilding to address certain identified gaps in the prevailing approaches. The multivocal and dialogic form of theatre is particularly suited to express conflict complexities and to establish communication between conflict parties. Facilitating this multivocality and the dialogic through its form, peacebuilding through theatre can prepare the ground for and garner support for the continuation of a peace process, while ensuring that the community itself is included as part of the process. Prevailing approaches to peace have repeatedly failed in establishing this groundwork, though it is central to the success of a peace process. Using theatre as a specific form of art, this book illustrates that art can play a key role in building a people's movement for peace: a movement that resists prevalent conflict narratives and mainstream peacebuilding through local strategies that urge conflict parties to seek sustainable peace. It pushes the existing boundaries of peacebuilding and conflict resolution to open up and draw from other relevant disciplines such as performance studies and mobilisation. Theatre for peacebuilding incorporates the questions of ethical values, emotions and creativity as an approach located within and engaging with the people and their everyday lives at a local level. Peacebuilding through the arts can become a platform that opens up alternative local solutions for conflict that is outside the realm of prevalent approaches to peacebuilding. As this book has shown, accessing the alternative local spaces is where the prevalent peacebuilding approaches are lacking the most, and it is here that incorporating peacebuilding through the arts can make a significant contribution in conflict transformation.

Notes

1. Sarwanam and Jana Karaliya mingle among the audience after the performances when they travel. Their accessibility is somewhat limited at the conventional stage performance, due to the constraints of the model.
2. Parakrama Niriella, interview with the author and Harshadeva Amarathunga, Thambuttegama, February 22, 2008.

Index

A

A Story of One Girl (Jana Sanskriti), 176
Abeysiriwardene, Sunil, 119
Abhina (Sri Lanka), 119
Achel Natya Samuha (Nepal), 197
agitprop, 19
Agniko Katha (Aarohan), 196. *See also* Subedi, Abhi
Amnesty International, 114, 192
Andara Mal (Jana Karaliya, Sri Lanka), 138
Antigona, 67
applied theatre, 10, 71, 73–75, 78, 122
art
   appreciation of, 236
   and dialogue, 130
   and emotion, 80–81
   and healing, 66
   and hope, 1
   and peacebuilding, 7–9, 12, 19, 22, 154, 233
   for peacebuilding, 12, 22, 87, 92
   political significance of, 2, 8, 9, 66, 67, 75, 82, 88, 91, 127, 239, 240
   theatre as an, form, 66–67, 76–78, 80, 90–92, 135, 157, 195, 234–236
art-based approaches, 9, 80

B

Bakhtin, Mikhail, 18, 90
Bandaranaike, Dharmasiri, 118. *See also The Trojan Women*
Band Pather (India), 157
Bertelsmann Stiftung, 193
Bhabha, Homi, 86
Bhitta (Aarohan), 196
Bleiker, Roland, 80, 93, 138
Boal, Augusto, 16, 71, 75, 160–161. *See also* Theatre of the Oppressed (TO)
The Brick Factory (Jana Sanskriti), 164–168
British, 116, 157

empire, 108
Raj, 188
see also colonial

C

ceasefire, 107, 110, 189
  internationally mediated, 14
  period, 118, 210
  see also Cease Fire
    Agreement (CFA)
Cease Fire Agreement (CFA), 110
censorship, 68, 139, 157
  self-imposed, 142, 237
  state, 67, 195
Centre for Performing Arts (Sri
  Lanka), 119
Ceylon Workers' Red Flag Union, 138
Chandler, David, 45
Charandas (Jana Karaliya, Sri Lanka),
  135, 138, 140
Chautari Natak, 10, 196. *See also*
  Playback theatre
civil society, 13, 34, 44–47, 49, 82,
  115
  capacity of, 44–46
  and democracy, 44
  elite-driven, 45–46
  groups, 196
  layer of, 46, 82
  role of, 3, 45
coexistence, 46, 112, 173
  and ethnic harmony, 15, 235
Cohen, Cynthia, 9–11, 87
colonial, 52
  India, 68
  legacy, 109–110, 188
  oppression, 157
  period, 67, 110, 157, 158
  see also British, Raj
communicative action, 46
communicative reason, 46–48

Communist Party of India (Marxist),
  174
Communist Party of Nepal (Maoist)
  (CPN(M)), 16, 189–190,
  193–194
community-based, 46
  approaches, 2, 51
  groups, 46
  initiatives, 7
  see also grassroots; ground level
Comprehensive Peace Accord (CPA),
  16, 189, 193, 194, 200
conflict
  cultural residues of, 42, 44, 54
  emotional cultures of, 47, 50,
    79–82, 143
  local complexities of, 3, 5, 18,
    42–43, 65, 75, 84, 86, 90, 234,
    236
  memories, 70, 82–86
  narratives, 78, 82, 84–85, 87, 127,
    132, 136, 139, 141, 142, 197,
    235, 240
  resolution, 5, 10, 91
  transformation, 5, 7, 37, 67, 69, 78,
    79, 81, 114
  see also War
conflict resolution, 5, 88
  and dialogue, 91, 196
  and peacebuilding, 12, 47,
    51, 240
  process, 81, 91
  and theatre, 10, 90
  see also conflict resolution;
    reconciliation
conflict transformation, 5, 7, 37, 67,
  69–71, 78–79, 81, 114
  and peacebuilding, 12, 233, 240
  process, 37
  and reconciliation, 67, 70, 137
  in South Asia, 233
  and theatre, 69, 73, 75, 90, 233

see also conflict resolution; reconciliation
Constituent Assembly (CA), 189–190, 194, 221
culture
  and art, 8, 76, 91
  and conflict, 85, 110
  and conflict resolution, 5
  of dialogue, 16, 136, 160
  emotional, of conflict, 47, 79–82, 143
  group, 202
  and history, 85
  local, 6, 34, 39–40, 82–83, 164, 188, 207–208
  monologue, 16, 160
  of peace, 4, 37, 156
  and peacebuilding, 6, 8, 34, 38–40, 50, 55, 82–84, 121, 134–136
  Sinhala and Tamil, 15, 121, 124, 134–135

D

Dalit Panthers (India), 158
dalit theatre movement, 158, 173
dance, and theatre performances, 67, 69, 77, 161, 180
  Kali Tandav, 219
democracy, 1, 45
  and dialogue, 160
  and liberal values and policies, 4, 32, 35–40, 42
  Nepal, 188, 189, 214, 222
  People's Movements for, Nepal, 195, 215
  in Sri Lanka, 108, 111
  struggle for, Nepal, 16
  and theatre, 18, 198, 200, 204, 206
  values of, 178, 224
  at the village level, 170–172, 189
  see also democratic procedures

democratic procedures, 3, 6, 35–38, 55, 93
  and democratisation, 36, 37
  see also democracy
Derrida, 66
dialogic
  form of Jana Sanskriti, 161, 162, 175
  form of theatre, 3, 17–19, 65, 88–91, 107, 127, 131, 133, 143, 153, 165, 178, 181, 233–236, 238
  of Jana Karaliya, 123, 128
  and multivocality, 3, 13, 17–19, 21, 65, 88, 91, 121, 123, 126, 128, 143, 161, 165, 168, 187, 224, 234, 236
  of Sarwanam, 198–199, 211, 216–220, 224
  of theatre, 13, 18, 21, 236
domestic violence, 156, 161, 168, 175–181. *See also* gender-based, violence; structural violence, and gender

E

Ek Rath (Sarwanam), 203
emotions, 1, 69, 131–133. *See also* conflict, emotional cultures of
  anger, 79, 85, 131, 132, 180
  and art, 80, 180, 209
  collective emotions, 79, 81, 131
  empathy, 80, 133
  grief, 79, 80, 132, 133
  and identity, 79, 80
  and memory, 85
  and peacebuilding, 81, 132
  social and political role of, 80
  and theatre, 70, 74, 216–222, 224, 240
  and transformation, 81

Ensemble Kashmir Theatre Akademi (India), 158
Enthayum Thayum, 135. See also Shanmugalingam, Kulanthei
everyday
  lens, 159
  life, 7, 11, 15, 66, 83, 89, 92, 155
  peacebuilding, 7, 50
  politics, 8, 9, 44, 48–50

F
Forum Theatre (FT), 71, 122, 160, 196, 234
  and the dialogic of theatre, 161, 165, 181
  see also Theatre of the Oppressed; Kachahari theatre
Fox, Jonathan, 69
Friere, Paulo, 18, 90

G
Gadjan, 161
Galtung, Johan, 156
Ganguly, Sanjoy, 12, 15, 173. See also Jana Sanskriti
Gayer Panchali (Jana Sanskriti), 170, 171
gender-based
  discrimination, 155
  violence, 155, 156, 188
  see also domestic violence
Ghosh, Girish Chandra, 157. See also *Siraj-ud-daula*
Government of Sri Lanka (GoSL), 107
grassroots, 2, 5, 33, 46, 51, 54, 153.
  See also community-based; ground level
ground level, 2, 5, 8, 20, 46, 48, 89, 93, 108, 111
  changes at the, 118, 238
  community at the, 36, 37, 41, 42, 46, 48, 158, 173
  cultural residues of conflict at the, 38, 42
  dialogue at the, 47
  legitimisation, 47, 111
  peace initiatives at the, 37, 42, 67, 94, 115, 118, 124, 194
  realities, 36, 49, 54, 110, 141, 191
  voices from the, 12, 192
  work at the, 13, 22, 48
  see also community-based; grassroots
Guernica, 66

H
Habermas, Jürgen, 46–48
Hashmi, Safdar, 158. See also Jana Natya Manch
healing
  and art, 66
  and community, 142
  and expression, 18, 90, 119, 138
  and reconciliation, 10, 18, 68–70, 87
  and rituals, 11, 67
  and theatre, 10, 20, 68–70, 84–85, 158–159, 237
Human Rights Watch, 112, 194
hybrid
  local-international, 52–55
  mechanisms and peacebuilding, 52–55, 114, 234

I
identity, 13, 154
  and emotions, 79, 80
  and ethnic conflict, 47, 124, 129, 194
  and peacebuilding, 83, 87
  and protracted conflict, 4, 35, 134

and religion, 117
imaginary, 46, 208, 239. *See also* imagination
imagination, 8, 33
  moral, 11, 87
  and theatre, 69, 74
  of theatre, 76, 78, 79, 82, 85, 233
  see also imaginary
  indigenous, groups, 158, 190, 195
  theatre, 66, 158
The Institute of Human Rights Communication in Nepal, 192
institution building, 4
  and state-building, 35–36
  and the United Nations, 3
  see also peacebuilding, as statebuilding
Integrated Rural Development Program (IRDP), 170, 171
Inter-Act Art (Sri Lanka), 119
Itihasko Banki Pristha (Sarwanam), 187, 216. *See also Remaining Pages of History*

J

Jana Karaliya, 12, 14, 15, 18, 21, 107, 119–136, 138–142, 180, 234–237. *See also* Niriella, Parakrama; mobile theatre
Jana Natya Manch or Janam (India), 158. *See also* Hashmi, Safdar
Jana Sanskriti, 12, 15–17, 21, 153–155, 157, 159–181. *See also* Ganguly, Sanjoy
Janatha Vimukthi Peramuna (People's Liberation Front), 140

K

Kachahari theatre, 71, 196. *See also* Forum Theatre

Kalakshestra Manipur (India), 158
Karusoo, Merie, 85
Kattaikuttu (India), 157
Koiv, Madis, 85
Kooththu, 2, 118. *See also* theatre, Tamil

L

Lederach, J.P., 8, 33, 86, 157. *See also* imagination, moral
Lennon, John, 66
Lessons Learnt and Reconciliation Commission (LLRC), 111, 113
liberal
  democratic, 4, 5, 32, 34–36, 38, 40, 42, 44, 55
  economic policies, 4, 35, 37–38
  frameworks, 38–40
  peace, 39–41, 52–54
  peacebuilding, 35, 37, 39–41, 45
  practices, 38, 43, 52
  values, 6, 35, 36, 38, 39
Liberation Tigers of Tamil Eelam (LTTE), 14, 92, 107, 109–113, 129, 132
local agency, 5, 7, 53, 54
Local Peace Committees, 195

M

Mac Ginty, Roger, 39, 40, 53
Madalenas Nepal (Nepal), 196
Mahabharata, 208, 211, 212, 214–216, 224
Mahinda, S., 67
Makkal Kalari, 12, 14. *See also* Jana Karaliya; Theatre of the People
Malla, Ashesh, 16, 195, 197, 198, 200, 201, 218. *See also* Sarwanam
Manch Rangmanch (India), 158
Mandala theatre (Nepal), 197

246 INDEX

Maoist insurgency, 13, 17, 188–192, 194, 206, 207, 213, 216, 217, 220, 224
Menon, Sadanand, 67
Meti Karattaya (Jana Karaliya, Sri Lanka), 135. *See also Mruchchakateeham*
Mithila Natyakala Parishad (Nepal), 196
mobile theatre, 14, 15, 121, 123, 126, 236, 237. *See also* Jana Karaliya
Maunaguru, Sinnaiah, 118. *See also Ravanesan*
Mruchchakateeham (Jana Karaliya, Sri Lanka), 135. *See also Meti Karattaya*
multiple voices
  expression of, 89–90, 91, 92
  space for, 17, 122, 123, 126–128, 153, 161, 166, 220, 221, 236
multivocality
  and dialogic, 3, 13, 17–19, 21, 65, 88, 91, 121, 123, 126, 143, 161, 165, 168, 187, 224, 235, 236

N
Naari (Shilpee Theatre), 196
Nalapana Jathakaya (Jana Karaliya, Sri Lanka), 135
Natrang theatre group (India), 158
Nāṭyaśāstra, 157
Naya Nepal (Achel Natya Samuha), 197
Nepalese peace process, 16, 189–191, 195, 197, 198, 210, 224, 239
Nicholson, Helen, 74, 75
Niriella, Parakrama, 14, 15, 120, 122, 125, 129, 134, 138, 139, 141, 238. *See also* Jana Karaliya
Nussbaum, Martha, 80

O
Office of the High Commissioner for Human Rights (OHCHR), 190
oppression
  and structural violence, 160, 164, 165, 172, 178, 180
  and theatre forms, 71, 72, 138, 157, 196, 197
origin myths, 79

P
Panchayat
  in India, 164, 166, 170, 175
  in Nepal, 16, 188, 196, 199
Paris, Roland, 32
peacebuilding
  and art, 7–10, 12, 19, 22, 154, 233
  art for, 2, 12, 22, 86, 93
  and conflict resolution, 12, 47, 51, 240
  and conflict transformation, 12, 233, 240
  and culture, 6, 8, 34, 37, 39, 40, 50, 55, 82–84, 122, 134–136
  and emotions, 81, 93, 132
  everyday, 6, 7, 50
  hybrid, 52, 53, 55, 114, 234
  and identity, 83, 87
  liberal, 35, 37, 39–41, 45
  as resistance, 163–169, 235
  as societybuilding, 6–7, 31, 43–55, 234
  as statebuilding, 6–7, 31, 33–43, 48, 51, 55, 234
People's Movements in Nepal (also *Jana Andolan*), 21, 189, 195, 215
Perera, H.A., 12, 120. *See also* Jana Karaliya
performance(s)
  and censorship, 67, 68, 139

and conflict, 11, 66, 83, 118, 119, 124, 125, 199, 206
and politics, 67, 141, 154, 159
and reconciliation, 15
and ritual, 11, 66, 159
space(s), 19, 74, 86, 88, 118–120, 179, 197, 203
style, 198, 204, 206, 223, 224
and transformation, 15, 16, 83, 127–129, 161–178, 196
Picasso, 66
Plato, 66, 68
Playback theatre, 10, 69, 70, 196
Pokharel, Sunil, 195, 196. *See also* Aarohan
political theatre, 19, 158, 159, 162
Prabhakaran, Velupillei, 111
Public Performance Board of Sri Lanka (PPB), 139

R
Ramayana, 119, 157
Rangkarmi (India), 158
Rathnawalli (Sri Lanka), 119. *See also* Abeysiriwardene, Sunil
Ravanesan (Sri Lanka), 118. *See also* Maunaguru, Sinnaiah
reconciliation
  collective, 47, 84, 136
  and conflict transformation, 67, 70, 137
  and healing, 10, 18, 68–70
  obstacles to, 112, 114
  and performances, 15
  and performance traditions, 15
  post-conflict, 84, 89, 111, 139, 199, 221
  and theatre, 67–70
Red-Flag Women's Movement, 138
religion, 5, 68, 155, 171, 173, 179, 199

Remaining Pages of History (Sarwanam), 187, 204, 208, 216–218, 220–224. *See also Itihasko Banki Pristha*(Sarwanam)
Richmond, Oliver, 3–5, 7, 45–46, 49, 51, 52, 54
Riefenstahl, Leni, 92
ritual(s), 2, 11, 67, 69, 85, 141, 217
Rosa Cuchillo, 67

S
Sadbhawa theatre (Nepal), 196
Sakuni Pasa Haru (Sarwanam), 187, 207
Sakuni's Tricks, 187, 208–216, 224. *See also Sakuni Pasa Haru*
Sarama (Jana Sanskriti), 168
Sarwanam, 3, 12, 17, 21, 188, 197–209, 216–218, 221–225
  alternative theatre of, 13, 17, 198, 204–205
  national tours, 198, 205–206
  and struggle for democracy, 17, 195
  theatre approach, 198–199
  theatre hall, 197
  see also Malla, Ashesh
Sekkuwa (Jana Karaliya, Sri Lanka), 138
Seven Party Alliance, 189–190
Seven-Point Agreement, 17
Shanmugalingam, Kulanthei, 135. *See also Enthayum Thayum*
Shilpee Theatre (Nepal), 196. *See also* Yubaraj, Ghimire; *Naari*
Shonar Meye (Jana Sanskriti), 168, 177
Siraj-ud-daula, 157. *See also* Ghosh, Girish Chandra
Sithamparanathan, K., 20. *See also* Theatre Action Group (TAG)
Sri Lankan peace process, 110–112, 115

cease-fire, 14, 92, 107, 110, 113, 118, 189, 210
Stages Theatre (Sri Lanka), 119
stereotype(s)
  challenge, 47, 126–129, 136
  construction of, 116
  ethnic, 117, 124, 143
  gender, 192
  negative, 70, 76, 116, 131
street theatre, 14, 17, 122, 158, 195, 198, 205, 208
structural violence
  and gender, 163–167, 175–178
  and peacebuilding, 3, 16, 117, 153, 155–157, 159
  in politics, 154, 155, 168, 169, 171–174
  see also domestic violence; gender-based, violence and women
Subedi, Abhi, 196, 199. *See also Agniko Katha; Thamelko Yaatra*

T
Tagore, Rabindranath, 67
Tamil theatre, 20, 118, 123, 135–136. *See also* Sithamparanathan, K.
Thamelko Yaatra (Aarohan), 196. *See also* Subedi, Abhi
theatre
  being co-opted, 92, 143
  and conflict resolution, 10, 90
  and conflict transformation, 67, 69, 70, 73, 75, 90, 233
  and dance, 67, 69, 77, 161, 180, 217, 219
  and democracy, 17, 198, 200, 204, 207
  and emotion(s), 69, 74, 220, 224, 240
  and empowerment, 70–75
  folk, 157
  and healing, 10, 20, 68–70, 84, 158, 159, 238
  and history of political scripture, 67, 68
  and imagination, 69, 74
  imagination of, 76, 78–79, 82, 85, 234
  indigenous, 66, 158
  mobile, 121, 123, 236, 237
  propaganda, 19, 93, 160
  pro-war, 19–20, 119
  and reconciliation, 67–70
  and resistance, 72, 153, 177, 178–181, 235, 239
  space, 73, 83, 89, 121, 126, 179, 200, 203, 211, 233, 237, 238
  traditional, forms, 122, 161, 204
  tribal, 157
Theatre Action Group (TAG), 119
Theatre for Development, 197
Theatre of the Oppressed (TO), 10, 14, 16, 71–73, 75, 89, 160. *See also* Forum Theatre; Kachahari theatre
Theatre of the People, 14, 119. *See also* Jana Karaliya; Makkal Kalari
The Trojan Women (Sri Lanka), 118. *See also* Bandaranaike, Dharmasiri

U
undefined, 118, 194
UN Human Rights Council, 111, 114
United Nations Mission in Nepal (UNMIN), 16, 190
United Nations Peacebuilding Commission, 4
UN Working Group on Enforced or Involuntary Disappearances, 113
Upreti, Bishnu Raj, 189, 194, 210

V
victor's peace, 14, 111

W
War, 8, 14, 19, 66, 80, 89, 91, 92, 107, 111–114, 118, 140, 208, 210, 213, 214, 237. *See also* conflict
Where We Stand (Jana Sanskriti), 172–175

Y
Yubaraj, Ghimire, 196
Yuyachkani, 67

CPSIA information can be obtained
at www.ICGtesting.com
Printed in the USA
LVOW13*1534100518
576718LV00002B/2/P